Procurement
Quality
Control

4th Edition

Procurement Quality Control

4th Edition

American Society for Quality Control Vendor-Vendee Technical Committee

Edited by James L. Bossert

ASQC Quality Press
Milwaukee

ASQC
Quality Press
611 East Wisconsin Avenue
Milwaukee, Wisconsin 53202

ACKNOWLEDGMENTS

Many people contributed to the writing of this handbook. The efforts of some deserve special recognition. Art Blank and Brian Margetson wrote one of the best general guides for developing a supplier rating system. It took them a long time and this is reflected in its quality.

Dick Laford, our ship-to-stock expert, assisted me in the chapter that included the evolution from ship-to-stock to just-in-time.

Dave Files contributed to the distributor portion of Chapter 3.

I was constantly reminded of my responsibilities by John O. Brown. Whenever things slowed down, there was a note or a phone call from John asking how things were coming. His "gentle reminders" kept me going. He contributed definitions, artwork, and support.

Elizabeth Nicholson patiently deciphered my writing, checked my spelling, and did a super job typing the manuscript. Without her help, I'd still be typing it.

Finally my wife, Nancy, and daughters, Lindsay and Ashley, deserve recognition. Without their patience and support, I never could have completed this. Many an afternoon and evening were given up so that this could be completed on time. Thank you all.

James L. Bossert

TABLE OF CONTENTS

FOREWORD

In today's global marketplace, goods and services are obtained with little, if any, regard to their point of origin. The predominant factor in any buyer-seller relationship today is value and hinges on the quality of what was purchased and sold. *Procurement quality control* has become synonymous with total customer satisfaction. Suppliers are now recognized as major influences as well as strategic partners in ever-changing competitive arenas.

The science of procurement quality control has evolved from a lot-to-lot approval process to an expert- and technology-based use of resources. This evolution will yield improvements to many facets of the procurement process and, in many instances, change existing ideas and methodologies. This edition of *Procurement Quality Control* acknowledges the existence and practicality of change within the buyer-seller relationship, and has in itself benefitted greatly from the previous editions, which include the diverse, professional experience of this committee's membership, both past and present.

The task of revision was initiated in 1985 during the chairmanship of Richard J. Laford. Project leader, James L. Bossert, has attempted to quantify the totality of change in this field of endeavor. His vision will challenge the reader to pursue new ideas and broaden the scope of procurement program development throughout industry. The entire committee hopes that this edition will be a valuable reference to the quality professional and enjoy the same success in the quality community as the previous editions.

Barry S. Lawrimore, Chairman
Vendor-Vendee Technical Committee

CHAPTER 1

WHY PROCUREMENT QUALITY?

Key Words: Quality, Supplier, Buyer, Inspection, Procurement Quality

Summary:
- **The evolution of procurement quality**
- **The "new" role of procurement**
- **The basic requirements**

Today the word quality appears on almost every product we come across — food, appliances, automobiles, software. No matter where you turn, you see or hear about quality. In fact, we demand a certain level of quality in everything we buy. This is evident in the increase of consumer complaint features in newspapers and on television.

What is meant by the word "quality?" The American Society for Quality Control defines quality as "the totality of features and characteristics of a product or service that bear on its ability to satisfy given needs."[1] The features and characteristics of any product are how we as consumers evaluate how "good" that product or service is. For example, in a restaurant, the amount we leave as a tip is a direct reflection of the quality of the service we have received. Satisfying given needs can include the quantity, price, or purity of something. It is what we as consumers have defined as our minimum acceptable standard. If, for example, there is a need for a chemical with a 99.9 percent level purity, but that level cannot be obtained unless we pay an exorbitant amount, that need may have to be redefined to a level which is more cost effective. So the need for good specifications is established. These specifications will give the supplier the performance features which the buyer requires. The ASQC states that "specifications for the manufacture of a product or the delivery of a service are a translation of features and characteristics onto manufacturing or performance terms. The features and characteristics are often considered in relationship to design and specification of the product or service; to the conformance of the product or service to specifications and to the compliance of the supplier of the product or

1

service to requirements."[2] This approach serves as a reminder of the distinction between the functional and implemented aspects inherent in the design concept and specifications, and in the conformance and compliance aspects of the product and implementation process.

So now our definition of quality has expanded beyond the traditional designing and conformance aspects to the implementation and delivery of the product. Where does the product fit? How do we perceive it? How can we buy it? How do we know what we are buying? We need to answer these questions before manufacturing the product in the design reviews. Then and only then should we have confidence in what we are purchasing.

The Traditional Role of Purchasing

Years ago, before the industrial revolution, products were made by skilled craftsmen. Only the highest quality was made and sold to those who could afford those products. The feedback to the manufacturer was immediate because he could see by the expression on the consumer's face if the quality was unacceptable. Only when Eli Whitney developed the concept of interchangeability of parts did the need for procurement quality begin.

As the complexity of products has increased so has the need for quality. With this, purchasing agents have assumed the added burden of quality assurance. Traditionally, the role of the purchasing agent has been one of getting the product at the lowest cost. Potential suppliers were evaluated on terms of their ability to provide the following:

1. The desired quality defined as the suitability of product or service of use as intended.
2. The total number of products required including the schedule by which the product or service is required.
3. Tangible and intangible services which are benefits over and above quality and price.
4. Price, which is a measure of value.

Purchasing agents also took into account additional factors that supplemented the above requirements. These included such things as geographic location, labor relations, the supplier's internal facilities, the supplier's reserve or back-up facilities, the capability of the supplier's management services, the supplier's service capability, and the supplier's financial status.

Once this information was compiled, the purchasing manager would conduct plant visits for the prospective suppliers. This would be done only after the number of suppliers had been reduced to a manageable number. This on-site visitation would be used to appraise factors such as production control, cost control, morale, and the quality of the materials management activities.

Purchasing agents were also asked to evaluate or rate suppliers. Supplier rating can take many forms, some simple and some complex. In Chapter 8, supplier rating will be examined more closely. When analyzing supplier performance, a purchasing agent is evaluating how a supplier measures up to the defined performance standards the purchasing agent applies to all suppliers. This enables a differentiation between good and marginal suppliers. A good system has guidelines that provide assistance in scoring all areas of resource selection. Any past experience with a supplier's quality and delivery performance is important because it is quantifiable data. Any past experience with technical, financial, and managerial services can also help in making an assessment. Price is not considered at this time. In fact, any quoted prices must be referred back to quality and delivery performance to have any validity. We need to know what to expect to determine the total cost of a purchased product accurately.

Performance standards reflect the cost that purchasing agents must incur in the satisfying of user requirements. For example, suppliers may be rated on quality in terms of three categories: cost of defect prevention, defect detection, and defect prevention. The sum of these costs for each supplier can then be expressed as a percent of the total value of materials purchased from that supplier.

Delivery performance may be expressed in terms of acquisition and availability costs. These costs may represent follow-up time, expediting time, telephone expenses, field surveillance costs, premium transportation costs, in addition to manufacturing losses due to late deliveries.

Traditionally, this kind of information is then put into each supplier's overall rating. This composite score is made available to all purchasing agents in the organization. The rating can increase or decrease the amount of business a supplier receives, so the evaluations must be done carefully. The purchasing agent has fulfilled his or her traditional role; however, times are changing and now there is more emphasis on quality. The amount of technical knowledge needed to assess the adequacy of each manufacturing operation has caused a move towards the team approach for supplier rating. This will be discussed further in Chapter 8.

What is procurement quality? We have talked briefly on the traditional role of procurement and the changes occurring in that area. Is procurement quality a measure of how good the procurement organization performs? Is it a measure of the quality of the products purchased? Is it somewhere in between? The true answer lies somewhere between the two extremes. There is a need to purchase high quality materials, but there is also a need for a high quality organization to purchase the products. Procurement quality is any and all aspects that deal with the purchasing of products. It sounds simple but it really is a complex definition. The definition assumes that there are well-defined specifications for the design of the product being purchased. This implies that we have defined what conformance means in the product, that the measurement requirements are identified, that the reliability and maintainability of the product has been determined, that the delivery and packaging requirements are met, and that liability and environmental concerns are addressed. The communication that takes place among purchasing agents is critical in maintaining a favorable outcome.

There is a series of required steps to ensure good communication. First, purchasing agents need to develop good sources of information. There are many ways to obtain information: purchasing directories in magazines, industrial journals, catalogs, books, advertisements, handbooks, and purchasing bibliographies. These show the purchasing agent what is out there, and what suppliers are trying to sell. Another way is to interview salesmen. Salesmen can tell you what the competition is doing and they can give leads to other potential suppliers. Some salesmen may have examples of comparative studies which have been done either by their company or by other independent concerns.

It is also a time to look at establishing productive relationships with our suppliers. Through site visits and design reviews, the purchasing agent can obtain information on the acceptability and capability of potential suppliers. As the process progresses, the purchasing agent will be able to develop a relationship with the supplier in which both the user and the supplier work together to solve problems.

Second, site inspections allow the purchasing agent to determine the capability of the supplier to provide the material and to convey the seriousness of the potential of doing business with the supplier. The site visit also serves as a means to impress on the supplier that the user expects the supplier to provide exactly what the user wants.

Third, the purchasing agent needs to evaluate the supplier in an objective manner. The intent of any evaluation system is to examine all suppliers according to criteria important to the users. The purchasing agent will then take the top three or four to evaluate more closely. This is intended to determine the strengths and weaknesses of each candidate. It allows the purchasing agent and the user to decide which supplier has the most promise for providing the required product.

The fourth step is the selection of the best candidate to provide the product. This is more than determining the lowest bidder. All the information collected needs to be reexamined. All references need to be contacted to obtain other viewpoints: technical competence, delivery performance, good will practices, statistical process control implementation, laboratory/measurement capabilities, financial outlook, service availability, and capacity. The intent is to obtain a supplier that will provide the specified quality, at the prescribed time, at a reasonable price. The supplier will provide good service when changes are necessary, take the initiative for technical innovations, provide advance notice for process changes, and work for the mutual user/supplier benefit.

This is a lot of work for a purchasing agent to do alone. The purchasing agent's new role is to be a facilitator who obtains the necessary experts to evaluate and decide as a group which supplier has the best potential. There are a number of combinations of people that can comprise this team. It can include people from the development community who have developed the product from an idea; it can include people from the manufacturing area who have to use the product as it comes in the door; it can include people from laboratories who have developed testing methods and need to determine the capability of the supplier; and it can include a person from the quality profession to evaluate the level of process control in the supplier.

This team is pulled together when the product is ready to go from the design phase to manufacturing. In the initial meeting the team will cover what the product is, what the intended use is, and what the timeframe is with which they have to work. At subsequent meetings, the team can look at the preliminary list of potential suppliers and the initial quantities needed for scale up. After the evaluations have been made and the supplier is selected, the team must document the reason for the selection in a report kept on file for future reference. This team will continue to meet for up to one year to review the supplier's performance. If any problems arise, it is up to the team to work with and assist the supplier in providing the product. At the end of a year, the team will either disband or continue to audit the supplier semiannually. A copy of any reports written at this time should be given to the supplier to keep the supplier informed. It is encouraged that, where possible, the supplier participate in these meetings either through conference calls or by visits to the user.

Bibliography

Glossary and Tables for Statistical Quality Control. Milwaukee: American Society for Quality Control, 1983, p. 4.

CHAPTER 2

STRATEGIC CONSIDERATIONS

Key Words: Strategy, Continual Improvement, Long-Term Commitments, Distributors

Summary:
- **Primary business goals**
- **What does strategy mean**
- **Supplier strategy**
- **Benefits achieved**

When trying to decide how to work with suppliers, it is imperative that company directions and goals be taken into account. The bottom line is simple: The main goal of any business is to make money. The way to get there can take many forms. The best way for long-term stability and profitability is to produce the highest quality product at the lowest possible cost. The procurement organization is given the task of developing a supplier base that allows this to happen.

Supplier programs with a distributor tend to be more difficult to set up because the distributor has no control of the manufacturing process. The most common way to set up a supplier program is to have distributors work only with "certified" manufacturers for the products they handle. This can be accomplished in two ways: Distributors can get their manufacturers together and work with users to certify the manufacturers, or users can recommend suppliers who have already been certified so distributors can establish contracts with those manufacturers.

A distributor supplier program has five basic components: a manufacturer audit system, a shipping/packaging control system, a storage control system, a specification program, and a quality information system. The manufacturer audit system is a systematic way of assessing the quality program at the manufacturer. The purpose of this is to evaluate, document, and assure that the product produced is of the quality level the customer desires. The shipping/packaging control system is a way of ensuring traceability and lot integrity from various suppliers, and that the quality is not compromised in the repackaging operation. The storage control system ensures that the product maintains its quality while in the distributor's possession. The specifications program is the maintenance of up-to-date specifications for all of the distributor's customers and, when necessary, documentation of who at the manufacturer's facility has a copy of the specification. The quality information system is a system that maintains information from the supplier on the user's most requested quality characteristics. This would be sent with every shipment containing that lot/batch of materials.

In addition, distributors may be evaluated on the technical support and service they provide. There are times when distributors will be contacted for quality problems that occur in the products they supplied. The technical expertise distributors possess or have access to can be critical in the resolution to the problem. It is also critical how quickly distributors respond to the problem. The level of satisfaction with a distributor is directly related to the quality of the response and the time taken to respond.

What is a Distributor?

A distributor is a nonmanufacturing source of product. Generally the distributor does not change the product itself. The distributor may change the packaging to meet the customers' needs, but only in rare cases does the product change. The chemical industry is one of the rare cases where some distributors may mix chemicals together to form a new product. There are three types of distributors: a surrogate sales force for a manufacturer, a repackager and surrogate sales force, and a manufacturer/distributor.

A surrogate sales force for the manufacturer serves as the marketing function for the manufacturer. They take a product from the manufacturer as is. The manufacturer has responsibility for product quality since the user receives the package in the original condition from the manufacturer. The distributor is trained by the manufacturer when necessary in the proper handling and storage needed to maintain the quality of the product while it is in the distributor's possession.

The repackager and surrogate sales force receive the product in large quantities and repackage the product to sell in the customer's desired quantities. Here the distributor and the manufacturer work together to make sure that nothing compromises product quality in the repackaging phase. The manufacturer/distributor performs a similar function to that of the repackager. However, the manufacturer/distributor also produces a new product by the addition of other ingredients.

Supplier Strategy

Strategy means many things to many people. In its simplest form, it is a way of maximizing the actions you have control over and minimizing those you do not. This means that for any business, there has to be a set of guidelines that dictate where we want to be at a given point and that this is clearly understood by everyone. For example, if it is stated that the business wants the highest quality attainable, then there has to be a definition of "highest quality." It could mean that certain physical characteristics are met consistently; it could mean that the product is recognized by others as being the best in the field; or it could mean that the product attains an increase in the market for your product.

There is another aspect to this that directly impacts the business. If the supplier consistently provides the highest quality, there will be significant gains in the productivity of the manufacturing operation resulting in reduced internal costs. The business can control the quality of the product coming into the plant and the communications between it and the supplier, and it can establish mutually beneficial policies that provide incentive to the supplier to provide the highest quality. This is the foundation for the development of a supplier strategy.

Today there is an increased need to develop a supplier strategy. With the increase in technology, there are many small shops that provide highly specialized services/products which answer a specific need in the marketplace. These shops can be considered the "new" guilds. These are the craftsmen of today who provide a high quality product for a select customer. They work hard to maintain their status as being on the "cutting edge" of their technology.

Many companies are looking at how to shorten the development cycle to bring new products into the marketplace sooner. One way to achieve this is to bring in critical suppliers during the development process and enlist their assistance. A critical supplier is one whose product is necessary for the production of a new product. Many times suppliers are aware of new technologies in their field. They are also aware of the capabilities and limitations of the current products they provide. As they learn what the expectations are for the product they are providing, they can recommend changes in the product that will enhance its performance. For example, a certain plastic part was to go into a copier. The supplier was brought in and found out that the part was to be located near a heating element which would cause the plastic part to warp over time. The supplier recommended a different composition of resins which would have higher heat resistance. This resulted in an improved product and a significant savings in potential redesign and service costs.

Many businesses are looking at ways to reduce inventories. Traditionally, inventories have been maintained to provide protection against unforeseen incidents. This gave the user a constant supply source. A supplier program can reduce the risk involved because there is routine communication between the supplier and the user. Some of the communications can include revised forecasts covering long-term and short-term needs, and updates on the present performance of the supplier. This allows the supplier to provide the product on a "just-in-time" basis if that is the way the business is operating.

When suppliers know what is expected of them and how they are evaluated, they can focus on reduction. The cost reductions will enable suppliers to enter into longer term contracts without threatening their goal of making money for their company. At the same time, suppliers are assured of a longer term partnership with the user, a benefit to both. Many companies have successfully reduced costs through the implementation of statistical process control (SPC) techniques. These techniques are simple to use and place the responsibility for quality on the worker. The purpose of SPC is to prevent poor quality from occurring by controlling the process. This is different from the traditional concepts of inspection and sorting to maintain the desired quality level.

The implementation of SPC is an evolutionary process. The supplier and the user have to establish a time line to measure the progress of the SPC implementation. This allows both the supplier and the user to be fully aware of the expectations of each organization. It also gives the user an opportunity to assist the supplier with resources to accomplish the agreed upon goals. As the supplier attains SPC on his processes, the user can initially reduce any incoming inspection with the intent of eliminating all inspection when the supplier achieves statistical control.

There are various strategies that have been used by businesses. The most common one is that of giving the supplier increased responsibility in terms of the product. The strategy here is that the supplier is certified, which means that no incoming inspection is performed on a product or grouping of products. The certified supplier may be entitled to a variety of benefits: increased opportunities for new business, long-term contracts for product, cost rebates for consistently meeting requirements, and so on. However, there are also risks involved: The supplier commits to an SPC program as a way to operate to keep costs down, the price is fixed for the duration of the contract, and raw materials may be required to be purchased from another certified supplier. These things must be considered since the supplier will, in many cases, be held accountable for any loss incurred through the shipment of out-of-spec parts.

Another strategy is where the supplier is made part of the design team developing a new product. Here the supplier is expected to lend expertise to a new design. It is a mutual commitment since both the user and the supplier will benefit from the results. The user gets the latest technology in the supplier's specialized area, and the supplier gets an opportunity to improve relations with the user and to increase business. Here the supplier is expected to participate in design reviews, specification development, prototype products, measurement assurance, and life testing. The supplier is given unique opportunities to have some control in new products.

Another strategy is the practice of improved forecasts for products. Basically what happens here is that the supplier receives updates on a routine basis of the production schedule. This way the supplier is continually updated on both the short-term and long-term schedules. This enables the supplier to adjust the schedule and maintain as little inventory as possible. With the advent of computerized telecommunications this is becoming a preferred way of doing business.

The various strategies discussed here work well with all types of suppliers, including those who manufacture a product, those who supply common items such as desks, office supplies, etc., and to distributors. The strategies have been developed with the manufactured product suppliers in mind, but with a little modification the others can be brought under the supplier program umbrella.

Procurement Quality Control

CHAPTER 3

THE PSYCHOLOGY OF SUPPLIER RELATIONSHIPS

Key Words: Partnership, Behavior, Objectivity, Mutual Understanding, Integrity, Proprietary Information, Respect, Safeguard of Reputation

Summary:

- **Traditional buyer/supplier relationship**
- **Development of a partnership**
- **Informal code of ethics for procurement quality**

When dealing with suppliers, the most important thing people must remember is: "What would I be doing if I was in the supplier's place?" This type of thinking will assist members of a procurement team in conducting themselves in a manner beneficial to both companies' interests.

This has not always been the case. Traditionally the buyer/supplier relationship has not been one of consideration, but one of dictation. The buyer dictated to the supplier exactly what the buyer wanted. No deviations were accepted. If the supplier did not want to do business, there were plenty of other suppliers who were interested. Consequently, supplier relationships were one-sided. The suppliers also learned quickly how to get deviations from the specifications. The simplest way was to announce a price increase shortly after obtaining the contract. The buyer would call to tell the supplier that the price increase was out of the question. Then the supplier would tell the buyer the order could not be met. The buyer would inquire why and the supplier would tell the buyer that under the current specification, a certain dimension could not be met consistently. To ensure that the specification be met, a price increase was necessary. Then the buyer would ask the question the supplier had been waiting for: "What if we can get you a deviation from the specification?" This was exactly what the supplier wanted. The supplier knew from the beginning that the specification was unrealistic. The supplier also knew that if a deviation or change in the specification would have been asked for at the beginning, the supplier would have been eliminated from getting the contract. So the supplier waited until the contract was his before making a move.

The traditional relationships were based on a carefully executed program of moves similar to a chess game. Neither side was willing to be completely open. The difficult dimension was recognized by the supplier (the expert in the field) but the buyer's company recognized no experts but its own. If the design engineer put the dimension on the specification, then it was correct. Supplier expertise was viewed as inferior where it may have been just the opposite. The supplier understood that the best way to get the change made was to speak in terms that the buyer would understand: dollars. If the buyer accepted the price change, the supplier had enough money to either improve the process or to hire more inspectors. In either case, the supplier won.

The buyer on the other hand had a problem: A specification deviation or change was necessary if the parts were to be delivered on time. If the change/deviation was not possible, then the buyer's company will pay more for the product than was originally contracted. Either way, the buyer looks bad, as if enough research was not done during the supplier search. The idea that the design was wrong never occurred to anyone.

So here is a classic situation of mistrust on both parties' accounts. This has resulted in increased product costs, high waste, and, in some cases, field failures. The buyer's company lost its reputation for providing a high quality product that took years to reestablish, because the buyer's company did not acknowledge that there were any experts except its own.

Today competition has forced this situation to change. As major companies shrink both their employee and supplier bases, the concept of partnerships has grown. A partnership grows with time. The development can be likened to an interpersonal relationship resulting in marriage. When first meeting with a potential supplier, it is like going on a date. Both parties try to put their "best foot forward." As the selection process ends, a supplier is given an initial contract. This is the "going steady" phase. Both parties are making a limited commitment to see if the initial impressions are true. This can lead to the engagement phase where longer term contracts are considered based on past performance. The marriage occurs with the long-term contract and the approach to the supplier for assistance in new product development. All new product development is confidential and both parties agree to not divulge any information to other companies. The honeymoon phase occurs when everything is "rosy" between the buyer and the supplier. This can last a long time (up to a year) or be very brief (one week). Once the honeymoon is over, the true partnership begins. This is when both parties work toward mutual benefit.

When a problem occurs, both parties work together to solve it. This may mean traveling to each facility to discover possible solutions. It may mean a redesign of the part or process to correct some unanticipated defect, or a mutually agreed upon absorbence of costs to alleviate short-term setbacks. Whatever the problem is, it is worked on and solved together. There is no assigning of blame.

The key elements of a partnership can be summarized into an informal code of ethics. This code was originally developed by the Vendor-Vendee Technical Committee of the ASQC. The motivation behind it was the understanding that both the buyer and supplier have an interest in attaining the same objectives. There are 12 elements to the code:

1. *Personal Behavior.* All dealings between both quality control functions should be conducted in a manner to credit the companies and individuals involved. In contacts between quality control functions of both the supplier and the buyer, it is necessary to avoid compromising relationships.

   Essentially, this says that we should act in the manner in which we would like to be treated. This reflects well on ourselves and the company we represent.

2. *Objectivity.* Both the buyer and the supplier should address the fulfillment of all contractual requirements and objectives. The legal aspects of a contract cannot be ingored. But, there is also a moral obligation to achieve a satisfactory end product. It is to the mutual advantage of both parties that the objective attained is accompanied by a fair and equitable cost distribution.

   In this case, the buyer and the supplier need to focus on what is required by each to achieve the desired outcome. If the buyer is asking for some requirements requiring additional expenses, the buyer should expect to pick up part of those expenses.

3. *Product Definition.* The buyer should furnish a complete description of the quality requirements in writing for the procured item, including minimum workmanship standards. The buyer's quality organization is morally obligated to assure that all requirements are clear, complete, nonconflicting, and correct. Assistance in the interpretation of requirements should be readily available to the supplier.

   Simply stated, all specifications should be understood by everyone, and any additional information to help clarify the specifications should be freely given.

4. *Mutual Understanding.* Direct communications between quality functions should be implemented at the initiation of all contracts and continue through the life of the contract. Direct communication assures professional maintenance of the mutual obligation by the respective quality managements. To allow quality functions to be handled through default by others will result in product quality degradation and a loss of reputation for the profession.

Let the quality people talk to the quality people. Let the operators talk to the operators. Keep the communications as direct as possible; avoid all middlemen.

Quality Evaluation. It is the buyer's responsibility to appraise the supplier's quality performance fairly and it is the supplier's right to be aware of this appraisal. The supplier has the benefit of knowing what his comparative quality position is with the customer, since it is this factor that predicts the supplier's future. Common benefits are derived by working together. It is important to commend a supplier when consistent, satisfactory performance is achieved.

Evaluate the supplier with a consistent rating system. Let the supplier know what the rating is. Discuss possible areas of improvement and, where applicable, ways to achieve improvements.

Product Quality. Suppliers should honestly and fairly inform buyers of the quality status of delivered items. Delivery implies that contractual objectives have been met. Certifications that fail to indicate deviations or omissions are misleading and demonstrate poor practice or lack of good faith. Unintentional discrepancies that could jeopardize a buyer's program should be clearly communicated to responsible individuals to assure maintenance of the supplier's quality and ethical reputation.

When there is a problem with a shipment, notify the buyer. Data should be sent with every shipment if that is part of the contract. If a deviation has been granted, then it should be noted on the data sheet.

Corrective Action. Corrective action should be actively pursued and implemented by both the supplier and the buyer. The acceptance of this responsibility by both demonstrates good faith in the contractual relationship as well as quality discipline and technical competence.

Working together to solve problems when they occur saves time and money. It also fosters the partnership between the two companies.

Technical Aid. Technical support should be provided by the buyer when requested by the supplier. Care must be exercised since such efforts may confuse the question of responsibility. Technical support activities must be conducted with mutual respect for the competence of both the supplier and the buyer, in their respective specialties.

When there is a request for technical support, the buyer has two options: to provide someone from his company or to recommend an independent source. This does not mean that the buyer assumes resonsibility for the product the supplier provides. It simply means that the buyer is willing to help the supplier on

16

a specific problem.

9. *Integrity.* Facilities and services should be used by the visiting party only to the degree of the contractual obligation or as volunteered by the supplier or the buyer. Inspection, laboratory facilities, and equipment must be provided to the extent specified in the contract. The supplier must permit the buyer access to facilities where the buyer can perform source inspection and/or other associated functions involved with the assurance of contractual obligations. The supplier should normally permit the buyer to observe inspections or tests and to review the resultant data. The visitor must not accept gifts, entertainment, or other preferred treatment of any nature, thus eliminating any unethical behavior by which the level of quality may be compromised.

   Do not do anything that could embarrass you or your company.

10. *Rewards.* Supplier quality management should encourage its purchasing agent to use only qualified suppliers. Quality management should compile and maintain a current list of qualified suppliers based on performance. The use of the most qualified suppliers from a quality control viewpoint should be considered in the selection of suppliers, rewarding those suppliers that consistently produce conforming products.

    Establish a list and use it when selecting suppliers.

11. *Proprietary Information.* Both parties should refrain from divulging proprietary information obtained in confidence. Divulging privileged information violates ethical and moral standards and certainly is not in the best interest of either party.

    Betraying a trust is destructive to business relationships.

12. *Safeguard of Reputation.* Both parties should avoid making false, unsupported, or misleading statements. Integrity and professionalism are paramount in every business relationship.

    There must be an open, honest relationship established if a partnership is to grow and develop. Anything less than that works against everything you are trying to accomplish.

Procurement Quality Control

CHAPTER 4

BASIC ISSUES: SPECIFICATIONS

Key Words: Specifications, Properties, Sampling, Product Specification, Process Specification, Analytical Specification, Raw Material Specification, Standard Terms, Process Capability Index, Test Capability Index

Summary:
- **What is a specification**
- **What are the types of specifications**
- **What are the components of a specification**
- **How should specifications be determined**

A specification is a grouping of specific parameters required to assure the success of a product to perform as designed. This is sometimes a difficult set of expectations. Many times it is the capability of the manufacturing process that is the critical factor resulting in deviations to specifications. In fact, industry recognizes that changes are necessary in the development and implementation of specification change and deviation procedures. It is a challenge to the design community to develop specifications that are meaningful and within the manufacturing process capability.

There are four basic types of specifications:

1. *Product Specifications.* This type is the most common and defines what is required for a product to perform as expected by the consumer.
2. *Process Specifications.* This type of specification defines the parameters of the manufacturing process that must be controlled to produce a product.
3. *Analytical Specifications.* Where applicable, this type of specification defines what is necessary for an analytical laboratory to measure to a required level of sensitivity.
4. *Raw Material Specifications.* This type of specification defines what is acceptable as raw material coming into a manufacturing process.

Procurement Quality Control

Generally, product specifications are determined first, followed by process specifications, analytical specifications, and raw material specifications. These specifications enable the design and manufacturing people to communicate in common terms. These terms are the requirements at every level of the manufacturing process. Specifications provide manufacturing checkpoints for product quality.

There are common components to all specifications. First, there is a description of the product. It can be verbal, or if a manufactured part, a profile. After the description, the required characteristics are listed. These characteristics include the upper and lower tolerance limits, how the product is to be measured, the units of measurement, and, in the case of chemical tests, the test method procedure.

The third component is the sampling and packaging requirements. These identify how the product is to be sampled and how it is to be packaged. This is also where any special handling concerns are addressed. From this, different industries attach various information such as test method descriptions, environmental testing requirements, shelf-life restrictions, certificate of analysis information, process control requirements, safety requirements, and various governmental regulatory requirements.

Besides these common elements, product specifications should include the following (ANSI/ASQC Standard Q94-1987 p. 9):

- Reliability, serviceability, and maintainability requirements.
- Permissible tolerances and comparisons with process capabilities.
- Product accept/reject criteria.
- Installability, ease of assembly; storage needs, shelf life, and disposability.
- Benign failure and fail-safe characteristics.
- Aesthetic specifications and acceptance criteria.
- Failure modes and effects analysis, and fault tree analysis.
- Ability to diagnose and correct problems.
- Labeling, warning, indentification, traceability requirements, and user instructions.
- Review and use of standard parts.

By including these components, product specifications will contain the information necessary to minimize liability issues.

Process and analytical specifications also have some unique components (ANSI/ASQC Standard Q94-1987 p. 9):

- Manufacturability of the design, including special process/analytical needs, mechanization, automation, assembly, and installation of components.
- Capability to inspect and test the design, including special inspection and test requirements.

Basic Issues: Specifications

- Specification of materials, components, and subassemblies, including approved supplies, and suppliers, as well as availability.
- Packaging, handling, storage, and shelf-life requirements, especially safety factors relating to incoming and outgoing items.

There are many ways to develop specifications and everyone has an opinion on how specifications should be developed. Some work on hunches, some just "trust their instincts," and some use statistics. Obviously, the "best" specifications come from the use of statistics. Now another potential problem occurs: Which statistical tool should be used? Histograms? Designed experiments? What about just using a mean and standard deviation? Is one more correct than another? In many cases, no. The only difference in using statistical tools is how fast you can get to the "final" specification. Is there any final specification? A specification can be thought of as an evolutionary document which provides checkpoints at parts of a continuing cycle. The popular word today is "continuing improvement." What this means is that all products can be improved, and that if our company is to remain competitive, then we must find ways to improve. A specification is a plateau where the evolutionary climb has established a base. This base remains until there is enough information to establish a new base. So we can consider specifications as both a stabilizing influence and a dynamic document.

In developing specifications, simple tools like histograms, means, and standard deviations can provide great insight with small amounts of data. One of the most common ways is to calculate an index known as the Process Capability Index (PCI). PCI tells the development personnel how much of the specification range is taken up by the manufacturing process. The formula used is:

$$PCI = \frac{Upper\ Spec\ -\ Lower\ Spec}{6\ SD}$$

This is sometimes written as Cp. The inverse of this index tells the percent of specification:

$$\frac{1}{PCI} \times 100 = percent\ of\ specification\ taken\ up\ by\ the\ process$$

There are variations of this that can further refine the use of these indices (see Appendix).

Recently, another statistic has been used for analytical testing. This is known as the Test Capability Index (TCI) which is used similarly to the PCI. The TCI is calculated as follows:

$$TCI = \frac{\text{Upper Spec} - \text{Lower Spec}}{6 \text{ SD of Testing Method}}$$

This provides information as to the adequacy of the testing methods on the product being developed. The inverse of this provides information as to how much analytical variability takes up the specification range.

PCI and TCI enable the design personnel to develop estimates that can evolve into specifications. The next step, the specification team, is where the "final" specifications come out. The specification team consists of development personnel, the material supplier, and the manufacturer. This team looks at the data design personnel has utilized, data on the manufacturing capability, and data from the supplier's capability, and develop a specification over a period of time. This team may also include other personnel, such as an analytical representative if laboratory testing is involved. This team works to develop specifications that are realistic and that reflect product use.

Government Quality Specifications and Standards

Those working with government agencies have another set of criteria contained in the Government Quality Specifications and Standards. Government quality documents normally begin with a specification of quality program requirements. This requires a documented program for all activities necessary to attain continuous control of product quality during manufacturing. Usually this program will be reviewed and accepted by buyers after they are satisfied that the necessary activities do exist and are being performed effectively. The quality program specification, or the contract, will typically refer to other government documents to which compliance is also required. These secondary documents may refer to still other applicable documents that establish the requirements of additional program and product details. The second level of quality documents may specify equipment calibration systems, sampling procedures, product detail requirements, and analysis of all raw material.

Government documents may be obtained through the procuring activity, the government contracting officer, or directly from the U.S. Government Printing Office. Those documents pertaining to other governments must be obtained from the appropriate governmental agencies.

A few of the basic government quality program specifications are listed as follows:

- DOD MIL-Q-9858A Quality Program Requirements
- DOD QRC-82 Quality Program Requirements Supplement to MIL-Q-9858A

- DOD MIL-I-45208A Inspection System Requirements
- DOD ISR-1 Inspection System Requirements Supplement to MIL-I-45208A

The local government contract administrating offices will help suppliers in setting up procedures that comply with government requirements. In addition to surveying facilities to determine quality program compliance, they also advise on how to comply. Specialists in a wide variety of technical subjects are available to help interpret details and establish procedures to provide required control.

Government quality requirements are more detailed than most commercial requirements. The extensive details included in government documents have evolved from quality experience in the past. It is mandatory to the success of aerospace projects, military endeavors, and the preservation of human life that a deficient level of conformance be eliminated. Therefore, government documents have become concerned with both program concepts and product details so that quality is thoroughly defined. Product specifications and standards are also necessary to provide interchangeability of products from more than one source.

Continuous source inspection, surveys, and audits are frequently used. Government contracts rely on source inspections, quality program audits, and surveys to assure that end items have incorporated the requirements specified at all levels of procurements. Resident government representatives are assigned when the frequency of shipments, the complexity of the product, and the criticality of performance require constant surveillance at the manufacturing facility. Their primary responsibility is to assure product conformance when shipped. In addition to outgoing inspection, they also perform continuous audits of control procedures to assure that quality programs are maintained.

The supplier should become acquainted with all requirements included in the specifications and standards. The total performance and documentation requirements are not apparent from a single or a few specifications listed in a contract. The supplier should also review and be informed of all program requirements, product specifications, and documentation details that apply in the referenced documents before being committed to a government contract. If the supplier does not become familiar with the specifications imposed, he may learn too late that costs were greater than expected and the product cannot be shipped because of standards which were not met.

Modifications to government documents may be included in contract conditions. Changes to the pertinent specifications and standards are not possible for individual procurements. Hence, justified changes must be made as additions or exceptions in the contractual agreement. Identification and clarification of questionable details must be completed before the contract is signed. This assures performance on schedule and avoids delays that can be costly to both supplier and buyer.

The supplier and buyer should be aware of added cost factors resulting from the conformance requirements to government documents. Some may not be apparent unless all specifications are reviewed in detail. The additional work required can affect costs significantly and should be considered in pricing.

Some of the cost factors are certifications from subcontractors, inspections to approve quality programs, certification of specific processes, additional documentation required to provide objective evidence of compliance to details, changeovers to military type materials and finishes, additional environmental testing, and time required by program reviews.

Reference

ANSI/ASQC Standard Q94-1987. *Quality Management and Quality Systems Elements — Guidelines.* Milwaukee: American Society for Quality Control.

CHAPTER 5

BASIC ISSUES: RECORD KEEPING

Key Words: Part Number, Nonconforming Materials, "P" Charts, "C" Charts, Control Charts, Variables Data, Attribute Data, "NP" Charts, "U" Charts, Mainframe, Personal Computer

Summary:
- **What types of data are important**
- **What types of reports can be set up**
- **What types of system concerns need to be addressed**

One of the first questions buyers must ask themselves is, "What information do I want from this supplier?" From this a series of secondary questions can spring up, but the primary question is what will be addressed here. When trying to decide what information to receive from suppliers, buyers must determine how they will use that information. For example, if a particular dimension is critical, the buyer may want the supplier to plot that dimension on a control chart. This accomplishes two things:

1. The supplier will establish some long-term information about the critical dimension.
2. If the supplier is not using SPC techniques, the supplier will have to begin supplying the data.

Data in which some characteristic can be measured are called variables data. These data lend themselves to control charts and histograms easily. The collection of these data can be time consuming for some characteristics. These data can be useful in the development of specifications.

Another type of data is called attributes data. These are counting data. This information can also be control charted. It is generally obtained from go/no go gages or appearance defects. The number of rejects is counted and compared to the total number of pieces in either the lot or those inspected. These data are relatively quick to obtain.

There is a third group of data which, in some respects, is the most important: lot traceability information. Located in this grouping are part

25

number or characteristic identification, the supplier identification, the number of parts shipped, and so on.

From this the buyer then decides how to track the characteristics of interest. The best way is through the use of control charts. The ASQC defines control charts as "a graphical method for evaluating whether a process is or is not in a 'state of statistical control.'" A process is considered to be in a "state of statistical control" if the variations among the observed sampling results from it can be attributed to a constant system of chance causes" (*Glossary and Tables for Statistical Quality Control* pp. 30-35). All this simply means that the data are plotted on a graph and decisions are made based on the graph. There are six types of control charts that are commonly used from this information: two types for variable charts and four for attribute charts. The two variable charts are:

1. X-bar and Range/Standard Deviation
2. Individual with a Moving Range

The four attribute charts are:

1. "P" Charts (Percent Defective Charts)
2. "C" Charts (Defect Charts)*
3. "NP" Charts (Number of Rejects Charts)*
4. "U" Charts (Defects per Unit Charts)

An X-bar and Range/Standard Deviation Chart is used when there are subgroups of collected data. This is the most sensitive of all the control charts listed here. Sensitive means that any unusual occurrences that can cause an "out of control" condition will be picked up quickly on the chart.

An Individual Chart is used when subgrouping data are not feasible. This can be due to a time restriction, excessive costs in obtaining the data, or a lack of materials. In this case, a Moving Range Chart is used to "artificially" create subgroups to estimate control limits and determine the "state of control."

The "P" Chart is used to estimate the percent defective of all lots shipped. It is not as sensitive as the prior two charts, but it does enable the buyer to make some determination of consistency.

The "C" Chart measures the number of defects in a lot. There is a restriction of a constant subgroup size for this type of chart.The "NP" Chart serves as a similar function and has the same restriction on subgroup size.

The "U" Chart measures the number of nonconformities per unit. This can be extremely useful in products that can have multiple defects in the same unit, ranging from complex machinery (copiers) to sensitive, complex products (film) where destructive testing takes place.

---

*Must have constant subgroup size

Another source of data is the certificate of analysis, which is sent by the supplier to the buyer for each lot. These data are usually laboratory-tested results, which are on the characteristics of interest.

This information can be sent by the supplier to the buyer, who then places the data into some overall reporting form. There are many ways to report data. Generally, a graph works best if it is kept simple. Only data that are necessary for a clear interpretation of information should be included. The information should be in a logical sequence. Present summary trend reports first with detail reports following. The summary trend reports should indicate supplier quality levels for a given period. The detail reports allow the operating personnel to select products that need some corrective action. This selection can be based on volume, frequency, or cost of nonconforming parts.

There are four basic types of reports: (1) percentage, (2) cost, (3) significant problem, and (4) personnel or gage control.

1. *Percentage Reports.* This type of report is designed to show supplier or in-house quality as a percentage relationship of nonconformities to inspections, operations, or man-hours expended (Table 5.1).
   Advantage: Report is easy to prepare and comprehend.
   Disadvantage: Percentage nonconforming may be inappropriate if used to compare supplier to supplier (or department to department) unless each is producing equally complex parts.

Supplier or Department	Parts Inspected	Nonconformities	Nonconforming
WXY	10,000	10	0.1%
XYZ	50,000	100	0.2%

Table 5.1 Percentage Report

2. *Cost Reports.* A cost report shows supplier and in-house costs incurred due to improper quality (Table 5.2).
   Advantage: Cost has greater impact on management and is a good basis for determining when corrective action should be applied.
   Disadvantage: Accurate dollar values are extremely difficult to obtain.

Supplier	Product Cost	Quality Cost	Quality to Product Cost
WXY	$ 25,000	$5,000	20.0%
XYZ	$150,000	$5,000	3.3%

Table 5.2 Cost Report

3. *Significant Problem Reports.* This technique points out the most significant problem or operations by listing items in rank order with the highest percentage listed first. Details are required on major items only (Table 5.3).

Advantage: The most significant nonconformities are selected and efforts are directed toward attaining the most effective corrective action.

Disadvantage: Establishing criteria for selection from among critical problems is difficult.

Total Nonconformities			1,200	
Total Different Supplier or Operations			50	
Part Number	Supplier	Operation	Nonconformities	Total Nonconformity
1234	WYZ	10	500	41.7%
4567	WXY	75	300	25.0%
Remainder of Problems			400	

Table 5.3 Significant Problem Report

4. *Personnel or Gage Control Records.* This technique is generally used to indicate requalification date of personnel or recalibration date and inventory data on gaging (Table 5.4).

Name	Department or Supplier	Type Test	Due Date
John Doe	123	XYZ	4-07-85
Jane Doe	234	WXY	4-12-85

Gage Number	Department or Supplier	Due Date
123456	Department 12	4-08-85
234567	Department 15	4-09-85

Table 5.4 Personnel or Gage Control Report

When setting up an information system, the first question is, "Should this system be a PC or mainframe system?" A PC system is most practical for low volume, multiproduct operations and for high volume single product operations. The amount of data to be collected is much less than for mid-to-heavy volume, multiproduct operations which can be more efficiently collected on a mainframe system. However, it is not only the amount of data but also what you want to do with it that dictates what type of system to be used. Some graphs and data reports require that a mainframe system be used from a time factor. If it takes one hour to generate a report on a PC (and you have to wait until it is done before you can do anything else) and 15 minutes on a mainframe system (where you can do other things while the report is being generated), then a mainframe may be more cost effective.

Once you have decided on what type of system, then how can these data be input? Years ago, keypunched cards were the only way. Now a floppy disk can contain all the information already input into the desired format, or data can be transmitted over the telephone lines directly into the database, or data can be stored in a data collection device and sent to the computer at regular time intervals, or data can be punched in as

28

they are received. The options are increasing every day so ask the computer experts what is avaialble.

The data that should be input depends on what type of report you want to generate. At the minimum, the input should include the supplier identification, the part identification, the lot number, the quantity and the date received, the quantity rejected (if any), the nonconformity description, and the resultant corrective action. This information along with any control chart data will be the foundation for the routine reports for management.

In attempting to set up an information system, all anticipated and potential users must be contacted. Explain what you want to do and ask for suggestions. Once this list of suggestions is developed, determine the most critical components. Design a system that is simple to use and adaptable. This is generally done by developing a system in a series of modules that arc linked together through a series of menus. Each menu would be linked by common identification like the part identification and the supplier identification. In this way, the system can start out small and grow as necessary.

Reference

ASQC Statistics Division. *Glossary and Tables for Statistical Quality Control.* Milwaukee: American Society for Quality Control, 1983.

CHAPTER 6

BASIC ISSUES: SITE INSPECTION

Key Words: Acceptance, ANSI/ASQC Standards Q90-Q94 Series, Design, Economy of Resources, Metrology, Process Evaluation, Procurement, Product Evaluation, Program Evaluation, Quality Management, Surveillance

Summary:
- **Why evaluate**
- **Types of surveillance**
- **Basic principles**
- **How to do an evaluation**

Whenever a buyer is ready to place a contract with a new supplier, it is a common practice to make a site inspection to evaluate the extent to which the supplier's quality program conforms to the ANSI/ASQC Standards Q90-Q94. This series defines the "guidelines for the selection and use of a series of standards on quality systems that can be used for external quality assurance purposes" (ANSI/ASQC Standard Q90-1987 p.1).

The primary reason for evaluating a quality program is to make sure that the program is accomplishing its intended function effectively and economically. This evaluation can be useful internally as well as externally. Management can rapidly determine inefficient operations when using an evaluation as a self-audit.

This is critical because every organization relies on a quality program to some extent. An intolerable situation would quickly develop if each buyer insisted on specifying the supplier's quality program in detail. Conflicting requirements would make compliance virtually impossible. So the quality program evaluation needs to focus on basic principles and leave the details to the supplier. This means that the quality program evaluation is concerned with management control of the factors that can affect the quality of product. The simplicity or complexity of controls and the specific methods of operation are the supplier's management prerogatives. The function of the evaluation is to ascertain that an adequate quality program has been established and that it is effectively operated.

This is a strategy that considers the supplier's quality program as an extension of the buyer's program to minimize or omit all receiving inspection of products that have been certified by the supplier. This does not mean that the buyer does not perform periodic audits to verify the incoming product.

There are three types of evaluation that are commonly used:

1. *Program.* This judges the effectiveness of a program on the basis of conditions in which it operates. This is used primarily in supplier selection. It entails consideration of such things as space, facilities, and the number and type of employees. Program evaluation assumes that at least a satisfactory level of quality is present if the facilities, personnel, and the program itself are operating effectively.

2. *Product.* This consists of gathering evidence that indicates the product's degree of conformance to the stated design. This is useful for nonproduction involving a large volume of identical products over a long period of time.

3. *Process.* This emphasizes what the manufacturer, the worker, and the machine do to achieve an end product. It involves assumptions that certain methods of operation will lead to desirable results, and that such results can be most effectively obtained when activities are directly related to goals and objectives. A process evaluation requires the examination of the overall program for evidence relating to: (a) the setting of process performance goals, (b) the existence of adequate procedures for attaining the goals, (c) the implementation of control procedures, (d) the determination of the extent to which the goals are achieved, and (e) the improvement of the procedures when a need is indicated.

Underlying Principles

It must be remembered that evaluation is the systematic gathering of evidence concerning selected parameters of the quality program and making a decision on the basis of the evidence collected. This involves three distinct steps:

1. Selecting and defining parameters to be evaluated.
2. Developing and applying measurement to those parameters.
3. Assigning appropriate values to the evidence obtained to achieve a sound basis for decision making.

The objectives of the program must be known to carry out these steps. This is compared to the results of that program. Explicit statements of objectives are essential because they are the basis for formulating, operating, and evaluating the program. A simple example is baking a pie. The objective is to make the pie. The formulation phase is where all the ingredients are put together on a table where the manufacturing will be done. All the components are put together and placed in the oven in the operating phase. The evaluation phase is where the result is tested and compared to the objectives. How well was the objective met?

The program evaluation is a joint supplier/buyer activity. When the evaluation is properly accomplished, it is mutually beneficial for all parties. It is essential that the evaluation recognizes and encourages continuation of those activities done well, and that it specifically identifies how improvements can be made in areas of less than optimum performance.

Simply put, the best way to control and improve quality is to prevent nonconformity. The successful prevention of defects is not a chance occurrence, but rather the result of an aggressive, tough-minded insistence that the product be manufactured correctly the first time.

Realistically, no single program can accomplish this for all products in all types of organizations. There are eight basic principles that are the foundation for every successful program. How effectively these principles are applied determines the success of a program.

1. *Control of Quality Management.* There must be adequate planning, forceful direction, and control in how the operators measure and evaluate the product. The quality organization must be equal in authority to other organizations with direct responsibility and accountability to top management. Quality begins with planning and continues through product delivery.

2. *Control of Design Improvement.* A system that assures that all specifications are current is essential to the control of the product. This is also known as document control.

3. *Control of Procurement.* The end product is only as good as the raw materials that go into it. Suppliers should look into establishing their own supplier program.

4. *Control of Material.* It is not enough that the correct material has been specified and purchased. It must also be properly identified, stored, issued, and used.

5. *Control of Manufacture.* The control of processes is necessary for the production of a conforming product. Uncontrolled processes result in waste and excessive variability. With some products, the only time particular characteristics can be verified is when the product is made. This is common with sealed or "blackbox" devices, or with products like film or light bulbs where evaluation after the product is made destroys it.

6. *Control of Acceptance.* Verification that the finished product

meets the design intent. This is sometimes called the inspection and testing component.

7. *Control of Measuring Instruments.* Inspection and testing is only as good as the precision, accuracy, and reliability of the measuring instruments.

8. *Use of Quality Information.* All quality oriented information should be directed toward the product. This means placing it where it has the most impact, on the product floor.

Evaluation

There are many techniques for conducting quality program evaluations. The simplest is to walk through the plant and allow general impressions to accumulate into an opinion of the quality program. The dangers of this method are obvious: Superficial and showy examples may oversell the entire program, or some small deficiency may disproportionately reflect on an otherwise satisfactory program. Generally, more reliable results are obtained if a more formal technique is used to compile objective information in an orderly manner.

Questionnaires, checklists, survey forms, rating systems, and other tools of the trade vary widely. Much has been written about the advantages and disadvantages of these tools, and the interest in such systems is often far greater than merited. More important is a basic understanding of the fundamental principles that must be applied to consistently manufacture conforming products. Successful quality program evaluation systems invariably use professionals as evaluators, and major reliance is placed on the evaluator's judgment rather than on a stereotypical technique. No two quality programs are the same. Each is the product of different environments, different personalities, and different problems. A model program in one plant might not work in another. The evaluation of a quality program is thus a review of a one-of-a-kind set of policies, procedures, and operating practices. Effective application of the eight basic principles set forth is what should be measured. The particular administrative method used in applying these principles is not of concern so long as the principles are applied in a manner that will assure conformity. Evaluating is a viable means to assure the supplier and buyer that program, process, and product requirements are satisfactorily achieved and maintained.

Professional societies, industry associations, and various international governments have long sought ways of standardizing methods of maintaining surveillance over quality programs. The goals have been to make such surveillance more effective and to minimize replication costs by both the buyer and supplier. One factor which has tended to defeat efforts at standardization is the fact that virtually every buyer has attempted to impose his own unique "program requirements." These unique requirements have, in turn, given rise to the development of lengthy and detailed questionnaires and checklists which tend to oversimplify actual situations. Finally, wide differences in the professional and technical competence of evaluators, and variations to their ethical standards have made buyers reluctant to rely on evaluations by others. With the advent of ANSI/ASQC Standards Q90-Q94, *Quality Management and Quality Systems Guidelines,* some of the benefits of standardization may be realized.

Before conducting an evaluation, considerable effort should be made by the evaluator to become familiar with the product or products involved. Drawings and specifications should be studied to determine which requirements are critical, major, and minor. Inspection records, reliability test results and, if available, customer service history should be examined for possible items of particular concern.

Prior to any evaluation, there will be communication of intent made to the supplier identifying the specific nature of the visit. This communication will advise the supplier as to the purpose of the evaluation, specifically what is to be evaluated, and an acceptable date to both the supplier and buyer. No attempt to evaluate any supplier should be made before an agreement is obtained and an invitation has been extended.

The evaluation should begin at the supplier's facility with the contact organization and other supplier-selected representatives in attendance. The scope of the evaluation, enumerating the specific area or areas that will be observed, should be discussed. At this time, all questions should be answered. After the conclusion of this preliminary conference, the evaluation will be conducted. It is suggested that a representative of the supplier accompany the evaluator or evaluating team at all times during an evaluation.

Much time should be spent during an evaluation observing normal operations to obtain objective evidence to support subsequent ratings, evaluations, and conclusions. It is important that the value decisions of the evaluator be based on actual observations of operations, rather than implied examples of performance or procedures. Throughout the observation of operations, the evaluator should be accompanied by a supplier management representative. Comments and questions directed to management personnel and to other employees must be carefully considered and clearly stated so that they in no way create an impression of disagreement with, or disparagement of, operations. It is equally important that any differences of opinion among visiting evaluators be kept objective and inconspicuous.

An evaluation represents a best judgment after all evidence has been considered. Included as evidence should be the results of observations of operations, discussions with supplier personnel, and considerations of data provided by the supplier. Individual value decisions should be reviewed by the evaluator and the management representative in preparation for a report to management. Ordinarily, there should be agreement between the individuals concerned, but if such cannot be reached, the respective positions should be clearly and objectively defined. It should not be assumed that the need for knowledge, experience, and associated good judgment can be overruled by technique. A competent evaluator must invariably use a checklist or evaluative criteria to assure the completeness and objectivity of the evaluation.

As the evaluator observes performance, the questions included in applicable sections of the objectives should be kept in mind. The objectives documents should neither be in constant evidence as though they were absolute references, nor should they be used conspicuously so as to create an impression of being used to evaluate individual job performances. The important considerations relate to the nature of the quality program, as it is compared with the statement of principles that precedes each set of objectives. Sufficient notes should be made during the course of the evaluation to provide information for rating purposes and for composing statements describing explanatory or supporting evidence.

An evaluator is expected to verify by direct observation, to his own satisfaction, the degree of conformity of the supplier's practice to the general principles stated in the criteria, by relying on the evaluator's own experience and knowledge to determine the adequacy of actual operations. From this information, the evaluator can prepare a written report for the closing conference including pertinent commendations and recommendations.

A closing conference, conducted in the same cooperative spirit that has characterized the entire evaluation, should provide an immediate basis for growth and improvement of the quality program and improve the relationship between the supplier and buyer. Participation in the closing conference should include management and any experts, consultants, or other advisory personnel who have participated in the evaluation. The evaluator should present a written report and orally discuss activities, areas covered, procedures used, findings in particular areas, and considered conclusions. Any member of the closing conference should be allowed an opportunity to present evidence appropriate to items being discussed and to question any evaluation. The results of the final review should represent the best judgment of the evaluator. If areas of disagreement exist and a common understanding cannot be obtained, a clear explanation of the factual basis for divergent opinions and conclusions should be recorded and appended to the report. In the event that the evaluation concludes that there are areas of deficiency to be presented in the program, recommendations should be presented.

By far the most important part of an evaluation is the action taken upon its completion. If unsatisfactory conditions are not corrected, then both the evaluator and the group evaluated have wasted a lot of time and money. No action may give an indication of what to expect in future dealings with this. The recommendations of the evaluator should provide a good starting point for revising and improving the overall quality plan. Proper application of this revised plan should result in more effective control.

The buyer should expect some benefits from an evaluation of a supplier quality program. If the evaluation has been conducted and concluded in a professional, objective manner, it should be expected that improvement in the quality of delivered products or services would be realized. Such a result cannot be anticipated, however, if the closing conference and final report of the evaluation are, in effect, an endpoint or termination of the supplier/buyer relationship. The buyer must maintain communication with the supplier especially when recommended changes require action on the part of the supplier.

Once a supplier exhibits a satisfactory quality program as concluded by the evaluation, the buyer may reduce receiving inspection or other verification activities without significantly increasing practical risks. When deficiencies are noted, the buyer possesses sufficient evidence to strengthen inspection requirements of products received from this supplier. Occasionally, an entire quality program may be deemed unsatisfactory. This may prompt immediate action by the buyer including such actions as rejection of product, management meetings, and possible contract cancellation.

Reference

ANSI/ASQC Standard Q90-1987. *Quality Management and Quality Assurance Standards — Guidelines for Selection and Use.* Milwaukee: American Society for Quality Control.

Procurement Quality Control

CHAPTER 7

BASIC ISSUES: PRODUCT AND PROCESS MONITORING

Key Words: Audits, Control Charts, Preshipment Samples, Product Evaluation, Receiving Inspection, Repeatability, Source Inspection

Summary:

- **How to monitor special processes**
- **How to monitor product**
- **How to obtain data about the supplier**
- **The types of data available**
- **An overview of source inspection**
- **An overview of audits**

Special Testing

Most companies rely on an outside source for a required service that is not available within its own facility. This stems mainly from economic limitation rather than lack of technical ability. Special testing examples of this are heat treatment, plating, sterilization, magnetic particle inspection, liquid penetrant inspection, X-ray inspection, and chemical testing. In many cases, special testing is required by the buyer because conformance to a specification can not be verified through normal inspection methods. This is used to verify what is known as a special process. A special process is a method in which a material undergoes a physical, chemical, or metallurgical transformation. Process control efforts tend to be concentrated on the operating condition of the process. Are the facilities, setups, adjustments, and services in accordance with the development determined to produce the required results? For example, in a welding operation, are the electrodes, dwell time, and current settings as prescribed? In heat testing, are the belt speed, manifold temperature, and atmosphere in accordance with specifications?

Testing for special processes can take two forms:

1. Nondestructive testing such as radiographic inspection (X-ray), magnetic particle inspection, penetrant inspection, ultrasonic inspection, and eddy current inspection.
2. Destructive testing such as chemical analysis, salt spray analysis, tensile and shear strength analysis, and impact testing.

These types of tests tend to be expensive, so when a buyer requires this type of test, it is to eliminate doubt in the supplier's capability. It is a common practice to rely on the supplier's integrity and accept a certificate of compliance which lists not only the desired materials, but also the impurities. But there are other alternatives for certification. A buyer can certify the capability of the equipment as measured by a specific test as defined in the specification. In this way, the buyer has assurance that the equipment can consistently manufacture the product if properly set up.

A buyer can certify the training and abilities of the people who perform the tasks and inspections in accordance with the requirements in the specification. So the buyer is now confident that the supplier's personnel has the minimum skills necessary to produce the product.

A buyer can certify the limit of nonconformity of major or minor items. This is seen frequently in automotive requirements where critical parts allow no nonconformance to the specification and minor parts may allow one or two per lot. As a general trend, most companies are requiring 100 percent conformance to specification; in a few years, all companies will require 100 percent conformance. Certification can be on a lot-to-lot basis, but it can also be used for continuous production if there is a start and expiration date.

After a procedure has been established by a company for special processes and the personnel is certified, an audit should be performed by a team from the buyer's facility. This team has three purposes:

1. To provide for a periodic review of the special processes to see that the special process instructions are available to the people running the process, that the instructions are current, and that the instructions comply with the quality and contractual requirements.
2. To verify that manufacturing and quality control practices are in accordance with the established procedures.
3. To witness or perform a retest of the accepted product to assure repeatability of results. This audit should be performed annually at a minimum.

If the company does business with the government, then there are contractually imposed government specifications for special processes. These special process specifications have been established by certain industries, commercial standards associations, and engineering associations, such as the American Society for Testing and Materials, the American

Society for Nondestructive Testing, and the American National Standards Institute.

All military specificatons are listed in a publication entitled, *Index of Specifications and Standards.* Part I is alphabetical, Part II is numerical. They can be obtained by subscription. These and individual specifications may be purchased from:

The Superintendent of Documents
U.S. Government Printing Office
Washington, DC 20402

Routine Testing

However, not all products require special testing. There are many products that can be monitored routinely with common tools, such as SPC, preshipment samples, and raw material inspection. Careful analysis and planning are necessary by the buyer before implementation of any inspection plan to assure the highest degree of conformity. Process control at the supplier's facility provides the best protection, but there are many cases where some type of incoming inspection is required.

Inspection performed to assure the conformity of purchased materials, parts, assemblies, and supplies is commonly referred to as receiving inspection, incoming inspection, or purchased parts inspection. Whereas the latter clearly refers to inspection of purchased parts and assemblies only, the terms receiving inspection and incoming inspection are generally used interchangeably to refer to inspection of all incoming material. In some companies, however, incoming inspection refers strictly to inspection performed on incoming raw materials such as strip, tube, rod, chemicals, and powders for casting or molding processes, etc. This inspection usually consists of fairly simple checks with possibly some routing of samples of the material for analysis and is performed by the same personnel that does the actual receiving and handling of material. In other companies, receiving inspection means the inspection of purchased parts and assemblies that ordinarily require personnel with a considerable amount of more training. These inspections may include any or all of the usual types of checks or tests — dimensional, visual, chemical, physical, electrical, etc. — and any special ones that may be devised.

The optimum organization of a receiving inspection department will vary depending on the volume, variety or mix, complexity, number of suppliers, the quality and services supplied, as well as the scheduling requirements within the buyer's plant, and the caliber of the buyer's quality control personnel. The usual and recommended practice is to establish a central receiving inspection department separate from other inspection functions within the company. There are several reasons for this:

1. Incoming material is usually physically received at one central station in the company due to special requirements such as receiving docks, traffic arrangements, and material handling equipment.
2. Documentation and routines associated with purchased material have unique features compared to those required in other inspection areas, and must be uniform within the company.
3. Dealing with suppliers produces special and complex problems compared with those encountered within the buyer's company. These differences become increasingly important because of the trend toward supplier certification programs.

The completeness and clarity of specifications are of particular importance in the procurement activity. There seems to be no limit to how nonconformities can occur or to the questions concerning the characteristics of purchased material. Certain areas, such as visual requirements and workmanship, are of a subjective nature. These can be troublesome unless prior discussions between the buyer and supplier result in agreement upon objective standards to define requirements.

The pertinent drawings and specifications should clearly define the characteristics of the material so that the supplier fully understands what is required and what will be enforced. Specifications should be free of ambiguities that could lead to differences in interpretation by the supplier, the receiving inspector, and the designer.

Material specifications should specify end requirements that must be met. In some instances, the buyer may specify raw materials and methods of manufacture, but must then assume responsibility for results. This manner of specification excludes the supplier's technical contribution and should be avoided wherever possible.

There are some companies whose receiving inspection consists merely of checking the package contents and packing slip for agreement between the material's identification and purchase order requirements. This may be adequate depending on the type of material purchased, the buyer's subsequent manufacturing operations and inspection, the supplier's quality program, and the quality history of the supplier. Generally, the degree of inspection is directly related to the risk the buyer assumes. If a supplier has a good history of conforming materials, the risk may be low and inspection reduced. If, however, the materials are critical or complex in nature or the supplier's conformity history is substandard, 100 percent inspection may be required. These elements must be considered to yield an effective and efficient inspection program.

The most effective and economical inspection is attained through the use of statistical sampling plans. These provide the greatest assurance, over a lengthy period of time, of economically determining whether submitted material meets the buyer's quality requirements. Sampling schemes, such as MIL-STD-105D, are commonly used for this purpose. These describe systems of classifying nonconforming material as critical, major, or minor, and provide sampling plans for a wide range of acceptance criteria which might be assigned to each class of defect. This standard provides routine procedures for shifting between normal, reduced, and tightened inspection in response to the quality of lots submitted.

Initial lots shipped by a new supplier, or initial lots of material manufactured to a new design by an established supplier, are often inspected to tighter levels than shipments received after the supplier's quality level has been determined. This is known as first article inspection. It should be comprehensive in nature so as to determine conformity requirements.

In some instances, the buyer furnishes the raw material, parts, or assemblies for subsequent supplier operations or processes. It is important that the purchasing agreements establish the supplier's responsibilities to: (1) receive, inspect, account for, and store such material, (2) contact the buyer regarding disposition of any furnished nonconforming material prior to using it, and (3) determine the total cost of such material which may be unacceptable after the supplier has performed work on it.

The amount of receiving inspection required for material purchased from another division of the same company depends on the degree of centralization and uniformity of policies and quality standards that prevail within the company. This situation provides an opportunity for improved efficiency and cost savings.

The company system may use laboratories not responsible to the supplier manufacturing division to provide quality assurance to the buyer division. In some instances, the relationship may be no different from dealing with an independent and possibly unknown supplier. Material found to be conforming by receiving inspection should be so identified and promptly moved from the receiving inspection area into a storage area. This policy will help maintain physical segregation from material that has not been inspected to optimize flow for production schedules and to minimize storage space in the receiving inspection area.

Nonconforming material should be identified promptly and moved to an area separated from other material pending material review. The purpose of reviewing nonconforming material is to determine causes of nonconformity and to obtain corrective action on serious or repetitive defects. The quality control, design, engineering, or marketing departments, or a Materials Review Board may determine the disposition of nonconforming material.

Disposition may be to use as-is, screen, repair, scrap, or rework nonconforming material in the buyer's plant or to return material to the supplier for screening, rework, credit, or replacement. In the event the decision is to accept the nonconforming material, concurrence of production, engineering, and manufacturing may be obtained as required by company policy and customer specifications.

Feedback of information and samples of defects are of utmost importance to eliminate any misunderstanding on the part of the supplier and to obtain corrective action by the buyer.

Costs incurred by receiving inspection will vary depending on lot size, the number of lots, the product mix, product complexity, special laboratory test requirements, specialized gaging, test equipment, inspection methods, and skills. Continuing pressures to reduce costs tend to optimize these factors for increased efficiency.

Receiving inspection costs have traditionally been accumulated and apportioned among all products as a part of general overhead. However, the charging of receiving inspection costs directly to specific products is advantageous in determining true costs of each product, particularly when there are relatively large differences between the sales volumes, profits, and costs of the various products. The costs of collecting direct charges must be weighed against the anticipated advantages in controlling these charges.

The costs for shipping rejected material back to the supplier for screening, rework, or credit are usually billed to the supplier.

Costs of screening or reworking by the buyer to meet production schedules can usually be recovered from the supplier provided these are negotiated for in advance between the supplier and buyer. Certifications may be in the form of labeling or written statements, and may be useful in reducing receiving inspection.

The labels attached to the product or lot package are intended to be informative and can include a description of the product, various product data, instructions for its use and maintenance, and safety precautions. These may be so worded as to imply that the supplier guarantees that the product conforms to the label. Another step of labeling is certification labeling which, in addition to describing the product, bears statements attesting that the product is free from specified hazards. Certification labeling is ordinarily based upon testing done by an independent testing laboratory. For example, Underwriters Laboratories, Inc. develops and publishes standards for materials that comply to protection from fire, burglary, hazardous chemicals, etc.

Certificates of certification may come in various forms. The one which is probably most familiar is the Certificate of Measurement which is issued by standards laboratories when they calibrate instruments and gages. A number of companies have found it a wise practice to require that the supplier furnish certification of critical and major characteristics from an independent laboratory particularly when the supplier's quality history is not established or well known.

The form of certification will vary depending on the material and its critical and major characteristics. Certificates of Analysis, Certificates of Test, and Certificates of Compliance are commonly used. The buyer may find it desirable to furnish a form with blank spaces to be filled in by the supplier. Certification data required from the supplier may be in the form of characteristic frequency distributions, indicating results of the supplier's inspection of the lot shipped.

Another method is for the supplier to ship the control charts used during the manufacture of the product. This is preferred since any unnatural variation in the process can be readily observed and can be a warning of potential problems in the lot.

Supplier Certification

In some cases, companies will certify a supplier. The use of this type of certification has increased particularly as a result of the surveillance procedures of the U.S. Government. This type of certification requires contractual agreement between the supplier and buyer on:

- Classification of critical, major, and minor characteristics and the acceptable quality levels for each.
- Specifications, procedures, and inspection methods.
- Acceptance inspection plans to be used.
- Acceptance by the buyer of defective material that may be in the shipments accepted through the agreed acceptance inspection plans.
- Credit by the supplier for shipments rejected by the buyer according to the acceptance inspection plans agreed on.
- Specific inspection data furnished by the supplier with each shipment, and certification that the data are representative of the subject material and were taken according to the contractual agreements.
- Intention of the buyer to waive receiving inspection when the supplier meets requirements during a trial period, with the buyer being entitled to resume receiving inspection if the quality deteriorates.

Supplier certification is particularly advantageous when there are repeat purchases of the same material. The buyer is able to eliminate or reduce receiving inspection and, hence, lower inspection costs through the use of supplier quality data. The buyer has greater assurance that quality and delivery requirements will be met and may improve production schedules. The supplier's competitive position is improved by recognition of quality accomplishments, and the supplier has greater assurance of acceptance of shipments by the buyer.

Source Inspection

Source Inspection: Inspection by the buyer's designated representative to confirm a product's compliance to contractual obligations prior to shipment of the material. Source inspection does not necessarily eliminate receiving inspection.

Engineering Coordinated Inspection: Source inspection involving quality control and engineering. Engineering usually is responsible for technical performance, and quality control is responsible for configuration and workmanship details. This type of source inspection is used for research and development-type products of limited quantities and complex assemblies.

Preproduction Inspection: Review and inspection of first samples prior to production run approval. Preproduction inspection is not a facility survey.

Acceptance at Source: Inspection and acceptance at the supplier's facility prior to shipment to the extent that no further inspection is required at the receiving point. Billing may be accomplished after this type of inspection.

Acceptance at Destination: Inspection may be performed at the source, but final acceptance of the material will be done at the destination. This may be specified because of special requirements that can only be performed at the destination.

Preshipment Samples: A sample of product is shipped to the buyer for inspection. If the sample is acceptable, the lot is shipped to the buyer.

Table 7.1 Definitions

Source inspection has some benefits: The buyer saves money on equipment that does not have to be purchased since the supplier does the testing; the buyer utilizes the expertise of the supplier in the product the supplier is providing; and if a nonconforming product is formed, the supplier can correct the problem prior to shipment.

However, this is not without disadvantage: Source inspection places the buyer at some risk if the buyer cannot verify the supplier's quality due to a lack of equipment and personnel. The buyer needs to establish a long-term relationship with the supplier to have confidence in the supplier's capabilities.

Source inspection can take place for three types of materials or assemblies:

1. *Complete Assembly/Material.* A product which will be used without further processing or modification. The need for source inspection should be predicated on the ability of the buyer to determine, at the buyer's point of receipt, the supplier's compliance to the purchase documents, specifications, and agreements as economically and completely as necessary to establish the acceptability of the delivered material. In some instances, it is impossible to perform a meaningful evaluation without destroying the product, or at minimum, making it unfit for use by the buyer. This must be included in the cost. Some items may be of such a delicate nature that both the supplier and buyer agree that handling must be kept to a minimum and, by mutual agreement, decide that inspection at source is indicated.

Some items may be of such a complex nature requiring adjustment, calibrations, tests , or combinations of subassemblies, that it would be impossible to check them without upsetting or destroying all of the supplier's settings or impossible to check them in any manner. Here it is apparent that source inspection would be of considerable value to the buyer because of the participation by the inspector in the supplier's procedures. Some items may be of such a nature that the failure of the assembly to meet the specification could result in the loss of human life, the loss of equipment life, and the loss of governmental projects or missions (military and/or scientific), as well as endangering public health and safety. No economy can justify inspection cost-saving programs against the possible danger factor.

2. *Subassemblies/Materials.* A product that will be used in conjunction with one or more other subassemblies, components, or processes to make a deliverable product. Subassemblies would have all of the same considerations applied in determining the "why" of source inspections as do complete assemblies, plus the added requirement of compatibility and assembly feasibility with other subassemblies, components, or processes which they may be subjected to by the purchaser.

   • Would the subsequent assembly procedures affect a delicate or complex subassembly or, more importantly, the completed assembly? This could be monitored closely on the source inspector's own assembly lines by virtue of the inspector's knowledge of the subassembly acquired during source inspection.

   • A safety sensitive subassembly, in addition to the above, could also be monitored on the buyer's assembly line to assure that nothing is done in the subsequent assembly or processing that might result in an unsafe product.

3. *Components.* A part to be used in conjunction with other parts and/or subassemblies to produce other subassemblies, complete assemblies, or deliverable products. For source inspection on components, the purchaser must consider all aspects as discussed under prior sections, as well as the relative importance of the individual components to the subassembly and/or completed deliverable product. For instance, how would an individual component affect a delicate, complex, or safety-type subassembly and complete assembly in the buyer's deliverable unit? Other things to consider for component source inspection are:

   • Is the item proprietary to the supplier or buyer? Who controls the design?

   • Is the buyer requesting modifications to an existing product to fit a specific need?

- Is the supplier new? Is the market new?
- Is the component a developmental or state-of-the-art item?

Source inspection should start in the preproduction phase of procurement. At this time the inspector can evaluate the supplier's methods, procedures, processes, personnel, and preproduction sample.

In the event of differences between the supplier's samples and the specification requirements, the inspector can provide an essential function by coordinating and aiding in the resolution of differences prior to official release for production. By the end of the preproduction phase all tools, processes, procedures, drawings, and specifications will have been tried, approved, and agreed on by all parties.

During the production phase the source inspector, in addition to the normal functions of determining the acceptability of the submitted material, performs other duties essential to the successful operation of the buyer's production line.

- Constant evaluation of the supplier's performance. Under this function, in addition to the quality evaluation, the source inspector becomes aware of any and all situations that may affect the production and delivery schedule and keeps management informed.
- Coordination with the supplier of all changes to specifications or the purchase order and report on the effectivity of implementation.
- Coordination of any problems the supplier's company may have with items purchased. If the trouble is within the supplier's realm, the necessary steps should be taken to preclude their repetition.
- Release for shipment only those items the supplier finds acceptable for use as defined by the specifications, samples, or purchase order.

The choice of a source inspector is a delicate and often critical decision. The effectiveness of the source inspector depends to a large extent on the inspector's ability to obtain the fullest cooperation from the supplier, while at the same time insisting that the product meet the required specifications.

The character and personal and professional habits of the inspector are equal in importance to the inspector's knowledge of the job. The ability to absorb information, observe operations, and make discreet investigations without being obvious is essential. The inspector must also be able to gain the confidence and cooperation of the supplier's inspectors and floor supervisors without becoming so personally involved that he can no longer make an objective judgment. The ability to make firm, positive decisions is also necessary. The source inspector must therefore combine the attributes of a technician, detective, politician, diplomat, baby-sitter, and disciplinarian. The amount of technical knowledge that the source inspector would be expected to have depends, naturally, on the type of inspection being performed.

One of the most critical functions performed during source inspection is that of record keeping. Accuracy is paramount. The minimum of information that is maintained is:

- Supplier's name and address.
- Drawing number, revision, and purchase order.
- Quantity inspected.
- Quantity accepted.
- Reasons for rejection.
- Contractor's personnel contacted with regard to rejects.
- Corrective action to be taken.

In addition, any shipping papers for all source-inspected items must reference the fact that the items comprising the shipment have been inspected, tested, and/or accepted at the source by an agent of the buyer's company. This is usually accomplished by the source inspector signing or stamping the shipping papers.

Too often the source inspector, particularly if a resident at the supplier's facility, is out-of-sight and out-of-mind, which is to say, regretfully, that he has been forgotten by his own company. This is an unhappy situation, to be sure, and it is therefore imperative that the source inspector be regularly informed of events at his home company. If there is an opening for advancement, the source inspector, if eligible, should be considered. When the source inspector returns to the company for any reasonable length of time, he should not be treated as an alien, but rather made to feel welcome and an essential member of the quality control group. The source inspector must be made aware of all changes in the scope of work by the supplier as reflected in revisions to drawings and/or purchase orders. The source inspector should be invited to all supplier/buyer meetings at the supplier plant which may impact the scope of work. If unable to attend, they should be on distribution of the minutes of the meetings.

The source inspector has responsibilities to his company that must not be overlooked. These include:

1. Advising management of conditions at the supplier's plant.
2. Maintaining accurate records and assuring their availability when required.
3. Working without interfering with the supplier's production.

4. Reporting to work at hours consistent with those of the supplier.
5. Remembering at all times that he is the buyer, and in many instances the sole representative of his company, who deals with line personnel at the supplier's plant. In this capacity, he should conduct himself so that he does nothing to discredit the company.

Product Audit

There is compelling logic in the contention that an adequate and competent supplier quality system can provide valid objective evidence of the quality of product which is equal in every respect to the data the buyer might obtain by inspecting the product. Substantial inspection economies result when the responsibility for verifying and certifying the conformity of the product to its governing specifications is transferred to the supplier. Source or receiving inspection of products so certified can be substantially reduced or even eliminated. To provide a reasonable basis for relying on supplier data, periodic product audits should be performed.

Quality audits have been likened to financial audits concerned not only with the accuracy of the books and the integrity of the bookkeeper, but with the adequacy of the accounting system as well. In like manner, the quality audit checks into the adequacy of not only the product and inspector, but also the facilities, the processes, and the quality program. Four basic types of quality audit are commonly found: (1) facility audits, (2) quality program audits, (3) process audits, and (4) product audits. Similar in many respects, the four types of audits differ in emphasis and timing. All have the objective of enhancing the assurance of quality and of minimizing costs. All usually embody some aspect of corrective action to improve the quality of product or the assurance of quality. All four types of quality audits are often performed with high reliability products involved. Normally, two or more types of quality audits are combined into a single audit function.

The product audit may vary in scope and complexity from a simple validation inspection of a small sample of product to an elaborate audit. The latter consists of a planned formal review of all factors affecting the quality of a particular product and involves evaluations of the extent of conformity of the product to design intent, satisfaction in service, adequacy of engineering information, and adequacy of inspection information and workmanship. A product audit usually includes inspection and laboratory testing of the product, and may become involved in the design and manufacture of the product. Product audits thus may vary from simple reinspection of the product to in-depth evaluations which may take a year or more to complete.

Basic Issues: Product and Process Monitoring

The purpose of the validation inspection is to determine the acceptability of the product, rather than the validity of the supplier's inspection of the product. For attributes sampling, MIL-Handbook H-109 provides an excellent plan for validation inspection. When variables data are available, it is possible to select a small sample and record variables data for each characteristic measured and to statistically compare the data with that provided by the supplier. Very small samples can be used when the comparison is made on a unit-by-unit basis. Somewhat larger samples are needed when the comparison must be made using grouped data on a lot-by-lot basis.

Determination of the conformity of the design intent is accomplished by thorough review of design, manufacturing, and inspection specifications, and an evaluation of the extent to which these documents provide economical and effective tolerances, process controls, and quality levels for the achievement of the desired functionality, reliability, and quality.

The adequacy of a production service may be determined by reviewing customer complaints, observing the product in service, or by conducting laboratory tests of a product under simulated service environments.

Conformity to design and manufacturing process may be evaluated by work sampling surveys. These are audits to determine the extent to which required controls are maintained over manufacturing operations. The availability and adequacy of specifications and work instructions at the point of manufacture are reviewed; the adequacy and accuracy of tools, gages, test, and processing equipment are evaluated; and small samples of product are often inspected.

Product audits normally require extensive planning. Each audit requires painstaking engineering review of the product requirements and careful selection of the characteristics to be audited. Normally, important characteristics that cannot be checked by nondestructive methods in the final product are closely examined during a product audit. (Characteristics normally inspected are also checked.) Each audit plan is unique, and seldom is applicable to more than a single product or family of closely related proucts. Whenever a product audit reveals substantial deficiency in either the product or the manufacturing process, many types of action are required:

1. Immediate steps must be taken to protect the buyer against inadvertently accepting and using an unsatisfactory product (e.g., screening of product, recall of accepted product, or scrapping of existing stocks).
2. The cause of the deficiency must be removed to assure that future products will be satisfactory.
3. An identification of the events leading to the immediate cause of the deficiency must be made and the supplier should develop a positive program for preventing a recurrence of the breakdown of his system.

CHAPTER 8

BASIC ISSUES: SUPPLIER RATING

Key Words: Quality Information System, Data Analysis, Performance Measures, Source Selection, Recognition, Supplier Reporting

Summary:

- **Reasons for rating**
- **Objectives**
- **Data collection**
- **Elements of rating**
- **Reporting**
- **Use of rating**
- **Potential rating problems**
- **PC example**

Reasons for Rating

Supplier rating has been a basic element of comprehensive quality programs for many years. Most major corporations have developed and implemented a form of supplier rating and as the "need to know" increases, many more organizations will be creating new systems of their own.

As new programs emphasizing ship-to-stock, Manufacturing Resource Planning II (MRP II), and just-in-time are implemented, there is an ever-increasing requirement for strong discipline in purchased material control operations. Information previously not considered significant has taken on new meaning and many elements of supplier performance previously ignored are now being monitored.

Maintaining satisfactory supplier performance is essential to all who purchase goods and services; therefore, it is necessary to continuously monitor supplier activities. Data must be collected and analyzed to establish trends and identify areas requiring further action. In order to be effective, a supplier rating must be an operating function in an organization and not just another report to show, "Look what we did."

Procurement Quality Control

The basis for effective supplier rating is a quality information system that allows the retrieval and analysis of data. It is also dependent on information from other operating systems to reach beyond the basic elements of scrap, rework, and deficiency reporting.

More often than not, the requirements for a rating evolve as a quality program matures and the need for more usable information relating to purchased materials is realized. This need is reinforced by various guidelines defining the elements of comprehensive quality programs; therefore, ratings are typically in use by major organizations who have developed sophisticated quality systems.

Governmental and regulatory agencies, as well as some industry groups, define requirements for control of purchase material, and a supplier rating program can serve to document trends in performance. The Automotive Industry Action Group's *Industry Guideline for Quality Certification* is one such document that applies to organizations desiring to attain certified supplier status. The guideline simply states, ''The supplier will be responsible for assuring continuous quality improvement of materials, processes, supplies, parts, and services that are purchased for use in the supplier's products, and must establish and maintain procedures related to this responsibility.''

Although supplier rating is not mentioned, an effective rating system can be the basis for establishing and measuring supplier performance. Through planned data collection and analysis a supplier rating can be an important function in assuring that continuous quality improvement is being achieved. Supplier rating is more than just a report or a measure of past performance. It is a major operating system essential to a disciplined purchased material control program.

Federal Motor Vehicle Safety Standards, Military Standards, Good Manufacturing Practices, and other source documents also dictate that strong control of supplier operations must be maintained. An integrated supplier rating system can be a real asset in the implementation of a comprehensive supplier assurance program.

Corporate requirements are one of the most common reasons cited for establishing a rating. In many instances the edict will be general in nature and only state that suppliers are to be rated. The development and implementation of the rating is then left to the discretion of the operating staff.

This has not always been the case. The other extreme is a situation where a rating package is handed down with ''Thou Shalt Do'' instructions. The user has little or no input to this type of program and operations have a tendency to become more busy work because ''corporate said so.''

Perhaps the best reason for implementing a supplier rating is that it allows a greater awareness of achieved supplier performance. When integrated with other operating functions, a supplier rating can serve many purposes from monitoring quality costs to tracking the timeliness of incoming materials. A strong rating can provide information necessary to effect change and contribute to the profitability of your organization.

Other than contractual requirements, perhaps the most important reason for implementing a supplier rating is that it can be effectively used to optimize purchased material costs. Through analysis of past and current performance it is possible to coordinate a planned supplier improvement program to reduce defect costs and advance toward the goal of on time receipt of defect-free product.

Even if you have an operational rating, the information contained in this publication may yield some new insights and ideas for improvement. As data gathering technologies and capabilities increase, the opportunities for system upgrade must be recognized and a continued quest for improvement maintained.

A comprehensive supplier rating program will provide the information necessary to plan and achieve the discipline necessary for continuous quality improvement. The following chapters will develop the various aspects of supplier rating and describe how the concepts may be applied to strengthen your supplier assurance program.

Objectives

The customer/supplier relationships of the past that operated in an adversarial environment are quickly becoming ancient history. Cooperation and integration are key elements of maintaining good working relationships and information needs to be shared if both customer and supplier are to grow together. Years ago, a supplier rating was considered only a tool to find the bad guy, but today it takes on new meaning.

Supplier rating involves many aspects of the purchased material control function and is an important management aid in optimizing operations. Supplier rating can be developed to perform as much or as little as wanted. Those that only want a rating to satisfy a requirement will do best to reconsider in view of the positive contribution that a rating can make to increasing the effectiveness of your supplier assurance operations.

The following objectives identify what can be achieved with a supplier rating:

Information System. A supplier rating is primarily an information system that permits the analysis of data to identify opportunities to effect change. Every organization maintains records essential to the performance of operations and the supplier assurance function cannot be an exception. Data must be collected to establish a history of what has occurred so that current status may be defined and measured versus goals and objectives.

You must have sufficient, accurate, and timely information available to make sound business decisions. Having data alone, however, will not prove useful unless it can be retrieved and analyzed. A supplier rating is a formal commitment to defining the needs of a purchased material control information system.

Measure Performance. Before quality improvement can be demonstrated, it is essential to establish and document current accomplishments. Goals may then be established for the various elements of supplier performance and achievements can be measured in comparison to expectations. Some of the more commonly evaluated elements are:

- Quality
- Delivery
- Cost
- Service
- Compliance

This allows the determination of which suppliers and products are in accordance with expectations. It also facilitates the identification of those areas requiring additional study.

Trend Performance. Collection of data and an initial analysis does not yield the entire picture of supplier performance. Trending is required to provide an indicator of change either positive or negative. A supplier's performance needs to be continuously evaluated in reference to past achievements.

Trending provides the capability to identify specific areas requiring more detailed evaluation. Significant changes in performance, whether positive or negative, dictate a need for a more detailed evaluation of the applicable data. Sometimes a "zero defect" performance is not a function of outstanding achievement by the supplier, but instead is the result of a glitch in reporting. The trending function identifies change and is a key aid in planning subsequent activities.

Source Selection. This element is primarily a purchasing function and use of a supplier rating is intended to allow buyers to make more intelligent decisions when sourcing new jobs or considering present jobs for resourcing. Quoted price alone is no longer a viable means of source selection because the elements of quality, delivery, and service overshadow the initial low bid. A product that is not delivered on schedule, or is defective, is not a bargain at any price.

The ability to compare suppliers within a commodity is a valuable aid in determining which supplier has demonstrated the best performance. Where multiple sources within a commodity are capable of furnishing a new product, an effective supplier rating can be used to aid in selecting the best source.

Another consideration involving source selection is a situation in which a supplier creates chronic and repetitive problems and is unable to achieve satisfactory performance. When there is no alternative, curtailment of business is the only means of correcting this situation. In this instance, the rating can identify specific jobs where supplier performance continues to be unsatisfactory.

Recognition. It is often desirable to reward those suppliers who have achieved outstanding status. Without an effective rating it is difficult, if not impossible, to determine objectively who your outstanding suppliers are. In many instances, a supplier who is considered ''best'' may not actually be providing the best performance. Unless there is an objective basis for evaluation, a recognition award may be no more than a good will gesture.

A Supplier of the Year Award based on subjective information has far less meaning than one which originates from demonstrated performance of a defect-free product supplied on time and at a competitive price. If you have the objective information available to make that statement, you have the information required for a supplier rating.

Open and current communications are essential to sustain growth and development of the customer/supplier relationship and a supplier rating provides the basis for the exchange of information. Regardless of what means is selected to recognize the supplier, it is important that both customer and supplier have a mutual understanding of what performance is expected and what has been achieved.

Initiate Action. Not all results of a rating will show improvement and some areas will indicate a deterioration of performance. When the status quo has not been maintained or there is continuous lack of improvement, an effective rating report can serve as an indicator to initiate a more detailed evaluation of a supplier's operation. As with any function, questionable performance is worthy of investigation if acceptable performance levels have not been achieved.

When working with a rating, it will become evident that not all problems identified will be the supplier's responsibility, so it will be necessary to evaluate your information before initiating action. A rating can only identify potential areas for action, so potential involvement is required to determine what must be done.

Negative performance is generally associated with unexpected or extra costs making it important to address problem areas as soon as they are identified. Problems that continue unnoticed for a prolonged period of time can prove extremely costly to both customer and supplier; therefore, timely action is needed to minimize costs.

Where problems have been identified, a coordinated effort by both customer and supplier can be undertaken to find the source of the problem and achieve lasting corrective action. Through a mutual effort, the customer and supplier can work toward the goal of continuous quality improvement.

Plan Activities. A supplier rating can prove beneficial in planning many segments of a purchased material control program. Product and commodity areas that require special manpower or equipment considerations can be identified and both short-term and long-term planning can be performed to meet the needs.

Audit and surveillance activities are a major element of purchased material control and considerable advance planning and scheduling are required to maintain the desired coverage. Through the use of rating information, products and suppliers that require auditing can be identified and future activities can be scheduled accordingly.

Meetings with suppliers are another important element of a business relationship and periodic performance reviews are necessary to ensure that communications remain open and objective. A buyer and salesman may communicate well together, but in most instances there has to be greater depth to the vendor/vendee relationship. Performance information must be communicated beyond the sales function and a mutual understanding of current requirements and achievements must be maintained.

In this manner, supplier rating information becomes the basis for planning and conduct of meetings with suppliers. All operations can be more effectively controlled when valid and timely information is available for planning — the objective of a good working supplier rating.

Data Collection. Data collection is the heart of a supplier rating and must be timely and valid. This is your history and only the information that is saved can be used to create the needed displays and reports. The collection of data can also be one of the greatest pitfalls of a rating in that one can become a slave to entering things that have little or no value for future use. There is a difference between "need to know" and "nice to know."

Before planning your rating it is best to determine what information is already available. The most effective ratings are those that are integrated with operating systems so that special or unique entry is minimized. Keep in mind that acutal operating data should be used whenever possible and duplication of efforts should be avoided.

If you are unable to access operating files and must create a unique rating system on a minicomputer, an example of a quality information and rating system using a minicomputer is addressed later in this chapter. The data used are basically the same as discussed here, but the opportunities for reporting and analysis are no where near as great as can be achieved when using an integrated program operating off a mainframe computer.

Ratings that are dependent on exclusive information for rating purposes only, are not desirable and should be considered as a last resort. Regardless of the type of systems available, the information needed to evaluate supplier performance is common.

Initially, you may not be able to achieve the ideal of integrating systems; however, it is necesary to understand the data requirements and know where the information originates. In order to determine what information applicable to rating is available within your organization, you will have to review each function from procurement to product shipment.

Individual departments may have the necessary information, but accessibility may present opportunities for your system people. The information that is essential to a supplier rating involves other operating functions and should not be a unique quality product.

Your goal in collecting data is to get what you can free without writing or special entry if at all possible. If sufficient information is not presently retained or available, then considerations will have to be made to establish the necessary database. Just because something is not available at the time of initial review, it should not become a roadblock to the development of your rating.

While you are in the early stages of investigation and brainstorming, it is best to do your planning along functional operations. Always keep in mind that each element of work must be performed as effectively as possible. The luxury of having several quality people in an office to enter data and shuffle papers to create a rating is a thing of the past. The information used for a rating is also pertinent to running your business, so there are strong incentives for development and improvement of data collection techniques throughout your organization.

A supplier rating should not be a function unique to quality or purchasing; use data from all operational functions. Duplication of efforts should be avoided and every effort made to incorporate as much available information as possible. If there is a lack of necessary information in your systems, you will have to draw on the creativity and ingenuity of your people to implement the necessary data collection operations.

Each organization will have different methods of operation regardless of how many elements of work are common. For the purpose of this discussion, the following elements are listed as a general guide to related functions:

- Inquiry
- Purchase Order
- Product Shipment
- Invoicing
- Receipt
- Inspection
- Stores

- Further Processing
- Assembly
- Testing
- Shipment
- Service

Although each element will not apply in every case, this is a typical procurement cycle in most instances. A product or commodity is purchased, further processed, and sold to someone else. What it is, how much it costs, or how many steps are involved in processing does not enter into considerations for this discussion.

A good place to begin your quest for data is with the purchase order information. This is the document identifying what is being purchased, the quantity, units of measure, expected delivery date, and purchase price. Once the product is received, additional data are generated relating to receipt date, quantity, etc. From the purchase order and receipt, the following can be identified:

- Supplier Name
- Part Number
- Part Name
- Issue/Release
- Quantity Ordered
- Unit of Measure
- Commodity
- Product Cost
- Date Due
- Date Received
- Quantity Received
- Lot Identity
- Quality Certification Requirement
- Quantity Inspected (if applicable)
- Name of Inspector
- Acceptance Status

Following the product into further processing or use will increase the amount of data available. Work orders, operation numbers, machine numbers, operator numbers, and other possibilities can be identified as they relate to work in process:

- Work Order Number
    -Operation Number
    -Machine Number
- Added Cost of Each Operation
- Quantity Processed

- Operator Number
- Made from Part Number

As with the purchasing information, the availability and detail of operating information is contingent on your methods of operation. The workers need to know what to do and how to do it, and have the necessary materials and equipment to perform the assigned task; therefore, in-process information should also be documented. In addition, there should be sufficient cost information to identify product cost throughout the manufacturing cycle. The data essential to a comprehensive quality information system should be available within your organization.

In the event of rejection or report of nonconformance, more data are created and your deficiency reporting system becomes involved. This expands the list of applicable information to include:

- Rejection Number
- Rejection Date
- Reason Nonconformance
- Quantity Rejected
- Number of Deficiencies
- Lot Number
- Last Operation
- Responsibility
- Disposition
- Scrap
- Rework
- Return
- Use As Is
- Material Review Board (MRB) Approvals
- Added Rework Costs
- Location of Product

A deficiency reporting system is a topic in itself; however, it is another major element of your quality program essential to a rating. Control of nonconforming material is stressed in all comprehensive quality programs and a strong deficiency reporting system is essential for the documentation of activities. Other information may be available, but for rating purposes the emphasis must be made to concentrate on the needs of those who will be working with the rating.

After processing, a product is either stored, assembled with other products, or shipped to the customer. More elements enter into the availability of data and deserve consideration for inclusion in the rating. Most of these relate to rejected products:

- Part Number of Assembly
- Serial Number of Assembly
- Added Cost of Rejection
    -Repair
    -Replacement
- Quantity Used

The options are infinite and limited only by imagination and the ability to collect and save data. Source inspection results, supplier meeting commitments, and product certification data are just a few of the many things to consider when planning your rating. Additional options are discussed later in this chapter.

Unique circumstances exist where high volume, low cost items are involved and data collection guidelines have to be developed accordingly. Since the purpose of a supplier rating is to provide a working system that is meaningful to those who will use the information, you must work with others to develop a compatible system. For this reason, a detailed investigation should be made to establish the needs of the users and the involved functions of those who will be sharing the data.

Timeliness is a major consideration when planning your rating and promptness of data collection must be stressed. When feasible, on-line data entry should be considered even if it is not available at the time of rating development. Old or incomplete information negates the effectiveness of any system and multiarea operations need to be linked via modern data communications technology to ensure timely update.

As with other major systems, the implementation of a rating can also be used to upgrade and improve data collection functions of your organization. Your ultimate goal is to increase the overall effectiveness of your company operations; therefore, the rating project should not be addressed as just another quality control system, but instead as a more effective method of operating.

If new equipment is contemplated, it is best to look toward the latest developments in data collection. Use of bar coding, magnetic tape, and other information coding systems are worthy of consideration to reduce manual entry requirements and preserve the integrity of data. Every effort must be taken in the planning stages to develop a system that will prove most effective in improving overall company operations.

Elements. Unless you have been given rigid guidelines defining what must be rated, you have several options to develop the elements important to your operations. The categories generally rated are:

- Quality
- Delivery
- Cost

Each has a unique meaning to the organization performing the rating. Since most ratings are conceived by quality assurance personnel, the element of quality generally receives prominence. With the advent of sophisticated materials systems and the dependence on "on-time delivery of conforming product," the element of delivery has taken on increased importance. The "who cares" attitude of the past has been replaced by the "need to know and improve."

Since a major objective of supplier rating is to measure performance, considerations need to be made with regard to availability of data and how it can be used most effectively. Once you have established what information can be obtained, you are in a position to determine the elements that you want to evaluate. One important rule that must not be overlooked is to keep it simple.

Computers can do many things quickly, but insignificant information generated at machine speeds produces only large quantities of useless information. Keep in mind that the program you are developing must be understood and accepted by those expected to work with it. Although you, as the program creator, may think it is magnificent, this does not ensure that your buyer or supplier appreciates your efforts.

All the rhetoric in the world will not help if your facilities and technology do not permit the necessary data collection and analysis. In past years it was common for quality personnel to spend many hours collecting information and organizing it for a report. Extensive calculations were often made and much clerical effort expended before a rating was completed. Unfortunately, those luxuries do not exist in today's business and the elements you choose for your rating must provide the greatest payback.

Quality. Quality improvement and defect-free performance imply a relationship between quality and deficiencies. The absence of reported deficiencies equates with desirable quality performance so that the measure of quality is directly associated with your deficiency reporting system. Your rating can only respond to the data available, and therefore if your reporting system is incomplete or flawed, your ability to achieve an effective rating will be severely hampered.

Some of the most common measurements of quality relate rejections to receipts. Quality performance is often expressed as:

- Percent defective (parts) = Quantity rejected/quantity received
- Percent defective (lots) = Number of lots rejected/number of lots received
- PPM (parts) = Number of units rejected/number of units inspected
- DPM (defectives) = Number of defects found/number of units inspected
- Quality = Number of units accepted/number of units ordered

Statistically oriented persons may suggest that a lot rejected based on a sample is not totally nonconforming and statistical calculations must be included in a rating to achieve a valid evaluation. There are positive aspects to detail statistical analysis, but the necessity for inclusion in a rating is subject to individual preference. If you believe that you need statistics and have the system capabilities to perform the calculations, then by all means include them.

Realistically, if your objective is to identify those suppliers who are responsible for problems requiring additional action, it can be done with simple ranking techniques. If a lot is returned or scrapped based on a sample inspection, the material is no longer available to production regardless of the statistics.

Another consideration is the use of weighted ratings, where each event is assigned a factor to indicate severity. In this manner, high cost events are generally carried at full weight and less significant nuisance type items are assigned low weight values. One of the drawbacks to this type of rating is that it requires an additional judgment to assign the weight factor and then requires more complex calculations when the rating is generated.

Excessive complexity does not ensure a good working rating. Performing calculations for the sake of demonstrating technical skills has no place in the development of a good working rating. Every effort must be made to keep things in terms of understandability and usability.

Consider the things you talk about when discussing supplier performance with purchasing, management, and suppliers themselves. The elements that address the most frequently asked questions are the ones that should be included in your rating.

Delivery. Delivery rating also has several interpretations and those most meaningful to you should be considered. There may be arguments that "the buyer knows," but experience dictates that objective information is far more reliable than memory. Some of the most common delivery considerations are:

- Percent of on-time deliveries
- Percent of early deliveries
- Percent of late deliveries
- Percent of over-order quantity
- Percent of under-order quantity

As emphasis on just-in-time operations increases, there is a necessity to maintain discipline in measuring delivery performance. If your materials system provides an adequate measure of delivery performance, it may be advantageous to use that information rather than create additional data.

An important consideration when dealing with all elements of supplier performance is to be able to break the information down to specific performance by part and event. This is necessary to allow a detailed analysis of what has occurred. Telling a supplier that 13 percent of shipments during the past six months were not on schedule is only a portion of the story.

It may be that only one product was responsible for the missed deliveries, so the reporting system must allow sufficient discrimination to facilitate a detailed analysis. A good working balance between summary and detail information must be achieved in all elements to provide a basis for an effective use of rating.

Cost. Cost is an important element worthy of inclusion in a supplier rating. It is perhaps the most universally understood unit of measure. A major criterion for supplier evaluation is the cost of doing business and quality cost information becomes very meaningful when measuring supplier performance.

The ASQC Quality Cost Committee has addressed this subject in the book, *Guide for Managing Supplier Quality Cost,* edited by William O. Winchell (ASQC 1987). Since there are many considerations beyond the scope of supplier rating, this book is suggested as a reference for more details regarding supplier quality cost.

A few of the more common cost items considered in supplier ratings are:

- Dollar value of purchase
- Dollar value of nonconforming product (includes scrap, rework, return, etc.)
- Dollar purchased/dollar rejected
- Dollar debited due to rejects
- Percent recovery = Dollar debited/dollar defect costs

Each product has an established price and in most instances the customer adds value to it. In the event of nonconformance, there are additional unanticipated costs that even further escalate the product cost. The costs of scrap, rework, return, and other associated quality costs provide a significant measure of supplier performance when compared to the cost of purchases.

Some may argue that cost information is only of interest to the accountants, but in reality, quality cost is an important element of management. All kinds of calculations can be made regarding the quality of material, but the bottom line question is, "What did it cost?"

Compliance. This element of supplier rating is more related to quality records and supplier reporting of quality information. Once again, each organization is going to have its own interpretation of what this element means. There is no common definition. It is necessary to know if and when purchased material must be accompanied by quality certification and a supplier's compliance with requirements is another element that can be measured.

Combining this element with other receiving data it is possible to develop a comprehensive overview of each receipt of purchased material. Increased emphasis is being placed on "ship-to-stock" and similar programs so there is a need to monitor the supplier's compliance with requirements beyond part number, quantity received, and date due.

Subjective Rating. The elements previously discussed are all considered objective since the information all relates to specific parts, events, requirements, etc. The applicable data would normally be obtained from current accounting, materials, and quality records. This adds credibility to the reporting as data will be consistent with operating records.

In addition to objective information, there are also subjective rating elements that may be considered. Ratings that take in to account service and supplier response are often used when quantitative information is not available. Examples of several subjective elements are:

- Supplier technical assistance
- Supplier response to schedule changes
- Supplier conformance to instructions
- Supplier service functions
- Supplier price quoting

Although meaningful to those who use them, subjective ratings generally require specific and unique data collection and do not always present a true measure of performance. Most are based on questionnaires that are completed from memory and serve to identify those suppliers who are best to work with. This is an important consideration, but nowhere near as meaningful as those elements based on objective information.

Other Elements. In addition to the previously discussed elements, many organizations find it beneficial to include data from their supplier quality surveys, source inspections, and other supplier-related activities. The need for comprehensive data collection becomes more evident as a purchased material control program matures. All of the above items are essential to the maintenance of a supplier qualification or certification program.

A well-planned supplier rating system can serve many purposes beyond providing the ability to rank suppliers. All elements of your supplier assurance program need to be considered when developing your rating, and plans must stress increasing operational effectiveness, not just adding a new report.

Reporting

Once the database has been established, considerations must be directed toward the type of output desired. In past years, everyone wanted a copy of a report so that they would have a piece of paper as recognition of their involvement. Many supplier ratings of the past evolved into gigantic paper mills as new report formats were generated on multipart paper. Selective retrieval of information was not commonly practiced and routine printouts were the prime method of obtaining information.

The printout still remains the most common means of data presentation, but consideration must be given to terminal display and use of microfiche. Printed reports should be kept to a minimum and as much of the rating information as possible should be obtained by terminal review and selective printing of retrieved information on a need-to-know basis. Historical information for reference purposes can be effectively retained on microfiche.

Some reports must still be generated on a regular basis; however, greater use of terminal retrieval will significantly cut down on the number of old and forgotten printouts that will have to be thrown away. Every effort must be made to optimize the effectiveness of your reporting.

The desired report format needs to be preplanned and different uses require different methods of presentation. Several summary levels should be considered based on the needs of the recipient. As an example, a management level report summarizing overall performance would not include the same amount of detail as would meeting with a supplier to review individual part performance.

As with most reporting structures, the higher the level, the less detail. When run on a mainframe computer, a lot of rating summaries are easily obtained; however, as with all operations, the cost of information generation has to be justified. Many different reports and formats can be created, but their utility has to be weighed versus their contribution to the success of the enterprise. In short if the report is not really needed, don't run it.

An important consideration when programming a new rating is to allow flexibility in retrieval of information. Being locked in to the routine monthly or quarterly reports should be avoided except where necessary to provide summary and trend information. Where detail information is involved it is often necessary to have up-to-date information which covers a different report period than routine reports.

In order to provide flexibility, it is suggested that a request/retrieval system is established where a report format can be selected and information obtained for a specified report period. This is primarily beneficial when conducting a detailed review of supplier performance, or investigating chronic and repetitive problems.

Some examples of working supplier rating reports are illustrated in Examples A through D.

Procurement Quality Control

Example A
- Summary of supplier performance
  - -Identifying suppliers requiring detail review
  - -Trending supplier performance

Example B
- Summary by commodity
  - -Comparing suppliers within commodity
  - -Identifying commodities requiring action
  - -Providing information to aid in source selection

Example C
- Summary by buyer
  - -Ranking suppliers within responsibility

Example D
- Detail supplier performance
  - -Identifying specific products requiring action

In addition to the major summary reports, there are many options for management reporting that can be developed for internal use. Everything need not be computer-generated and a combination of manual reporting and computerized reporting can be combined to report trends and accomplishments.

The emphasis on management reporting is generally placed on the economic factors of supplier performance. Several typical elements of management reporting are:

- Total supplier responsibility defect cost
- Total dollar value of purchased material
- Percent defect cost to dollar value purchased
- Total defect cost debited to suppliers (recovery)
- Percent defect cost recovered
- Number of lots received
- Number of lots inspected
- Number of lots rejected
- Number of supplier detail performance meetings
- Trends of defect cost and recovery
- Corrective action activity

As with other elements, your reporting must be developed to best utilize the available information. There is no best or only format so you will have to do some brainstorming with your personnel to determine their information needs. In addition to your own thinking, ideas can be obtained from rating reports that your customers use to measure your

"AVAILABLE S.I.C. REPORT"

DEFICIENCY REPORTS
SUMMARY SUPPLIER PERFORMANCE BY PART
07/01/79 THRU 07/10/80

(PART W/IN COMMODITY CODE W/IN VENDOR W/IN B/E)

PREPARATION DATE 01/22/80   PROGRAM HI80308H
REPORT HI80308R

CLASS	QUALITY 0/0 REJ.	DELIVERY 0/0 LATE	S.I.C.
A	.0 – .4	.0 – 4.9	.0 – .9
B	.5 – 1.4	5.0 – 9.9	1.0 – 2.9
C	1.5 – 3.4	10.0 – 17.9	3.0 – 5.9
D	3.5 – 7.9	18.0 – 29.9	6.0 – 9.9
E	8.0 – UP	30.0 – UP	10.0 – UP

(*SIGNIFIES NOT RATED)

PAGE 1
BUYER 60

PART NO.	PART NAME	QTY RECVD	QTY REJ	0/0 REJ	PURCH PRICE	STD COST	PRICE EACH	DEL	LATE	SIC	QDC	DEFECT COST	RECOVERY
VENDOR 123456A FANTASTIC CASTINGS													
COMMODITY 0846 CASTINGS, DUCTILE ACS5588													
0099003201	SUPPORT	435	249	57.2	6,137.85	14.11	16.02	6	100.0	13.6	E E E	834.06	537.21
TOTAL THIS COMMODITY		435	249	57.2	6,137.85			6	100.0	13.5	E E E	834.06	537.21
VENDOR 123456A FANTASTIC CASTINGS													
COMMODITY 0849 CASTINGS, DUCTILE ACS577B										BUYER 60			
0090681651	LOCK	179		.0	5,289.45	29.55	29.55		.0	.0	A * A		
0090681680	YOKE	616		.0	22,514.80	36.55	36.55	2	100.0	.0	AEA		
TOTAL THIS COMMODITY		795		.0	27,804.25			2	100.0	.0	AEA		
VENDOR 123456A FANTASTIC CASTINGS													
COMMODITY 0863 CASTINGS, GRAY ACS585										BUYER 60			
0099003199	SUPPORTCST	210	1	.5	3,299.10	15.71	15.82	2	100.0	.7	BEA	24.50	15.45
TOTAL THIS COMMODITY		210	1	.5	3,299.10			2	100.0	.7	BEA	24.50	15.45
VENDOR GRAND TOTAL		1,440	250	17.4	37,241.20			10	100.0	2.3	E E E	858.56	552.66

This report identifies all activity assignable to the applicable vendor code which is the responsibility of the buyer indicated at the top of the report. The part numbers listed are those purchased from the supplier even though the rejection may be written for a part made from the actual part number purchased. The computer carries the "made from" information and the rejection tag also has provision for indicating the defective component part number. In this case 250 parts were rejected for a defect cost of $858.56. By referring to the T.I.S. Detail report it is possible to see the specific rejections that were reported during the review period. This allows the supplier to see not only the quantity and cost, but the reasons for rejection.

Example A

"S.I.C. SUMMARY BY COMMODITY"

DEFICIENCY REPORTS
SUMMARY SUPPLIER PERFORMANCE WITHIN COMMODITY CODE
07/01/79 THRU 01/10/80
SEQ BY VENDOR W/1 DESCENDING SIC W/1 COMMODITY CODE
(*SIGNIFIES NOT RATED)

COMMODITY CODE 849 NAME-CASTINGS, DUCTILE ACS5778

PROGRAM H180308I
REPORT H180308M

DATE 01/19/80
PAGE 170

CLASS / QUALITY PERC DEFECT: A .0–.4, B .5–1.4, C 1.5–3.4, D 3.5–7.9, E 8.0–UP
DELIVERY AVE LATE: .0–4.9, 5.0–9.9, 10.0–17.9, 18.0–29.9, 30.0–UP
S.I.C.: .0–.9, 1.0–2.9, 3.0–5.9, 6.0–9.9, 10.0–UP

RANK	SUPPLIER NAME	VENDOR	QTY RECD	QTY REJ	O/O REJ	PURCH PRICE	DEFECT COST	RECOVERY	CLASS	DEL	LATE	SIC	ODC
1			60	275	458.3	3,894.60	890.92	3,291.44	A		.0	22.9	E*E
2			145	21	14.4	18,070.04	1,829.43	1,670.13	B	2	100.0	10.1	EEE
3			406	14	3.4	14,637.77	1,141.76	353.24	C	6	83.3	7.8	CED
4			497	17	3.4	6,193.68	443.87	499.85	C	2	100.0	5.4	CEC
5	FANTASTIC CASTINGS	123456A	795		.0	27,804.25			D	2	100.0	.0	AEA
6			100		.0	25,958.00				3	66.7	.0	AEA
7			929		.0	1,690.78				2	50.0	.0	AEA
	COMMODITY TOTAL		2,933	327	11.1	100,249.12	4,305.98	5,814.66		17	82.4	4.3	EEC

Example B

"S.I.C. SUMMARY BY BUYER/EXPEDITER"

DEFICIENCY REPORTS
SUMMARY SUPPLIER PERFORMANCE BY BUYER
07/01/79 THRU 01/10/80
(VENDOR W/IN VENDOR SIC W/IN B/E SIC W/IN BUYER SIC)
(*SIGNIFIES NOT RATED)

PROGRAM H180308V
REPORT H180308P

DATE 01/22/80
PAGE 20

CLASS / QUALITY PERC DEFECT: A .0–.4, B .5–1.4, C 1.5–3.4, D 3.5–7.9, E 8.0–UP
DELIVERY AVE LATE: .0–4.9, 5.0–9.9, 10.0–17.9, 18.0–29.9, 30.0–UP
S.I.C.: .0–.9, 1.0–2.9, 3.0–5.9, 6.0–9.9, 10.0–UP

BE	VENDOR	VENDOR NAME	QTY RECD	QTY REJ	O/O REJ	PURCH PRICE	DEFECT COST	RECOVERY	CLASS	DEL	LATE	SIC	ODC
6		***** BUYER TOTAL *****	681,440	18,993	2.7	19,138,778.94	257,998.97	279,211.40		2,085	75.9	1.3	CEB
60		*BUYER/EXPEDITER TOTAL*	93,275	3,370	3.6	1,526,663.95	44,319.89	40,356.86		359	78.6	2.9	DEB
			260	113	43.5	4,263.97	939.93	618.92	A	4	50.0	22.0	EEE
			25	7	28.0	12,013.50	1,625.23	1,617.63			.0	12.7	EAE
			2,704	161	6.0	139,534.65	13,744.73	11,098.10		21	76.2	9.9	DED
			6,967	73	1.0	52,036.53	4,675.23	3,428.15		6	66.7	9.0	BED
			15,537	258	1.7	59,422.11	4,038.62	3,086.38		19	84.2	6.8	CED
			3,594	621	17.3	37,294.85	2,324.58	1,034.16		13	84.6	6.2	EED
			1,093	10	.9	22,843.63	879.67	362.54		13	80.0	3.9	BEC
			928	280	30.2	42,288.94	1,324.20	3,517.97		6	100.0	3.1	EEC
	123456A	FANTASTIC CASTINGS	1,440	250	17.4	37,241.20	858.56	552.66		10	100.0	2.3	EEB

Example C

PROGRAM H180308P
REPORT H180408H

RUN DATE 07/19/80
TIME 08.5408

DEFICIENCY REPORTS
SUPPLIER RESPONSIBILITY REJECTS FOR 07/01/79 THRU 01/10/80
(PART W/I VENDOR W/I BUYER/EXPEDITER)

VENDOR COMP	PART NO COMP	PART NAME S/N UNIT	MADE FROM S/N	QTY	DR NO MATERIAL	DATE	DEPT OPER LAB/BURD	DEFICIENCY DESCRIPTION ADDED MATERIAL ADDED LAB/BURD	DISP	TOTAL	PROV D^2
123456A FANTASTIC CASTINGS											
						BUYER/EXPEDITER = 60					
	0079003199	SUPPORT	0099003199	1	215648	11/13/79 15.20	2312 014 9.30	POROSITY IN 126 MM BORE .00 .00	V	24.50	000000
	0079003201	SUPPORT	0099003201	7	215509	10/30/79 99.42	2312 017 92.77	POROSITY IN BORES .00 .00	V	192.19	000000
	0079003201	SUPPORT	0099003201	1	214793	10/05/79 14.20	2312 010 11.80	POROSITY IN BORE .00 .00	V	26.00	000000
	0079003201	SUPPORT	0099003201	232	215907	11/19/79 .00	2312 040 .00	COVE SAND INSIDE CASTINGS .00 109.42	W	109.42	000000
	0079003201	SUPPORT	0099003201	1	216878	12/12/79 14.20	2312 050 43.35	HOLE THRU CASTING .00 .00	V	57.55	000000
	0079003201	SUPPORT	0099003201	2	216226	11/29/79 28.40	2312 040 80.94	POROSITY IN DR HOLES .00 .00	V	109.34	000000
	0079003201	SUPPORT	0099003201	2	210598	06/22/79 28.40	2312 0400 80.94	POROSITY IN 22.020MM COUNTERSINK .00 .00	V	109.34	000000
	0079003201	SUPPORT	0099003201	1	211547	07/26/79 14.20	2336 F 43.35	POROSITY IN BORE 22.020 MM .00 .00	V	57.55	000000
	0079003201	SUPPORT	0099003201	3	214532	09/28/79 42.61	2312 041 130.06	PORC 'N REAM HOLES .00 .00	V	172.67	000000
	TOTAL FOR SUPPLIER			250		256.63	432.51	.00 109.42		858.56	

"T.I.S. DETAIL REPORT"

This report is used to supplement the S.I.C. Mailable in order to identify specific rejections. The DR number is the reject tag number and is used in all transactions regarding rejected parts. A copy of the DR is attached with the material it covers and serves to identify the details of the rejection. The original copy of the rejection is sent to Keypunch for adding the balance of information not entered at the CRT terminal where the part was rejected. In this manner it is possible to have immediate data entry for early identification of the rejection combined with added detail essential for subsequent analysis. This is the buyer/expediter format which facilitates sorting and use by Purchasing. A separate "supplier total" or specialized extract report is used by Supplier Assurance for defect cost reviews and corrective action meetings with suppliers. The normal time frame for this report is six months; however, any active file period may be reviewed by submitting the applicable control card code request. When meetings are held on a repetitive basis with a supplier it is common to use reports which pick up from the point that the last report stopped so that only new information is reported. The previous report is also used where unresolved problems are still being investigated. This avoids duplication of efforts and directs action to current problems.

Example D

71

performance. Regardless of origin, all worthwhile suggestions for building your own information system should be considered.

Development of a supplier rating is a cut-and-try process and the initial report generation and usage will no doubt yield some surprises. Experience with a system is the only way to determine whether or not it provides the information required. It is not uncommon for supplier rating programs to be updated as experience is obtained. Define your initial report formats, use them, and then upgrade as necessary to take advantage of systems and technology advancements.

Use of Rating

After the planning stages of your rating are completed, it is important to document what has been done and how the functions are to be performed. Even though a lot of the rating will be developed around information obtained from users and supporting functions, a comprehensive training program needs to be established. All involved persons will need a common understanding of the rating functions and how the program is to be used.

Even in smaller operations, it is essential to have a user's manual available explaining what the rating capabilities are and how operations are performed. Persons who will work with the rating need to be trained so that they will have a working knowledge of what and how things can be done. It is also essential that documentation remain up-to-date so that new persons can be trained when they too become involved with the rating.

Consideration also needs to be directed to information required for use with suppliers. Many initial supplier notifications of the rating will be done by mail so an understandable explanation of the rating needs to be prepared for submittal to suppliers. However, the ideal method of introduction is through a face-to-face meeting in which the rating can be explained and specific questions answered. Unfortunately, in today's business, this is not always feasible and many communications will have to be handled by mail or telephone.

Lack of familiarity or a negative outlook about your rating on the part of the persons attempting to answer questions about it can create many roadblocks to future use. To facilitate positive motivation, persons who are well versed in the rating should be designated as contacts for information, and all questions should be directed to them. When someone who knows little more than you do attempts to explain a subject you want to learn about, the result is usually a turnoff and something to avoid when introducing a new system.

The initial generation of the rating needs to be complete so that all the elements can be verified as operational. Even if everything worked properly during the software development and trial runs, the initial report still needs to be scrutinized in detail to assure that all the information is presented as desired and that all functions work. As with all system start-ups, the rating needs to be qualified before release to those who will work with it.

After the system is confirmed operational and everything is found to be as desired, what do you do next? The rating reports have been run and are ready for distribution and use. Everything is documented in the applicable procedures manual and user instructions so it should be a simple matter of doing it by the book.

Your initial runs are no time to compromise and your documentation of instructions is your guideline for performing the rating. If undocumented changes and variations are made when implementing the initial rating there is a strong potential for future problems. Some typical uses of a rating are discussed later in this chapter.

Performance Evaluation — Ranking. This element is performed in various stages and generally begins with an evaluation of overall supplier activity for the review period. It is advisable to establish a common time frame for this review that will provide both current and some historical information. Supplier performance should be ranked in terms of the category most important to you, with the supplier having the greatest potential for improvement ranked number one. The following is an example of this:

Report Generation: Monthly
Review Period: Current — two months
Historical — six months
Category: Supplier responsibility
Defect costs

This report can be used to identify suppliers that have been high-defect cost contributors during the current review period. Since only the past two months are covered in the current activity segment, a supplier will not be listed in the upper ranking for something that happened before the current review period.

One common problem arises from ratings that work on a long review period, such as a 12-month report. In this case, a supplier can continue to appear as one of the top contributors due to an isolated problem long after corrective action has been taken. When attempting to identify areas for further action it is best to work primarily with current information.

A supplier who is responsible for chronic and repetitive problems will generally remain in a place of prominence on a current rating report, whereas one who improves will soon be removed from the list. (Hint: When running a report used to find potential areas for improvement do not print information for those suppliers with "zero" contribution.)

Another method of reducing the volume of a report is to selectively report activity for those suppliers who contribute in excess of a predetermined amount. In the event of dollar measurement, it would be feasible to list only those suppliers who were responsible for defect costs over $200.

Whatever category is chosen for the ranking, it is the purpose of this evaluation to pinpoint areas requiring additonal action. Detail information is best omitted from the summary ranking to reduce paperwork and optimize the usability of the report.

Action Planning. Once the potential areas for improvement have been identified by the summary report or ranking, a more detailed analysis must be performed. The summary has told you which suppliers require a more detailed evaluation, and additional information is required to determine which parts and problems were involved. This is where data retrieval comes into use. Rather than generate detail information for all suppliers at the time of rating, it is best to obtain only that information required for further analysis.

As previously mentioned, a flexible data retrieval system is the most effective method to obtain information, and you will not be locked in to a fixed review period or other undesirable constraints. This is especially important when preparing for supplier meetings where it may be beneficial to have all information applicable to that supplier rather than be restricted to a specific review period.

To determine if action is required, the detail information for the supplier in question must be evaluated. This can be in the form of terminal review, printout, microfiche, or whatever means of data presentation you have available. The detail level of your rating should identify all activity that transpired during the review period so a determination can be made as to what was responsible for inclusion in the summary. At this point, the computer has done its work and the analysis by the user must be done.

What was responsible for ranking? Did one lot create the problem? Was it a series of unrelated events? What action can be taken to prevent recurrence of these problems? All these questions need to be asked and action initiated where applicable. In many instances the situation will already have been resolved and no further action will be required; however, it is often necessary to plan special quality audits or meetings with suppliers.

Meeting with Suppliers. Your rating system will open new channels of communication with your suppliers and provide a means to achieve a better understanding of mutual needs. When the need for special action with a supplier is indicated by your rating, you must collect the applicable detail information and make it available to the supplier so that preparations for a meeting can be made.

74

Basic Issues: Supplier Rating

Just as you performed your analysis to determine that action was needed, the supplier must have the details to perform an investigation and prepare an action plan. Supplier rating is not a game of, "Surprise — lookie what I found!" Both you and your supplier must work together and share information and technology to prevent recurrence of observed problems.

If this is to be the first product improvement meeting with a supplier it is often advantageous to work with an open file detail report. In this manner, all retrievable information can be reviewed rather than just the most recent information. The reason for this is that it will permit a broader review of past performance which will highlight the newly identified problem areas.

Where prior meetings have been held with a supplier, the circumstances are different and the most effective report is one that covers the time frame from the date of last review to present. Previous meeting information is essential for documentation of past findings and action, but up-to-date information is needed to identify current problems.

After adequate preparation by both parties, a face-to-face meeting with the supplier is the most effective means of establishing a mutual understanding of the reported problems. Each product and deficiency should be discussed and the results of applicable investigations and action documented. Not all problems will be the supplier's responsibility, and a strong rapport with the supplier is needed to work toward effective resolution of the deficiencies.

It is important to document the results of your discussions and, where feasible, follow up in the manufacturing areas to observe the changes and improvements that have been reported. An effective review meeting is a classic "show and tell" function rather than a front office exchange of reports. The paperwork is necessary to guide your meeting and document findings and commitments, but should be supplemented by review of the applicable products and processes.

In some instances, a detailed review with the supplier will reveal that revision of product design and specifications can improve producibility and significantly reduce quality costs. The combination of your rating information and supplier analysis and proposals can then be presented to engineering for consideration of design change.

Objective information is needed to make valid and timely decisions, and with a good quality information system you will be able to show cause for action. A call to engineering that says, "Charlie can't hold the 6.250 +/− .002 dimension. We need to open the tolerance;" will probably fall on deaf ears.

Instead, if you can present objective information illustrating the observed problems along with statistical process information from the supplier, your chances of securing technical assistance are much greater. The supplier assurance function is no different than any other phase of

75

your operations. Objective information is needed to make good business decisions.

Even though you performed a supplier survey and representatives from the supplier sales group call at your facility, the product improvement meetings open new avenues of communication and further bond the customer/supplier relationship. It is necessary to establish and maintain a good working relationship with your suppliers and during the product improvement meetings it is feasible to achieve a better understanding of each other's needs.

Product and Process Audits. In many instances it will become necessary to perform special audits to learn more about observed problems. These audits may range from piece part inspections up to and including detail process audits at the supplier facility. In either situation, they are functions above and beyond routing operations and require the allocation of added resources.

People, parts, and equipment will have to be coordinated as needed to facilitate a thorough problem analysis. Even if a problem is the supplier's responsibility, there has to be involvement beyond collecting parts and sending them back. In today's business, the customer and supplier must work together to minimize the impact of reported problems.

Special quantity planning may be required for control of interim shipments until lasting problem resolution is achieved. Some typical examples of special planning are the imposition of stringent supplier control and certification requirements, unique product identification, and tightened incoming inspection requirements. Audit and surveillance of supplier operations can also prove beneficial during the improvement cycle.

Many things can be done in the pursuit of excellence, but there has to be a justification for actions. Your supplier rating will identify potential areas for action, but you, the quality professional, will have to exercise sound judgment in deciding how the information is to be used. Not all reported problems need to be fixed, so priorities need to be established for optimum use of manpower and resources.

In some instances, neither you nor your supplier will have the capabilities to perform all the functions needed for analysis, and added contract work may be required. What began as a basic evaluation of supplier performance can develop into a comprehensive supplier assurance program. If no action originates from a supplier rating, then there really isn't much of a reason to have one.

Corrective Action Program. The supplier rating identifies problem areas and then becomes the responsibility of the supplier assurance function to use the information for improvement. As in any action-oriented program, the purpose of your rating is to effect change. When a rating is used as an operating quality information system, it can be far more beneficial than the ratings of the past that primarily compared suppliers to one another.

Not all problem areas warrant a meeting with the supplier or implementation of special action. Many, however, are significant enough to justify a request for problem investigation and report of corrective action. Suppliers must be kept informed of problems and a working corrective action system can be administered using data collected through your quality information system.

The corrective action request (CAR) is common to many quality programs and some organizations use the same form for both internal and supplier responsibility problems. The basic information relating to the problem is entered by the customer and the form is then mailed to the supplier for completion.

The objective is for the supplier to perform an investigation, describe the findings, and then relate what action has been taken to correct the problem. This is no different than what is expected during product improvement meetings with suppliers. The one exception is that the CAR is impersonal and frequently is considered more of a nuisance than anything else.

Unfortunately there is a tendency on the part of some suppliers to respond that the parts were sorted, the defectives repaired or scrapped, and the lot was returned. Corrective action told the operator, "Be more watchful next time you run these." There is a place for the CAR, but in many cases the administration of the program outweighs its benefits.

Although simple in concept, a CAR program can often create work that involves numerous people. A typical routine for a supplier CAR is listed as follows:

- Deficiency identified
- CAR written
- CAR logged in suspense file
- CAR sent to purchasing for mailing
- CAR mailed to supplier
- CAR received by supplier inside sales
- CAR delivered to supplier quality control
- CAR investigated by supplier quality control
- CAR form completed by supplier quality control
- CAR mailed back to purchasing
- CAR forwarded to originator
- CAR suspense file cleared

This may not be typical of all CAR programs, but unfortunately it describes many involvements that are common to many of them. The complexity increases when there is a delay in response and a follow-up mechanism is brought in to effect. More paper begins to move, telephones begin to ring, and a simple document can turn into a logistics nightmare.

It is necessary to have documentation of investigations and corrective action results, but the method by which the information is obtained needs to be well-thought-out to minimize unnecessary involvement. Open channels of communication between customer and supplier quality functions need to be maintained as effectively as possible.

Supplier Recognition. Current business trends are dictating the development of stronger customer/supplier relationships, and there is increased importance placed on continued quality improvement. It becomes necessary to demonstrate achieved performance, and an effective rating program is one means of documenting a supplier's accomplishments.

A supplier who has performed all the required functions to assure control of operations and has achieved Certified Supplier status will seldom be included in problem listings. Suppliers who have not been responsible for significant problems must also be evaluated, and it is important to monitor overall performance.

Comprehensive recognition programs generally include detailed audits of supplier quality programs and operating processes in addition to quality performance information. A supplier must not only supply defect-free parts on time, but in addition, must also demonstrate operational controls essential to assuring continued satisfactory performance.

Some sophisticated ratings incorporate the ability to combine audit results with achieved performance in a common report. This overall rating then is used to evaluate suppliers who previously achieved certified status or those suppliers who are candidates for certified status.

Most ratings, however, are applicable only to operating systems and an overall performance factor must be developed by combining audit results with achieved performance in an overall summary. Quality, delivery, cost, and systems capability must be combined to identify the outstanding suppliers. By maintaining common guidelines for evaluation, it is then feasible to document accomplishments and trend performance periodically.

Suppliers who continually demonstrate outstanding overall performance can then be identified for special recognition. This function of a rating is desirable for the promotion of good will, but is generally too complex for most organizations to undertake because of the support requirements. If the capabilities exist within your operation to perform an overall evaluation, then by all means do it.

The more you know about a supplier's capabilities and performance, the better able you will be to make sound business decisions. Lessons learned in the correction of today's problems can often be used in tomorrow's preventive planning. Fighting the same fires day in and day out is not profitable for either customer or supplier, and an effective quality information system and supplier rating can help reduce nonproductive effort.

Potential Rating Problems

This chapter is not intended as a scare tactic, but as an alert to some of the pitfalls that users of ratings have experienced. Everything will not always work as expected and not all persons will agree on how things are to be done, so you will have to judge for yourself and plan to prevent as many problems as possible. The following discussion will illustrate a few of the more common roadblocks to understanding and acceptance of a supplier rating.

The majority of problems to be discussed relate to existing ratings and were identified by involved members of the ASQC Vendor-Vendee Technical Committee. By being aware of these potential problem areas, you can plan avoidance when developing your own program. Many of these elements are interrelated and they tend to propogate with time if not addressed when they are first encountered.

System not Documented. This is a ground zero point and is frequently overlooked by those in a hurry to implement a new program. It is most common in smaller operations where the one or two persons involved in the project do not recognize an immediate need for documentation. Defining the system operations will be deferred until the initial bugs are worked out of the system.

Training is generally done by word-of-mouth and initially there is significant activity to use the rating. As long as operations continue satisfactorily, everything is believed to be under control until key personnel either leave or new persons are brought into the system.

"Charlie used to take care of that, and nobody else knows what it is all about" becomes a familiar phrase when Charlie is no longer available to baby-sit the rating. Suddenly, no one knows what the rating is all about and the program grinds to a standstill due to lack of knowledge and understanding.

Even basic elements such as data entry must be documented in detail so that someone can operate the system at times when assigned personnel are not available. It is necessary to maintain complete user documentation as well as systems documentation. When special programming is done to implement a rating, there should be complete and detailed systems information on record.

Supplier rating is no place to build a secret empire if the program is to remain operational. Total dependence on one or two people who have all the information in their heads is contradictory to the basics of sound operating systems. Instructions, guidelines, responsibilities, and procedures need to be documented and kept up-to-date.

An important item not to be overlooked when programming your own rating is the inclusion of "HELP" screens in the program. It is far more advantageous to have necessary instructions and information available by simply recalling a help screen. Make your system as simple and user-friendly as you can to optimize operating effectiveness.

Cluttered Reports. The format in which information is presented plays an important role in determining the usability of a report. Care must be taken to structure your reports for readability and ease of use. Your supplier rating is not the place to present all the information that has been accumulated.

There is no reward for using every available space on a printed page, and in many cases the understandability of a report will be impaired by too much information. Column placement, spacing, and report format are key elements to be considered when planning your rating. Excessive spacing also can be a problem. Reports with too much open area between entries can prove difficult to use. Trial formats need to be established and test runs made before finalizing the working reports. Similar considerations need to be applied when planning data entry. Clutter is not restricted to printed reports and terminal displays also must be designed for ease of use. Excessive use of instructions and unrelated placement of items on the screen can create entry problems.

Database Maintenance. In the quest to collect and save every tidbit of information there is often a tendency to require a significant amount of unique data to be collected for rating purposes alone. When programs of this nature are created, the data entry functions are often delegated to involved functions as a supplement to existing operations. This is generally satisfactory as long as there is available personnel; but when things get tight, there is a reluctance to continue the service.

Complex data entry is another potential problem area and every effort should be made to simplify this operation. Data entry will be the most frequently used element of your rating program and every effort must be made to make the operation simple and straightforward. Considerations need to be made regarding the information sources and logical entry sequences must be planned.

Credibility of data must be maintained and a good balance of program edits must be used to prevent the entry of totally erroneous information. On the other hand, edits must not be overly restrictive as to withhold everything on error lists, etc. Controls need to be in place to assure that erroneous information can be identified and purged from the system. Checks and balances need to be built into the system, but not to the point that the system ceases to function.

As stressed in other chapters, as much information as possible should be obtained from operating systems to minimize the unique entry for supplier rating. If other systems are not accessible and a unique program must be developed, the following chapter on mini-rating will provide more insight into creation of a quality information system.

Basic Issues: Supplier Rating

Timeliness. Being locked in to a quarterly report is one example where the frequency of report generation does not allow for timely monitoring of vendor performance. Problems are compounded when data collection is slow and incomplete. The effectiveness of your rating is directly related to the timeliness and completeness of the data.

In many instances a problem may recur a number of times before adequate data are collected and information is reported. Information should not be saved until every block on the form is filled in and guidelines need to be established to achieve prompt data entry. To be meaningful, the timeliness of rating information must be monitored and every effort made to expedite this function.

Lack of Discrimination. Ratings that are too general in nature are not effective in identifying areas for action. When only summary-type information is available, problems are often not identified by the rating. As with the situation of too much information, the effectiveness of your program can be impaired by too little information.

Other problems can be created when supplier identity cannot be associated with the product. This is especially meaningful when there are several sources for an item and the identity is lost during processing.

In many instances, data collection capability does not go beyond initial receipt and in-process information cannot be included in the rating. Due to the lack of available information and the inability to identify responsible suppliers, some ratings are unable to present a true measure of supplier performance.

Operational Problems. Implementation and maintenance of a supplier rating has to be an integrated effort within an organization. Operating departments need to be aware of each other's needs and share as much information as possible. Major system changes that no longer provide previously shared information can virtually destroy other programs. Thus, a continued awareness of overall operations must be maintained.

It is essential that quality maintain an open dialog with systems personnel and other functions in order to develop and preserve operating programs. As stated previously, supplier rating is a working program for continuous quality improvement and not just another report.

Excessively complex or diversified ratings are just another potential problem which relates to too much information. Many "ideal" programs have become victims of excessive run time and an over abundance of information. When your rating report is delivered by the box, you know that you have overstepped the bounds of utility.

Management Support. Perhaps the most detrimental factor in the development and implementation of a supplier rating is the lack of management commitment to the project. The need for a rating may be acknowledged and authorization provided to proceed, but beyond that, the program only receives lip service. In this instance a rating program is seldom accepted by others and, although tolerated, is not used productively.

Another instance of management not providing total support relates to a situation where systems people are instructed to create a rating program without involvement of the quality function. A significant amount of supplier performance relates directly to the materials function, but without the inclusion of applicable quality information, a rating cannot be complete.

In both situations, management support plays a major role in the acceptance and use of the rating. If there is a true management commitment to developing a supplier rating, there has to be recognition of the need and allocation of resources. You will require a commitment of people, time, and facilities to establish your rating. There will also have to be added commitment for support and use.

Mini-Rating

Although the majority of this book involves computerized, mainframe-based ratings, it is possible to implement a working rating with a minicomputer using software that will file data and allow the creation of reports. The rating that will be covered in this section was created with the following equipment and software:

- Apple II+ with 64K and two disk drives
- Epson FX-80 printer
- PFS File and PFS Report software (Software Publishing Corp., Revision E, August 1981)

By current standards, the system used for this exercise is out-of-date and is not as powerful or versatile as PCs in most offices today. It does, however, demonstrate that quality information can be retained and effectively used without resorting to state-of-the-art computers or extensive special programming. The concepts presented here are important, not the type of equipment or software used. Although this chapter deals with a unique quality information system, the best approach is still the integrated mainframe program and every effort should be made to develop integrated systems. If that is not feasible, a unique system is your only alternative.

This chapter is intended to offer ideas that can be developed into a working quality information system using a personal or office computer with spreadsheet or file type software. The important element in developing your system is knowledge of capabilities of your equipment and

ITEM	ELEMENT	DESCRIPTION
01	PART:	Part Number
02	QTYREC:	Quantity Received
03	NAME:	Part Name
04	LOT#:	Lot # of receipt
05	DATE:	Date of entry (YYMMDD)
06	ISS:	Issue or Release Number
07	CERT:	Supplier Quality Certification
08	VEND:	Supplier Name
09	DUE:	Day Number that shipment is due
10	REC:	Day Number that shipment received
11	RTR:	Retrieve Code, "V-VND, M-MFG, O-Other"
12	CMDTY:	Commodity of Part Family
13	INSP:	Name of Inspector
14	QINS:	Quantity Inspected
15	QDEF:	Quantity Defective in Sample
16	#DEF:	Number of Defects Found
17	DISP:	Disposition, "A"-Accept, "R"-Reject
A	RESP:	Responsibility for deficiency
B	RWK:	Rework
C	RTV:	Return to Vendor
D	SCP:	Scrap
E	UAI:	Use As Is
F	SRT:	Sort
G	REJ#:	Reject Number, use Disk#/Form#
H	DEPT:	Department where part was rejected
I	SHFT:	Shift
J	QTYR:	Quantity Rejected
K	ORD#:	Work Order Number/Job Number
L	OPER:	Operation Number at time of rejection
M	COST:	Total cost of deficiency, Mat, Labor, etc.
N	CODE:	Identity of Rejected parts (S/N, Code)
O	DEF:	Deficiency Detail
P	COM:	Comments, added detail
Q	MFG:	Manufacturing Approval
R	ENGRG:	Product Engineering Approval
S	QA:	Quality Assurance Approval
T	MFGENS:	Manufacturing/Process Engineering Approval
U	RMKS:	Remarks, additional comments

Table 8.1 Explanation of Exhibit A

software so that you can plan for effective data collection and use.

Since a rating is nothing more than an analysis of data, your first step is to create a database. The PFS user's manual identifies the initial step in this process as *creating a file*. This will be your first opportunity at creativity. What you set up will be what you will have to work with. When planning your file, you must remember that you will only create one form, but will enter many data elements as your system is used.

Think FUNCTION and data availability when setting up your file. The sequence of data entry and item placement on the form are prime considerations that must not be overlooked. Item placement should be planned to provide optimum readability and minimum entry gymnastics. Common information that is most frequently entered should be at the beginning.

If your initial form does not work out as expected, change to a better format. While you are in the planning stages it is best to work out the bugs rather than make do with something that will create future problems. A few extra hours redesigning a form prior to system use will be repaid many times over through reduction of data entry time and problems.

Optimizing the effectiveness of your operations is the prime objective of this project so this will be a good time to consider merging incoming inspection results and deficiency reporting into a common database. Exhibit A is a file created for this project and involves the information needed to record receipts, document deficiencies, and perform a supplier rating.

The examples discussed in the following review relate to a hypothetical operation. The names, part numbers, and all other details were created for demonstration purposes and similarity to any real persons, companies, or events is purely coincidental. This exercise is intended to be typical of a small manufacturing operation and illustrate the basics of a quality information system.

Exhibit A

Initially, you may only want to rate suppliers, but if you don't have a sound deficiency reporting system you can get a bonus from implementing a program of this type. See Table 8.1 to obtain a better understanding of the items included in Exhibit A.

The first reaction to this will probably be that it's an awful lot of junk to keep track of. This is true, but not all the elements are used for every entry. When you stop and think about your operation in terms of what happens in daily use, the format will begin to make more sense (Table 8.2). In terms of function, consider the following:

Receiving. When a shipment comes in from your supplier it will be accompanied by a packing list that should provide the following:

- Name of Part or Commodity
- Number of Part or Commodity
- Issue or Release Number
- Quantity Shipped
- Lot Number
- Supplier Name
- Quality Certification (if required)

The data received (item 10, Table 8.1) should present no problem. Keep a calendar handy with day numbers to provide a quick reference for this entry. The question of date due (item 09, Table 8.1) is the only real problem, and that can probably be obtained by a call to purchasing or checking a file. Basically, entering items 01-07 as applicable will provide a record of receipts including acceptance status, lot numbers, supplier

PART: _ 1 _____	QTYREC: _ 2 _____		
NAME: ____ 3 _____	LOT#: ____ 4 _____		
DATE: _____ 5 _____	ISS: 6 _ CERT: ____ 7____		
VEND: ____ 8 _____	DUE: _ 9 _____ REC: ___ 10 ___		
RTR: _ 11 _____	COMDTY: ____ 12 _____		
INSP: _____ 13 _____			
QINS: ____ 14 _____	QDEF: __ 15 _____ #DEF:__ 16 __		
DISP: _ 17 _____	RESP: __ A _____		
RWK: B RTV: C	SCP: D UAI: E SRT: F ____		
REJ#: _ G _____	DEPT: _ H _____ SHFT: _ I _____		
QTYR: ____ J _____	ORD#: ____ K ___ OPER:__ L ___		
COST: _ M _____			
CODE: ____ N _____			
DEF: _____ O _____			
COM: _____ P _____			
MFG: _ Q _____ ENGRG: _ R _____			
QA· ____ S _____MFGENG: ____ T _____			
RMKS: _____ U _____			

Table 8.2 Exhibit A

certifications, quantities inspected, etc.

You will still need a separate inspection plan system to provide instructions and other information necessary to assure that valid acceptance evaluation is performed, but that detail is not pertinent to this discussion. Not all materials will carry issue numbers, require certifications, or have lot numbers so all elements may not have to be entered.

If your materials people track receipt dates versus due dates you may be better off leaving the delivery information (items 09 and 10) to them. There is no reason to duplicate efforts and if the materials system can provide a valid evaluation of supplier delivery performance, it is best to let them perform that function. As long as supplier delivery performance is being monitored and the information is used for improvement, there is no need to do it over.

Performance of the function is the important element, not the generation of secondhand reports. Chances are there would be a reluctance to use "outsider" reports anyway if valid materials information was available. In this instance, the effectiveness of your quality information system won't be impaired by not including delivery information and it may even prove to be an asset by further reducing your data entry activity.

Rejections. Even in the best prevention-oriented system there will come a time when nonconforming material is encountered and deficiencies must be documented. Although this example is intended to demonstrate a supplier rating, the same file can store your deficiency report information. The key element here is the assignment of responsibility. When a nonconformance is identified it is necessary to collect some basic information.

The items of the form that are applicable to a rejection are item numbers 01, 03, 05, 06, 08 (if vendor responsibility), 11, and 13 through U. As with the receipts, not all times will apply, but they are included because each has an application. If you do not have written deficiency reports in use, you can enter the applicable information and then print a copy of the form to document the deficiency. This system can provide a bonus as it establishes a deficiency reporting system to aid in the control of nonconforming material.

Rework, return to vendor, and scrap rejections all have added costs associated with them. For the purposes of supplier rating it is important to identify these costs. Since the following examples are on a separate system that does not interface with accounting records or other records, you may have to calculate your own cost information if you cannot obtain the costs from another source. In this instance, accuracy to the penny is not essential; however, every effort should be made to use only factual information. Some examples include:

- Return to Vendor
  - -Unit cost × quantity rejected
  - -Including: added cost of rework/repair
  - -Cost of added operations
- Rework
  - -Added cost of rework/repair
- Scrap
  - -Unit cost × quantity rejected
  - -Including added cost of rework and repair
  - -Cost of added operations

Since the cost information will be used in subsequent reporting and analysis, it is important to keep the figures as factual as possible. Fudged factors and fictitious assessments should not be used. Guidance from purchasing and accounting will be needed to ensure that your information complies as closely as possible with actual costs. Your database must always remain objective and you must not forget the old adage "garbage in-garbage out."

This system will do no more than allow the collection and retrieval of data so that you can perform an analysis. You cannot expect to get anything worthwhile out of it if your entries are incomplete or erroneous. You can get no more out of the system than what has been entered.

Several examples of completed forms created for this exercise are shown in Exhibits B through G. Each is representative of typical receipt and rejection transactions. The examples are intended to illustrate use of available options for both supplier and internal responsibility deficiencies.

PART:	097436	QTYREC: 200	
NAME:	CLAMP	LOT#:	
DATE:	870223	ISS:	CERT:
VEND:	SUPER-SERV	DUE: 057	REC: 054
RTR:	V	COMDTY: HDW	
INSP:	D. GREEN		
QINS:	20	QDEF: 0	#DEF: 0
DISP:	A	RESP:	
RWK:	RTV:	SCP: UAI: SRT:	
REJ#:		DEPT: SHFT:	
QTYR:		ORD#: OPER:	
COST:			
CODE:			
DEF:			
COM:			
MFG:		ENGRG:	
QA:		MFGENG:	
RMKS:			

Table 8.3 Exhibit B

PART:	579310	QTYREC: 265	
NAME:	BRACKET	LOT#: C7-1	
DATE:	870302	ISS: 02	CERT: Y
VEND:	B&J MACHINE	DUE: 061	REC: 061
RTR:	V	COMDTY: MACH	
INSP:	H. WHITE		
QINS:	32	QDEF: 0	#DEF: 0
DISP:	A	RESP:	
RWK:	RTV:	SCP: UAI: SRT:	
REJ#:		DEPT: SHFT:	
QTYR:		ORD#: OPER:	
COST:			
CODE:			
DEF:			
COM:			
MFG:		ENGRG:	
QA:		MFGENG:	
RMKS:			

Table 8.4 Exhibit C

Exhibit B

This is a simple receipt of part not controlled by issue number or requiring quality certification (Table 8.3). The shipment was due on day 057, but was received three days early on day 054. There is no unique identification for this lot. The parts were inspected and accepted by D. Green on February 23, 1987.

Exhibit C

A form requiring greater information involves a part ordered to a specific issue number, which requires both unique lot identity and quality certification (Table 8.4). The shipment was received on the date due, sample inspected, and accepted.

```
PART:   919063                    QTYREC:  1300
NAME:   CONNECTOR                 LOT#:
DATE:   870213                    ISS:                    CERT:  N
VEND:   B&J MACHINE               DUE:  044               REC:   044
RTR:    V                         COMDTY:  HDW
INSP:   H. WHITE
QINS:   244            QDEF:  44            #DEF:  93
DISP:   R              RESP:  VND
RWK:           RTV:    SCP:        UAI:     SRT:  Y
REJ#:   AA025          DEPT:  REC           SHFT:  2
QTYR:   1100           ORD#:                OPER:  FIN
COST:   2464.00
CODE:
DEF:    438 HOLE NOT THRU, FLARE SEAT BAD
COM:    SORTED TO GET 200 PCS FOR PROD. FLARE SEATS DAMAGED DUE TO LACK OF
        ROT. PASSAGE NOT DRILLED THRU
MFG:                              ENGRG:
QA:     Y. QUALITY                MFGENG:
RMKS:
```

Table 8.5 Exhibit D

```
PART:   663407                    QTYREC:
NAME:   CASE                      LOT#:
DATE:   870215                    ISS:  05                CERT:
VEND:   JONES INC.                DUE:                    REC:
RTR:    V                         COMDTY:
INSP:   D. GREEN
QINS:   20             QDEF:  12            #DEF:  16
DISP:   R              RESP:  VND
RWK:    Y      RTV:    SCP:        UAI:     SRT:
REJ#:   AA078          DEPT:  MACH          SHFT:  3
QTYR:   12             ORD#:  B7-407        OPER:  010
COST:   76.44
CODE:   B87
DEF:    EXCESS STOCK AT LOCATOR & FINS
COM:    GRIND LOCATOR PAD FLUSH WITH SURFACE AND REMOVE FINS FROM INSIDE OF CASE.

MFG:                              ENGRG:
QA:     Y. QUALITY                MFGENG:  N. PROCESS
RMKS:   CORRECTIVE ACTION REQUEST SENT TO SUPPLIER 02/17/87
```

Table 8.6 Exhibit E

Exhibit D

Even though supplier quality planning has been performed prior to procurement, not all shipments will be found acceptable on receipt. Table 8.5 represents rejection of the lot at time of incoming inspection. The supplier was responsible and the disposition is return to vendor (RTV). The reject number was obtained from the disk identification and the form number displayed on the screen at time of entry. In this instance, disk AA was used and the sequential form number was 025.

Exhibit E

Nonconformance of material may not always be identified at time of incoming inspection, and it is sometimes necessary to reject purchased

```
PART:  633407                      QTYREC:
NAME:  CASE                          LOT#:
DATE:  87013                          ISS:              CERT:
VEND:                                 DUE:              REC:
RTR:   M                           COMDTY:
INSP:  D. BEST
QINS:  24                  QDEF:  2          #DEF:  12
DISP:  R                   RESP:  MACH
RWK:            RTV:       SCP:   Y    UAI:      SRT:
REJ#:  AA071               DEPT:  MACH        SHFT:  2
QTYR:  2                   ORD#:  A7-407      OPER:  050
COST:  43.10
CODE:  126A
DEF:   .438 HOLES DRILLED THRU & MISC DEF
COM:   STEPS IN 6.25 BORE, 9.75 DIM US.02 TOOL MARKS IN FACE. SET-UP PIECE WAS IN
       LOAD, OTHER PART-MACH WRECK
MFG:   R. FOREMAN                  ENGRG:
QA:    B. SURE                     MFGENG:
RMKS:
```

Table 8.7 Exhibit F

```
PART:  683044                      QTYREC:
NAME:  CABLE                         LOT#:
DATE:  870313                         ISS:              CERT:
VEND:  EXCELLENCE INC                 DUE:              REC:
RTR:   V                           COMDTY:
INSP:  T. BROWN
QINS:  1                   QDEF:  1          #DEF:  1
DISP:  R                   RESP:  VND
RWK:   Y        RTV:  Y    SCP:        UAI:      SRT:
REJ#:  AA036               DEPT:  ASSY        SHFT:  3
QTYR:  1                   ORD#:             OPER:
COST:  52.17
CODE:  86L
DEF:   CIRCUIT 4A TESTS OPEN
COM:   FOUND DURING SUB-ASSY TEST. REMOVE REPLACE, AND RETEST PER N. PROCESS

MFG:                               ENGRG:
QA:    Y. QUALITY                  MFGENG: N. PROCESS
RMKS:
```

Table 8.8 Exhibit G

material while "in process." Table 8.6 relates to some castings rejected due to a supplier responsibility deficiency while being machined. Since rework is required, the process engineer will provide the necessary instructions. Regardless of titles, it is important to have documentation of instructions and authorizations related to rejected product.

Exhibit F

Table 8.7 represents an overall quality information system. Not all deficiencies will be supplier responsibility. This example illustrates a manufacturing related rejection which adds the necessity to identify the department where the deficiency was detected, responsibility, shop order number, operation number, etc. This is the time to capture all the information that you will require for subsequent analysis and corrective action regardless of responsibility. One rejection alone may not be cause for action; however, chronic and repetitive deficiencies deserve special attention in order to prevent their recurrence.

Exhibit G

Table 8.8 illustrates the rejection of a part included in an assembly. Both rework and RTV are checked to indicate that added costs of rework were applicable to this deficiency. The S/N or Lot # of the rejected part is also listed as it is especially important when performing subsequent deficiency analysis and requesting corrective action by the supplier.

Establishing the Database. After the form has been planned and "saved," you are in a position to begin collecting the data. Ideally, the amount of writing should be minimized and direct entry is often best done at the time of transaction. Until you have information on file, there is nothing to retrieve or analyze so initially you will have to pay special attention to becoming acquainted with entry procedures.

You will have to be consistent in entering names, dates, and other information that will be used for sorting during future report preparation. It would be wise to create a "cheat sheet" with commonly used supplier names and responsibilities, etc., and have the information available at your entry terminal. There is no room for guesswork and a reference covering all aspects of your program should be on hand when working with the system.

Before going too far it is wise to run several test reports to see if your entry procedures are being performed effectively and that you can obtain the desired reports. Be sure your program works as expected before you become locked into a database. During the development of this project, several forms were created and tested before the final form (Exhibit A) was chosen.

The initial proposals lacked retrieval discrimination necessary to segregate responsibility areas. There were also some items overlooked which enhanced the capabilities of this minisystem so a considerable amount of cut-and-try was required before a final form was selected.

Exhibit A is not the ultimate format, but does satisfy the needs of this demonstration. The items included may or may not apply to your system, but the concepts will. It is up to you to identify the information that applies to your operation so that you can answer the "what, when, how, why, who, how much, etc." questions relating to quality performance.

Report Format. When your file form was created you established elements applicable to the functions of incoming records, deficiency reporting, and supplier rating. In short you have saved the information essential for the evaluation of performance. The information is on file so your next step is to retrieve it and use it effectively.

Your capabilities for reporting will be contingent on the features of your software. In this exercise, the PFS Report software for the Apple II + only allows a nine-column report and only sorts or ranks on the first two columns. Derived columns with calculations are feasible; however, there are constraints as to location within the report. Nonetheless, there are many options that can be selected.

One prime consideration is the ability to print enough information on one line to obtain a good working report. All the examples illustrated in this discussion were run by setting the printer in Condensed Mode thus making it possible to print a report with 132 characters per line on a standard sheet of paper. This is far more usable than the normal 80 character per line report, where it is difficult to get enough usable information on a page.

The exhibits prepared for this exercise were created from a test database which was made up using hypothetical names, dates, numbers, etc. The elements, names, and other items may not relate to your function directly, but keep in mind there are similarities!

- Everything has a name/description.
- Most products/commodites have an identifying number.
- Issue/release/specification numbers often apply.
- All products/commodities have a unit of measure.
- Most companies have departments/cells and profit centers.
- Many processes/manufacturing cycles etc. have distinct operations.
- Selected persons have authority for approval.
- Nonconformances will occur.
- Responsibilities are assignable.
- Added costs are incurred.

The item names on the file form may be different, but what you use in your program must be tailored to suit your needs. Set up what is important to you with your own vocabulary. Include the items essential to answering the most frequently asked questions about your products, processes, and suppliers. With the PFS Report, the item names are also used as heading names for subsequent reports so it helps to keep them understandable. Don't forget that other people will be expected to work with your report so an item name like "QTYR" used for quantity rejected may be meaningful to you, but a total loss to someone not familiar with the report.

Strive to keep your information as understandable as possible and by all means have complete and usable documentation on hand at your work areas. Quality information reporting is not a guessing game and should be supported by thorough planning and documentation.

The data for this exercise were collected and saved in files that consisted of 38 different items, any of which can be retrieved. The report format, however, limits each report to nine columns so a choice must be made as to what information is required. A multipage report which is predominantly "zeros" or "100 percent" is generally of little use, so it is important to establish formats that yield as much usable information as possible.

Retrieval of Information. Once information has been saved, it is similar to a written report that has been filed away. It is of little value unless it is retrieved and put to a productive use. Your computerized supplier rating is no different than a manual information system in that you must retrieve the information and use it as an aid in improving operations if you expect to derive benefit.

With the software used for this exercise, it is possible to use any one or combination of items to research the files. A few trial runs quickly point out the limitations of the system and the necessity for uniform data entry. Some of the key items selected for retrieval and comments about their application are as follows:

Item: Retrieval Specification

Part: >1 — This will print all requested information for files where the part number is greater than one. Exception: It ignores part with alpha characters included in the part number.

Date: >1 — Dates are reported as "YYMMNN"; therefore this will elect all files. Every transaction should be dated. This item is seldom omitted.

Disp: This item is basic to all entries and by definition must be either "A" or ACCEPT, or "R" for REJECT. Policy dictates that a transaction worthy of inclusion in the quality information system must have disposition and applicable authorization.

Resp: Names of functions were chosen for this item and included "VND" for vendor and "STORES," "MACH," "ASSY," etc. for applicable functions. Retrieval was based on the first letter of the name.

Vend: This is the only item for which a full item match was used due to the potential conflict in multiple names. Retrieving "JONES" would be meaningless if more than one supplier shared the same name (i.e., Jones & Company, Jones Inc., Jones Machine Works, and Jones Plating Ltd.). It is of little help when all you know is "Jones did it."

RTR: This field was added to aid in retrieval where it is necessary to segregate responsibility. "V" was used for supplier information, "M" for manufacturing, and "O" for other responsibilities. The RESP: item was too restrictive and would not allow an overview of manufacturing responsibility deficiencies.

Cost: >1 — This will select all entries that include defect cost data.

It is possible to prioritize by selecting > 500 which will only print those rejections with costs in excess of $500 so it is possible to exclude low cost items.

The opportunities are virtually endless and you can select any characters or numbers. This is when discipline in data entry becomes important because information must be in the expected form or it can not be successfully retrieved. In order to develop a successful reporting system you will have to cut-and-try until effective retrieval guidelines can be established.

Report Structure. Retrieval only tells the computer what forms to select and it also becomes necessary to establish a report format. Once again, any of the 38 items of Exhibit A can be chosen, but the example system will only create a report with nine columns and 132 characters per line. This is not all bad though because too much information makes the report difficult to use.

The structure of your report should be developed in accordance with the intended application. Priorities need to be established so that information will best serve the intended function. System capabilities play an important role in what can be achieved and common sense needs to be applied to get the most useful information possible out of your reports.

Although many calculations are possible, a report format can be made unusable by the inclusion of subcounts and subtotals, etc. This is especially noticeable where there are only one or two line items in each sort category. The added spaces and lines tend to spread the information out to the point that the report becomes difficult to read and interpret. The best way to find out what a report will look like is to run it. If it does what is intended, fine; if not change it until it accomplishes what you want.

The information to be included in a report is another personal judgment factor and each item must be considered on a functional need basis. It may even be necessary to run two separate reports using the same retrieval and sorting guidelines in order to get all the necessary information. Once again creativity plays an important role in getting the information put into a usable format.

The system created for this exercise was loaded with information typical of a manufacturing operation. Each entry simulated a receipt or rejection and an attempt was made to keep the numbers and data as close to a real world operation as possible. Unit costs were established for each part and added operation so that comparisons would be performed on a common basis.

The following reports were generated using the example database and are representative of some of the information that can be obtained.

COST	RESP	QTYR	PART	NAME	DATE	REJ#	DEF	VEND
5,542.50	VDN	150	633407	CASE	870106	AA008	NOT QUALIFIED, NO INSP REPORTS	JONES INC
3,360.00	PURCH	1,500	919063	CONNECTOR	870124	AA076	SPEC .750-16 THD, RECD .500-13	B&J MACHINE
2,464.00	VND	1,100	919063	CONNECTOR	870213	AA025	438 HOLE NOT THRU, FLARE SEAT BAD	B&J MACHINE
1,370.00	VND	200	87 YELLOW	PAINT	870313	AA026	TOO LIGHT, DOES NOT MATCH STD.	SUPER-SERV
1,329.00	PURCH	300	421588	ELBOW	870223	AA018	SPEC MALLEABLE, RECD GREY IRON	JONES INC
972.90	VND	115	579310	BRACKET	870108	AA004	.750 BORE .002 US, NO CHAMFER	B&J MACHINE
819.55	VND	185	421588	ELBOW	870302	AA047	.25 WALL MEASURES .12-.15	JONES INC
671.50	VND	17	633407	CASE	870320	AA048	HARDNESS CKS 3.5-3.7, SPEC 3.9 MAX	JONES INC
505.02	VND	114	421588	ELBOW	870310	AA013	SURFACE POROSITY AND LACK OF FILL	JONES INC
455.52	VND	146	086245	COVER	870301	AA043	WARPED, FLANGE .38 OUT OF PLANE	JONES INC
437.00	STORES	38	A566-C	FILTER	870118	AA039	WATER DAMAGE	
203.75	VND	163	086245	COVER	870312	AA044	FINS IN .62 CORED HOLES & SHIFT	JONES INC
194.50	VND	1	421588	ELBOW	870319	AA015	LEAKED THRU POROSITY IN RADIUS	JONES INC
164.40	VND	24	87 RED	PAINT	870306	AA057	MIXED COLORS, 2 CASES WERE 86 BLUE	SHIPFAST
158.62	VND	22	421588	ELBOW	870319	AA014	POROSITY IN 3.50	JONES INC
158.00	VND	4	633407	CASE	870216	AA079	CRACKED AT 8.25 BORE	JONES INC
130.50	STORES	87	421588	ELBOW	870226	AA017	RUSTED INTERNALLY, LEFT OUTSIDE	JONES INC
78.00	MACH	13	579310	BRACKET	870325	AA065	TOOL MARKS IN SEAL FACE AT 6.5 DIM	
76.44	VND	12	663407	CASE	870215	AA078	EXCESS STOCK AT LOCATOR & FINS	JONES INC
75.60	MACH	18	70622	SPACER	870221	AA080	MTG FACE ECCENTRIC TO BORE	
72.00	STORES	24	633407	CASE	870302	AA031	SURFACE FINISH DAMAGED, DIRTY	
64.75	ENGRG	35	086246	COVER	870114	AA075	INTERFERENCE WITH SHIFT LINKAGE	
61.50	MACH	1	086250	HOUSING	870225	AA081	4.00 BORE NOT FINISHED, MISSED OP	
58.80	VND	35	CF3	LEVER	870311	AA060	.753 DIA, CKS .768 & BURRS AT BORE	SHIPFAST
52.17	VND	1	683044	CABLE	870313	AA036	CIRCUIT 4A TESTS OPEN	EXCELLENCE INC
45.50	MACH	7	421588	ELBOW	870112	AA070	3.253/3.251 DIA CKS 3.247	
45.00	ASSY	1	633407	CASE	870302	AA019	THREADS STRIPPED AT FRONT COVER	JONES INC
43.10	MACH	2	633407	CASE	870123	AA071	.438 HOLES DRILLED THRU & MISC DEF	
42.00	VND	12	MP-304	STRAINER	870318	AA069	GAP IN WIRE AND SOLDER JOINT POOR	SUPER—SERV
35.84	ASSY	16	919063	CONNECTOR	870319	AA038	DAMAGED IN ASSY	
28.84	MACH	4	421588	ELBOW	870310	AA016	O'RING GROOVE .020 TOO DEEP	JONES INC
23.40	VND	900	250-1.75	CAPSCREW	870303	AA024	SPEC 1.75 LONG, RECD 1.25	SUPER-SERV
21.00	VND	7	683046	CABLE	080317	AA077	TERMINAL NOT SOLDERED, CAME OFF	EXCELLENCE INC
16.92	VND	2	579310	BRACKET	870305	AA005	.375 BORE NOT FINISHED, PIN NO FIT	B&J MACHINE
6.24	VND	2	086245	COVER	870326	AA045	BURNED IN SAND AT PORT	JONES INC
5.67	ASSY	1	683044	CABLE	870313	AA037	CUT LOOP TERMINAL IN ASSY	
1.68			CF3	LEVER	870219		ONE SAMPLE DAMAGED AS RECEIVED	B&J MACHINE
4.43	VND	1	421588	ELBOW	870313	AA054	MISRUN, FINS, SAND	POURQUICK
TOTAL: 19,795.64		5,260						

Table 8.9 Exhibit M

Exhibit M

Function: Identify high defect cost parts
Retrieve: Cost: >1
Sort: Column 1: Cost
        Column 2: Responsibility
Total: Cost, responsibility

The report (Table 8.9) lists all rejections in descending order of defect cost. It is intended to identify special parts that require more detailed analysis. Sufficient information is included to allow further investigation. All responsibility areas are reported since there is less than one page of information. In this instance there would be no reason to generate separate reports for purchased and manufactured parts.

VEND	COST	PART	NAME	QTYR	DATE	REJ#	DEF	CODE
					RATE87 VENDCOST			
B&J MACHINE	2,464.00	919063	CONNECTOR	1,100	870213	AA025	438 HOLE NOT THRU, FLARE SEAT BAD	
	972.90	579310	BRACKET	115	870108	AA004	.750 BORE .002 US, NO CHAMFER	L6-4
	16.92	579310	BRACKET	2	870305	AA005	.375 BORE NOT FINISHED, PIN NO FIT	L6-4
		086246	COVER	200	870311	AA068	NO RUST PREVENTATIVE	
TOTAL:	3,453.82			1,417				
EXCELLENCE INC	52.17	683044	CABLE	1	870313	AA036	CIRCUIT 4A TESTS OPEN	86L
	21.00	683046	CABLE	7	080317	AA077	TERMINAL NOT SOLDERED, CAME OFF	
TOTAL:	73.17			8				
JONES INC	5,542.50	633407	CASE	150	870106	AA008	NOT QUALIFIED, NO INSP REPORTS	116C
	819.55	421588	ELBOW	185	870302	AA047	.25 WALL MEASURES .12-.15	037A
	671.50	633407	CASE	17	870320	AA048	HARDNESS CKS 3.5-3.7, SPEC 3.9 MAX	1286
	505.02	421588	ELBOW	114	870310	AA013	SURFACE POROSITY AND LACK OF FILL	C7
	455.52	086245	COVER	146	870301	AA043	WARPED, FLANGE .38 OUT OF PLANE	027A
	203.75	086245	COVER	163	870312	AA044	FINS IN .62 CORED HOLES & SHIFT	037B
	194.50	421588	ELBOW	1	870319	AA015	LEAKED THRU POROSITY IN RADIUS	J6
	158.62	421588	ELBOW	22	870319	AA014	POROSITY IN 3.50	C7
	158.00	633407	CASE	4	870216	AA079	CRACKED AT 8.25 BORE	B87
	76.44	663407	CASE	12	870215	AA078	EXCESS STOCK AT LOCATOR & FINS	B87
	6.24	086245	COVER	2	870326	AA045	BURNED IN SAND AT PORT	C7-5
		086249	HOUSING	60	870326	AA046	CAST CODE OMITTED	
		633407	CASE	175	870219	AA042	1.5 DIA BOSS SHIFTED OFF CENTER	C87
TOTAL:	8,791.64			1,051				
POURQUICK	4.43	421588	ELBOW	1	870313	AA054	MISRUN, FINS, SAND	?
TOTAL:	4.43			1				
SHIPFAST	164.40	87 RED	PAINT	24	870306	AA057	MIXED COLORS, 2 CASES WERE 86 BLUE	016B
	58.80	CF3	LEVER	35	870311	AA060	.753 DIA, CKS .768 & BURRS AT BORE	
	0.03	188-10L	TERMINAL	2	870312	AA061	SPEC .188 DIA, RECD .12 MIXED	
TOTAL:	223.23			61				
SUPER-SERV	1,370.00	87 YELLOW	PAINT	200	870313	AA026	TOO LIGHT, DOES NOT MATCH STD.	C87
	42.00	MP-304	STRAINER	12	870318	AA069	GAP IN WIRE AND SOLDER JOINT POOR	
	23.40	250-1.75	CAPSCREW	900	870303	AA024	SPEC 1.75 LONG, RECD 1.25	
TOTAL:	1,435.40			1,112				
TOTAL:	13,981.69			3,650				

Table 8.10 Exhibit N

Exhibit N

Function: Supplier defect cost summary

Retrieve: RTR: ..V.., DISP: ..R..

Sort: Column 1: Supplier name

Column 2: Cost

Subtotal: Cost, quantity rejected

This report (Table 8.10) accumulates all deficiency report information which is supplier responsibility and presents it in descending order of cost for the applicable supplier. From this report it is easy to determine what suppliers are responsible for the greatest number of deficiencies and require special action. In each instance the cost represents product that was not available to production. Where costs of added operations and rework are not recovered by the customer, there is a substantial amount of money lost due to the deficiencies.

This report identifies areas where prevention of recurring problems can contribute significantly to the profitability of a company. Both high defect cost suppliers and parts are easily recognized.

						RATE87 VENDET		
PART	COST	NAME	DATE	REJ#	QTYR	CODE	DEF	COM
086245	455.52	COVER	870301	AA043	146	027A	WARPED, FLANGE .38 OUT OF PLANE	SEVERAL PCS ALSO CRACKED
	203.75	COVER	870312	AA044	163	037B	FINS IN .62 CORED HOLES & SHIFT	REWORK BY CORE DRILLING .62 HOLES AND GRINDING EXCESS STOCK FROM OD
	6.24	COVER	870326	AA045	2	C7-5	BURNED IN SAND AT PORT	PHONE REPORT TO JONES, SCRAP WAS APPROVED BY PURCH.
086249		HOUSING	870326	AA046	60		CAST CODE OMITTED	OK TO USE PER ENGRG
421588	819.55	ELBOW	870302	AA047	185	037A	.25 WALL MEASURES .12-.15	ONE SAMPLE CUT TO SHOW PROBLEM IS ON TOP OF LOAD, IS PAINTED WHITE.
	505.02	ELBOW	870310	AA013	114	C7	SURFACE POROSITY AND LACK OF FILL	THREE SAMPLES ALSO HAD FINS IN CORED PASSAGE.
	194.50	ELBOW	870319	AA015	1	J6	LEAKED THRU POROSITY IN RADIUS	REMOVE, REPLACE AND RETEST. UNIT S/N-4227
	158.62	ELBOW	870319	AA014	22	C7	POROSITY IN 3.50	CAN NOT REWORK PER U. DESIGN
633407	5,542.50	CASE	870106	AA008	150	116C	NOT QUALIFIED, NO INSP REPORTS	MACHINING LOCATORS OMITTED, NO EVIDENCE OF QUALIFICATION BY FOUNDRY CAN NOT USE PER N. PROCESS
	671.50	CASE	870320	AA048	17	1286	HARDNESS CKS 3.5-3.7, SPEC 3.9 MAX	CHECKED AT FLANGE AREA AS PER SPEC ALL CASES SAME CAST CODE
	158.00	CASE	870216	AA079	4	B87	CRACKED AT 8.25 BORE	DYE CHECK CONFIRMS CRACKS, VISUAL CHECK SHOWS PAINT IN CRACK
		CASE	870219	AA042	175	C87	1.5 DIA BOSS SHIFTED OFF CENTER	ENGRG AUTHORIZED USE BY DRILLING PORT IN CENTER OF BOSS. NO ADDED COST SPECIAL OPER M87-17 PER N. PROCESS
663407	76.44	CASE	870215	AA078	12	B87	EXCESS STOCK AT LOCATOR & FINS	GRIND LOCATOR PAD FLUSH WITH SURFACE AND REMOVE FINS FROM INSIDE OF CASE. INSTR 85-14 PER N. PROCESS
TOTAL: 8,791.64					1,051			

Table 8.11 Exhibit O

Exhibit O

Function: Performance review with supplier

Retrieve: Supplier name, RTR: ..V.., DISP: ..R..

Sort: Column 1: Part number

Column 2: Cost

Total: Cost, quantity rejected

After the major problem suppliers have been identified it is then possible to select a detail report which can be used for review with the supplier (Table 8.11). Even though parts may have been returned and purchasing has been in contact with the supplier, there may not have been any analysis performed or corrective action taken.

Using the information from this report and the analysis of rejected material, the supplier will be better able to audit the applicable processes and plan corrective action. By meeting with the involved suppliers and following up each of the reported problem areas, it is possible to develop a mutual plan for prevention of deficiency recurrence.

VEND	PART	DATE	RATE87 VENDPART QTYREC	QTYR	%DEF	DUE	REC	DELIV
B&J MACHINE	086246	870112	150			12	12	0.00
		870311	200	200	100.00	70	70	0.00
	579310	870108	125	115	92.00	5	8	−3.00
		870305		2				
		870311	200			75	70	5.00
		870211	150			43	42	1.00
		870302	265			61	61	0.00
	696514	870323	100			79	82	−3.00
	919063	870213	1,300	1,100	84.62	44	44	0.00
	CF3	870219	400			50	50	0.00
		TOTAL:	2,890	1,417				
CHIPMAKER	086246	870124	80			24	24	0.00
	579310	870310	300			69	69	0.00
		870123	150			23	23	0.00
	696514	870124	175			26	24	2.00
	919063	87015	450			17	15	2.00
	922404	870301	1,300			68	60	8.00
		TOTAL:	2,455	0				
EXCELLENCE INC	375R	870213	400			44	44	0.00
	683044	870313	250			75	72	3.00
		870302	150			61	61	0.00
		870313		1				
	683046	080317		7				
		870324	135			85	83	2.00
		870302	20			61	61	0.00
	686595	870302	140			65	61	4.00
		870213	40			44	44	0.00
		TOTAL:	1,135	8				
JONES INC	086245	870301	150	146	97.33	58	61	−3.00
		870312	180	163	90.56	71	71	0.00
		870326	35	2	5.71	82	85	−3.00
	086249	870326	60	60	100.00	85	85	0.00
	421588	870302	200	185	92.50	64	61	3.00
		870202	65			33	33	0.00
		870302	120			35	33	2.00
		870310	120	114	95.00	44	41	3.00
		870319		22				
		870319		1				
	633407	870216		4				
		870302	124			62	61	1.00
		870219	175	175	100.00	50	50	0.00
		870320		17				
		870106	150	150	100.00	6	6	0.00
		870115	225			16	15	1.00
		870124	170			23	24	−1.00
		870306	150			61	65	−4.00
		870114	85			14	14	0.00
	663407	870215		12				
	70622	870324	350			79	83	−4.00
		870123	500			23	23	0.00
		TOTAL:	2,859	1,051				
POURQUICK	086245	870114	75			14	14	0.00
	421588	870302	140			61	61	0.00
		870313	85	1	1.18	72	72	0.00
	70622	870304	100			64	63	1.00
		TOTAL:	400	1				
SHIPFAST	188-10L	870312	1,700	2	0.12	71	71	0.00
		870325	1,900			84	84	0.00
	375R	870317	1,200			79	76	3.00
	86 BLACK	870123	125			23	23	0.00
	87 RED	870313	150			72	72	0.00
		870306	96	24	25.00	62	65	−3.00
	919063	870321	400			79	80	−1.00
	CF3	870311	35	35	100.00	70	70	0.00
		TOTAL:	5,606	61				
SUPER-SERV	097436	870223	200			57	54	3.00
	250-1.75	870306	12,000			65	65	0.00
		870303	900	900	100.00	56	62	−6.00
	375R	870306	400			68	65	3.00
	87 YELLOW	870313	200	200	100.00	69	72	−3.00
		870323	199			70	82	−12.00
	MP-304	870318	30	12	40.00	75	77	−2.00
		870306	25			65	65	0.00
		TOTAL:	13,954	1,112				
		TOTAL:	29,299	3,650				

Table 8.12 Exhibit P

Procurement Quality Control

Exhibit P

Function: Quality/delivery performance
Retrieve: RTR: ..V..
Sort: Column 1: Supplier name
          Column 2: Part number
Subtotal: Quantity received, quantity rejected

This report is shown as an example of what some believe a supplier rating is supposed to be (Table 8.12). The delivery factor is included because the hypothetical company did not have any computerized materials system and this information was the only retrievable delivery information that was available.

This report uses two derived columns that were created using the following formulas:

$$Percent\ Defective\ =\ 100\ (QtyRej)/QtyRec$$
$$Delivery\ =\ Date\ Due\ -\ Date\ Received$$

A delivery ahead of schedule will be represented by a positive number and a late delivery will be negative. Although neither is ideal by today's standards, the information does provide a measure of how well the supplier complies with schedules.

The percent defective number is self-explanatory, but does not really present it a measure of significance by itself. It is an indicator of problems, but this report does little to identify any more than part number. If materials could produce valid delivery information, this format could be disregarded without a significant loss to the program.

Exhibit Q

Function: Supplier performance
Retrieve: RTR: ..V.., DISP: ..R..
Sort: Column 1: Supplier name
          Column 2: Part number
Subtotal: Quantity inspected, quantity defective, number of
          defects, cost

This format is included for those who like to look at numbers and see calculated values in reports (Table 8.13). The trend toward SPC has made many people amateur statisticians and it has been expressed that calculations are necessary for a thorough analysis of ALL operations. The factors of PPM and DPM were referenced in some of the information developed during preparation for this chapter so examples have been included to illustrate an application.

98

VEND	PART	REJ#	QINS	QDEF	#DEF	PPM	DPM	COST
				RATE87 PPM/DPM				
	086246	AA075	2	2	2	1,000.00	1,000.00	64.75
	086250	AA081	1	1	1	1,000.00	1,000.00	61.50
	421588	AA070	7	7	9	1,000.00	1,285.71	45.50
	579310	AA065	65	13	19	200.00	292.31	78.00
	633407	AA071	24	2	12	83.33	500.00	43.10
		AA031	60	24	24	400.00	400.00	72.00
	6833044	AA037	1					5.67
	70622	AA030	45	18	18	400.00	400.00	75.60
	919063	AA038	16	16		1,000.00		35.84
	A566-C	AA039	1	38		38,000.00		437.00
B&J MACHINE	086246	AA068	20	3	3	150.00	150.00	
	579310	AA004	13	3	7	230.77	533.46	972.90
		AA005	36	2		55.56		16.92
	919063	AA07	1	1	1	1,000.00	1,000.00	3,360.00
		AA025	244	44	93	180.33	381.15	2,434.00
EXCELLENCE INC	683044	AA036	1	1	1	1,000.00	1,000.00	52.17
	683046	AA077	20	7	7	350.00	350.00	21.00
JONES INC	086245	AA043	13	9	15	692.31	1,153.85	455.62
		AA044	20	3	7	150.00	350.00	203.75
		AA045	35	2	5	57.14	142.86	6.24
	086249	AA046	13	2	2	153.85	153.85	
	421588	AA047	20	5	5	250.00	250.00	818.55
		AA013	13	6	9	461.54	692.31	505.02
		AA014	22	22		1,000.00		158.62
		AA015	1	1		1,000.00		194.50
		AA016	7					28.84
		AA017	125	87	87	696.00	696.00	130.50
		AA018	1	1		1,000.00		1,329.00
	633407	AA042	20	5	7	250.00	350.00	
		AA048	65	17	17	261.54	261.54	671.50
		AA079	4	4	6	1,000.00	1,500.00	158.00
		AA008	13	13	18	1,000.00	1,384.62	5,542.50
		AA019	1	1		1,000.00		45.00
	663407	AA078	20	12	16	600.00	800.00	76.44
POURQUICK	421588	AA054	13	1	3	76.92	230.77	4.43
SHIPFAST	188-10L	AA061	125	2	3	16.00	24.00	0.03
	87 RED	AA057	24	24	24	1,000.00	1,000.00	164.40
	CF3	AA060	8	8	13	1,000.00	1,625.00	58.80
SUPER-SERV	250-1.75	AA024	8	8	8	1,000.00	1,000.00	23.40
	87 YELLOW	AA026	1	1	1	1,000.00	1,000.00	1,370.00
	MP-304	AA069	30	12	15	400.00	500.00	42.00

Table 8.13 Exhibit Q

PPM = 1,030 (QtyDef)/QtyInsp
DPM = 1,000 (Number of defects)/QtyInsp

The number of zeros does not match the technical writing that expresses the factors in PPM, but for purposes of this example, "parts per thousand" provides enough information to illustrate what the results will be. Adding extra zeros in this instance is of no significance and only extends the report width.

The cost factor is included as a reference and comparison to the other numbers. The database is the same for each of the examples and only the report formats have been changed to show what results can be achieved. You can judge for yourself which numbers present the greatest impact and measure of meaningful supplier performance.

					VENSUM COSTRANK				
COST	VEND	DATE	QINS	QDEF	#DEF	QREJ	PPM	DPM
8,791.64	JONES INC	8703	345	101	107	1,051	292.75	310.14
3,455.50	B&J MACHINE	8703	441	53	104	1,417	120.18	235.83
1,435.40	SUPER-SERV	8703	225	23	27	1,112	102.22	120.00
223.23	SHIPFAST	8703	484	34	40	61	70.25	82.64
73.17	EXCELLENCE INC	8703	108	8	8	8	74.07	74.07
4.43	POURQUICK	8703	59	1	3	1	16.95	50.85
0.00	CHIPMAKER	8703	220	0	0	0	0.00	0.00
TOTAL: 13,983.37			1,882	220	289	3.650		

Table 8.14 Exhibit Ra

					VENSUM QCOUNT				
VEND	DATE	#REC	QREC	QINS	QDEF	#DEF	QREJ	COST
JONES INC	8701	21	3,345	395	40	45	854	7,450.88
	8702	12	2,385	277	31	46	567	5,097.43
	8703	17	2,859	345	101	107	1,051	8,791.64
	8704	24	3,665	285	35	39	200	875.40
	8705	16	2,850	195	14	14	165	1,145.50
	8706	18	3,150	175	4	5	35	98.65
TOTAL: COUNT: 1		108	18,254	1,672	225	256	2,872	23,459.50

Table 8.15 Exhibit Rb

```
VEND: _____ DATE: _____
QREC: _____
QINS: _____
QDEF: _____
#DEF: _____
QREJ: _____
COST: _____   "VENTREND"
#REC: _____
#RWK: _____ FORM FOR COLLECTING
#RTV: _____ SUPPLIER PERFORMANCE
#SCP: _____
#UAI: _____
#PRT: _____
#CRT: _____
#STS: _____
#LOT: _____
MISC:_____
```

Table 8.16
Form for Collecting Supplier Performance

```
VEND: JONES INC        DATE: 8703
QREC: 2859
QINS: 345
QDEF: 101
#DEF: 107
QREJ: 1051
COST: 8791.64
#REC: 17
#REJ: 13
#RWK: 3
#RTV: 8
#SCP: 1
#UAI: 2
#PRT: 6
#CRT: 10
#STS: 2
#LOT: M
MISC:
```

Table 8.17 Monthly Supplier Performance

					VENSUM #COUNT			
VEND	DATE	#REJ	#RWK	#RTV	#SCP	#UAI	#PPT	#DPT
JONES INC	8701	7	1	5	1	1	5	14
	8702	7	3	4	0	0	5	8
	8703	13	3	8	1	2	6	10
	8704	4	0	2	1	3	6	19
	8705	2	0	2	0	0	6	13
	8706	2	0	1	1	0	6	14
TOTAL: COUNT: 1		35	7	22	4	6	34	78

Table 8.18 Exhibit Rc

Basic Issues: Supplier Rating

				VENSUM MONTHLY				
VEND	DATE	QREC	QINS	QDEF	#DEF	QREJ	%REJ	COST
B&J MACHINE	8703	2,890	441	53	104	1,417	49.03	3,455.50
CHIPMAKER	8703	2,455	220	0	0	0	0.00	0.00
EXCELLENCE INC	8703	1,135	108	8	8	8	0.70	73.17
JONES INC	8701	3,345	395	40	45	854	25.53	7,450.88
	8702	2,385	277	31	46	567	23.77	5,097.43
	8703	2,859	345	101	107	1,051	36.76	8,791.64
	8704	3,665	285	35	39	200	5.46	875.40
	8705	2,850	195	14	14	165	5.79	1,145.50
	8706	3,150	175	4	5	35	1.11	98.65
POURQUICK	8703	400	59	1	3	1	0.25	4.43
SHIPFAST	8703	5,606	484	34	40	61	1.09	223.23
SUPER-SERV	8703	13,594	225	23	27	1,112	8.18	1,435.40
TOTAL:		44,334	3,209	344	438	5,471		28,651.23
COUNT:	7							

Table 8.19 Exhibit Rd

Where sufficient valid information is available and the PPM/DPM numbers are meaningful, they should be used. This is another element that relates to the normal lines of communication you must maintain with your customers and suppliers.

Exhibit R

Function: Overall supplier performance for month
Retrieve: Date: 8703
Sort: Column 1: Cost:

This report is based on a separate file created for summary purposes due to the limitations imposed by the software used for the accumulation of data (Table 8.14). Exhibit Rb shows a completed form for one supplier (Table 8.15). This information is obtained from a summary of supplier performance generated from the detail data file.

A separate form must be created for each supplier for each month (Table 8.16). When there are not many suppliers involved, this is not a time-consuming project. Various additional summaries can then be prepared from this file and supplier performance can be trended on a month-to-month basis (Table 8.17). Exhibit Rc indicates the number of transactions (Table 8.18), and Exhibit Rd summarizes the quantities involved (Table 8.19).

Exhibit S

Function: Supplier performance within commodity
Retrieve: RTR: ..V..
Sort: Column 1: Commodity
Column 2: Part number
Subtotal: Quantity received, quantity inspected
Quantity rejected, cost

Procurement Quality Control

COMDTY	PART	VEND	RATE87 COMPART DATE	QTYREC	QINS	QTYR	COST	%DEF
	421588	JONES INC	870319		22	22	158.62	
		JONES INC	870319		1	1	194.50	
	579310	B&J MACHINE	870305		36	2	16.92	
	633407	JONES INC	870216		4	4	158.00	
	663407	JONES INC	870215		20	12	76.44	
	683044	EXCELLENCE INC	870313		1	1	52.17	
	683046	EXCELLENCE INC	080317		20	7	21.00	
			TOTAL:	0	104	49	677.65	
CAST	086245	POURQUICK	870114	75	13			
		JONES INC	870301	150	13	146	455.52	97.33
		JONES INC	870312	180	20	163	203.75	90.56
		JONES INC	870326	35	35	2	6.24	5.71
	086249	JONES INC	870326	60	13	60		100.00
	421588	JONES INC	870302	200	20	185	819.55	92.50
		POURQUICK	870302	140	20			
		POURQUICK	870313	85	13	1	4.43	1.18
		JONES INC	870202	65	13			
		JONES INC	870302	120	13			
		JONES INC	870310	120	13	114	505.02	95.00
	633407	JONES INC	870320		65	17	671.50	
		JONES INC	870124	170	13			
		JONES INC	870306	150	13			
		JONES INC	870114	85	8			
		JONES INC	870302	124	13			
		JONES INC	870219	175	20	175		100.00
		JONES INC	870106	150	13	150	5,542.50	100.00
		JONES INC	870115	225	13			
	70622	JONES INC	870324	350	0			
		JONES INC	870123	500	0			
		POURQUICK	870304	100	13			
			TOTAL:	3,259	357	1,013	8,208.51	
ELECT	188-10L	SHIPFAST	870312	1,700	125	2	0.03	0.12
		SHIPFAST	870325	1,900	200			
	683044	EXCELLENCE INC	870313	250	32			
		EXCELLENCE INC	870302	150	13			
	683046	EXCELLENCE INC	870324	135	13			
		EXCELLENCE INC	870302	20	8			
	686595	EXCELLENCE INC	870302	140	13			
		EXCELLENCE INC	870213	40	8			
			TOTAL:	4,335	412	2	0.03	
HDW	097436	SUPER-SERV	870223	200	20			
	250-1.75	SUPER-SERV	870306	12,000	125			
		SUPER-SERV	870303	900	8	900	23.40	100.00
	375R	SHIPFAST	870317	1,200	125			
		SUPER-SERV	870306	400	32			
		EXCELLENCE INC	870213	400	0			
	919063	SHIPFAST	870321	400	0			
		CHIPMAKER	87015	450	50			
		B&J MACHINE	870213	1,300	244	1,100	2,464.00	84.62
	MP-304	SUPER-SERV	870318	30	30	12	42.00	40.00
		SUPER-SERV	870306	25	8			
			TOTAL:	17,305	642	2,012	2,529.40	
MACH	086246	B&J MACHINE	870112	150	20			
		B&J MACHINE	870311	200	20	200		100.00
		CHIPMAKER	870124	80	0			
	579310	CHIPMAKER	870310	300	32			
		CHIPMAKER	870123	150	13			
		B&J MACHINE	870211	150	13			
		B&J MACHINE	870302	265	32			
		B&J MCHINE	870108	125	13	115	972.90	92.00
		B&J MACHINE	870311	200	0			
	696514	B&J MACHINE	870323	100	13			
		CHIPMAKER	870124	175	0			
	922404	CHIPMAKER	870301	1,300	125			
	CF3	SHIPFAST	870311	35	8	35	58.80	100.00
		B&J MACHINE	870219	400	50		1.68	
			TOTAL:	3,630	339	350	1,033.38	
PAINT	86 BLACK	SHIPFAST	870123	125	1			
	87 RED	SHIPFAST	870313	150	1			
		SHIPFAST	870306	96	24	24	164.40	25.00
	87 YELLOW	SUPER-SERV	870313	200	1	200	1,370.00	100.00
		SUPER-SERV	870323	199	1			
			TOTAL:	770	28	224	1,534.40	
			TOTAL:	29,299	1,882	3,650	13,983.37	

Table 8.20 Exhibit S

102

Although it is possible to compare performance within commodity, this report (Table 8.20) does not permit sufficient sorting to be effectively used. It is included only as a reference to illustrate another form of evaluation that may be performed to determine which commodities are the greatest problem contributors.

There are many other options and combinations that can be conceived for reporting, and experimentation will be required to determine which formats provide the most useful information. The system is flexible, but when working formats are established and proven successful there is little reason to change for routine functions.

The intent of this chapter is to provide an overview of a basic quality information system. The concepts are the important elements intended to stimulate thought and identify items worthy of consideration when planning new systems or modifying existing systems. What you incorporate in your operations must meet the needs of your business and provide optimum effectiveness. Through comprehensive planning and attention to detail a supplier rating program can become a successful aid in maintaining a strong purchased material control program.

CHAPTER 9

BASIC ISSUES: COMMUNICATIONS AND PROBLEM SOLVING

Key Words: Corrective Action, Rejection Reports

Summary

- **Types of communication**
- **Frequency of communication**
- **Problem identification and resolution**

Whenever two parties get together, there is a potential communication problem. Both parties have different ideas about what they want to get out of each meeting. What the buyer wants to do is to create an atmosphere of openness and interest so that the business at hand is accomplished as quickly and as graciously as possible.

When developing a partnership with suppliers, the buyer wants to establish how often he wants to communicate on routine issues. It is also a good idea to reinforce the issue of contacting the buyer as quickly as reasonable when a problem arises. So there are two basic forms of communicating with suppliers: (1) routine issues, and (2) problems.

Routine communication should initially take place once a month by both teams. This is so the teams can become familiar with each other. Until a level of confidence can be built up, openness with each other will be slow. In fact, in the initial meetings, most of the communication will be one-sided. The buyer will do most of the talking. If the buyer can quickly develop a trusting relationship, the progress to a meaningful partnership will be expedited. The first meeting of the teams should take place at the supplier's facility. This serves two purposes: (1) the buyer's team can see the facility, and (2) it sends a positive message to the supplier. The message is that the buyer is interested in the supplier and wants to help the supplier in any way. The buyer is meeting the supplier on the supplier's "turf." The supplier will be more comfortable in familiar surroundings, and this lends itself to more open communications.

It is necessary for the buyer's team to meet before the initial visit and discuss the purpose of the visit and the team's long-term goal. An agenda should be prepared jointly and sent to all team members. Generally, the initial meeting is one where the buyer talks about the relationship that is beginning and where the buyer hopes it will end. The buyer also has the opportunity to show where and how the product being supplied will be used. This creates an opportunity for the supplier to make alternative suggestions about other materials that may be more suitable for the intended purpose. This can lead to the acceptance of a better suited product if it can pass the accreditation testing. At the end of the initial meeting, a schedule should be established for future meetings. If the supplier is located nearby, the monthly meetings could alternate from the supplier's facilities to the buyer's facilities. If the supplier is not in the local area, then quarterly meetings should be set up at alternating facilities, and in between, meetings can be accomplished by conference call. This enables the buyer and supplier teams to talk routinely and keep costs down.

Before every meeting, an agenda should be sent to both teams so that everyone is prepared. Routine monthly meetings can last as long as necessary, but experience has shown that after a year, these can be cut back unless there are problems or special circumstances. Some examples of special circumstances include new people brought onto the teams due to retirements or personnel changes, new ownership, or a new location. A rule of thumb is to have each team visit the other facility at least once a year after the first year. This helps maintain good relations.

When problems occur at the buyer's facility, it is important that the supplier be notified as soon as possible. The buyer should clearly identify the problem. If a problem is stated in terms like "will not assemble" or "will not mate," the supplier will have a difficult time identifying the source of the problem. For example, if the problem is the result of the distance between holes that are not to the drawing, then the supplier can go back and rectify the problem. If the holes are to the specifications, then there may be a problem in the buyer's process. It is the responsibility of both teams to identify the problem sources at their respective facilities and work together to solve the problem. All corrective action needs to be documented so that if a similar problem occurs, there is some traceable starting point. This is accomplished in many companies through the use of a Rejection Report. It lists the cause for rejection and has room for the supplier to identify what corrective action has been taken. A visit to the supplier may be necessary to demonstrate the problem and determine the appropriate corrective action.

In summary, a good procurement quality program depends on good communication. Both teams need to establish trust and confidence with each other so that open intercourse takes place. The frequency needs to be established at the first meeting. When problems arise, the cohesiveness of the teams will enable a swift resolution.

CHAPTER 10

BASIC ISSUES: FROM SHIP-TO-STOCK TO JUST-IN-TIME

Key Words: Ship-to-Stock, Supplier Certification, Characteristic Accountability, Annual System Audit, Source Inspection, Just-in-Time

Summary

- **Evolution of ship-to-stock**
- **Supplier and product qualification**
- **Auditing the ship-to-stock system**
- **Advantages of a ship-to-stock program**
- **Relationship of ship-to-stock to just-in-time**

Shipping suppliers' products directly to stock is an alternative to the traditional method of assessing supplier quality by means of the incoming inspection process. The ship-to-stock (STS) program is a way to more efficiently and economically handle incoming material from high-quality suppliers. It requires purchasing and supplier personnel to talk, as partners rather than adversaries, about quality systems and product requirements. The principles were developed in a military environment and have since been implemented successfully in the commercial business world.

Traditionally, the purchasing company selected an approved supplier of material by evaluating the supplier's quality system, assessing financial position, and determining design and manufacturing capabilities. From that point on, the purchasing company monitored the supplier's product quality through incoming and source inspection.

The unintended results of this approach often were delayed in the supplier-to-user time cycle, duplication of effort and equipment, discovery of problems at the wrong time and place, untimely corrective action, and inefficient use of human resources. These serious drawbacks are strong incentive to consider a STS program.

The STS program can be divided into three phases: the candidacy phase, the qualification phase, and the maintenance phase. In the candidacy phase, past quality history indicates if a supplier's system is producing quality products, therefore making the supplier a potential candidate for the STS program. The supplier and the purchaser's STS representatives then establish the STS agreement criteria that will form the requirements for the supplier's qualification. The STS agreement also outlines the quality rating, audit, and inspection requirements needed to maintain the program.

Once the background data has been collected and the STS agreement defined, the information is evaluated by the STS coordinating committee, which decides whether to consider the supplier as a candidate. The committee is comprised of a cross section of major departmental functions and representatives from each manufacturing plant.

The qualification phase entails both supplier qualification and product qualification. The candidate supplier must undergo in-depth quality system and process surveys, which are performed with special attention to the supplier's adherence to process controls. These surveys, along with the quality history, form the basis for the decision to qualify the supplier for the program.

Since the STS program is based on supplier/product combinations, product qualification is also necessary for the success of the program. The product qualification process requires:

- A first article inspection and/or evaluation test.
- A characteristic accountability, which is the process of reviewing each characteristic on the engineering drawing/specification for the supplier's method of manufacture and frequency of inspection. This review documents the quality plan for the specific product.
- Successful completion of a minimum number of lot-by-lot inspections with a predetermined minimum quality rating.
- Product manufacture using a mature production process.
- Approval of the supplier quality control engineer who is responsible for monitoring the STS program with the supplier.

Once a product is qualified, that product may only be released and shipped by a designated supplier STS representative. The supplier STS representative audits each STS lot (after all processing and final inspection) to verify completion of all operations, verify critical and major characteristics, and assure the completion of all paperwork. The representative's stamp and signature on the packing slip attest that the lot meets the requirements of the STS program. The maintenance phase involves system audits, process audits, product audits, and inspections.

Annual system auditing verifies the effectiveness of the supplier's control of the quality system and process. It includes, but is not limited to:

- Drawing and specification control.
- Purchased material control.
- Measuring and testing equipment control.
- Process and product acceptance.
- Material review and corrective action.
- Finished material storage.
- Packaging and shipping.
- Record retention.
- Quality management and reporting.

System audits are much more strict than system surveys since they must assure that the supplier's system is still capable of producing an acceptable product.

The second type of audit is the process audit, which is periodically performed to assure that the quality parameters are adhered to during each process.

The third audit type is the product audit, which encompasses the following:

- One hundred percent dimensional inspection.
- Nondestructive testing (NDT), if applicable.
- Review of inspection, heat treat, plating, NDT, and material certification records.
- Corrective action on any deficiencies.

Product audits should be performed periodically, for example, each quarter, or every 1,000 products, or a frequency considered necessary by the purchaser and the supplier.

Periodic incoming or source inspection of the key product parameters is the fourth element of the maintenance phase of the STS program. Few commercial companies can afford the luxury of a staff of source inspectors or regional quality engineers located in various parts of the country, and they often have less expertise in supplier auditing than is found in military environments. Consequently, the focus of incoming quality engineering should make each engineer responsible for all products produced by assigned suppliers. This should be done to make the engineers supplier-oriented and force them to concentrate on the supplier's total program and quality yield. Otherwise, they tend to be narrow in focus, and as long as their products are trouble-free, they will be unconcerned about other products assigned to other engineers, which breeds a disjointed effort in supplier quality management.

With the particular focus in place, the engineer has total responsibility for assigned suppliers. The emphasis will shift from product/process to a total systems emphasis conducive to shipping products to stock.

Procurement Quality Control

The STS program may appear to be rather demanding on a supplier, but a close look will show that all the supplier requirements are already present in any good quality system. It is important that the supplier have an established quality system that contains the proper controls to continuously produce an acceptable product. With an established quality system, the purchaser need only audit the supplier to ensure continued conformance, and ship the product to stock.

The STS program described here has a number of advantages:

- Establishment of close interface between purchaser and supplier.
- Establishment of mutual trust between purchaser and supplier.
- Placement of total responsibility on the supplier, leading to enhanced pride.
- Encouragement of other companies to do business with the supplier.
- Reduction of inventory levels.
- Reduction of dock-to-line time.
- Replacement of incoming/source inspection activity with scheduled audits.
- Reduction of the need for specialized test equipment.
- Reduction of rejections by placing emphasis on quality early in the process.

If a supplier has effective and proven control systems producing good quality products, it is redundant and perhaps foolish to perform incoming inspections on a lot-by-lot basis. Quality management's responsibility is to seek out alternative cost saving methods, and of course, a viable STS program is an excellent example.

Just-in-time (JIT) is a concept that can be broken up into two segments: JIT procurement and JIT inventory. JIT procurement involves scheduling and receiving purchased goods in such a manner that the customer carries almost no purchased goods inventory. JIT inventory relates to work-in-process inventory at a near zero level and does not relate to STS, which focuses on the reduction of material acquisition costs related to the quality function. STS operates under the premise that an effective total quality control system yields products that fit the customer's needs (Laford p. 29).

STS qualifies a product by verifying the design and the process that makes the product and then emphasizes auditing and periodic inspections to verify that the process does not change. STS further emphasizes that the cost of qualification and preventive audits is less costly than the traditional methods of after-the-fact appraisal inspection. JIT procurement focuses on these elements, but also includes rigid forecasting and scheduling, inventory carrying costs, traffic and transportation costs, etc. STS is a forerunner to JIT procurement. With STS in place, the company can then focus on other issues involving JIT (Laford p. 29).

Reference

Laford, R.J. *Ship-to-Stock*. Milwaukee: ASQC Quality Press, 1986.

Procurement Quality Control

CHAPTER 11

BASIC ISSUES: DATA EVALUATION

Key Words: Average, Bossert Charts, Control Charts, Histograms, Standard Deviation

Summary:

- **Descriptive statistics**
- **Plotting the data**
- **KIS**

Every day data are received from various suppliers. Depending on the company, these data can go directly into a file in the purchasing department, can be sent to the using area, or can be plotted. As more and more purchasing agents learn about quality and statistics, the data are going to be looked at more closely. This chapter focuses on some basic statistical tools that will enable the buyer to make decisions based on what the data are saying.

Today, data come in many forms — certificates of analysis, raw numbers, histograms, and control charts, to name a few. Suppliers are deluged with requests for data in a variety of forms. For some it is not a difficult task; for others it appears like a mountain. The question each supplier should ask is: "What are you going to do with the data?" The answer received can determine what the long-term plans are for that supplier. For example, I had to develop a program for implementing SPC in the plant where I worked. I had five different supplier programs that had to be satisfied. Some supplier programs wanted control charts, some wanted histograms, and some just wanted raw data. I ended up developing a program that satisfied the most stringent requirements. The data were collected in the same manner throughout the plant. These data were put into control chart form for in-plant purposes. The suppliers who wanted control charts got them, and so did everyone else. All the buyers who came in and asked about data were shown the program and told what they would receive. Everyone was happy: We had an SPC program that met our needs, and our customers received good information on our process. The point is that if suppliers have a well-documented plan for collecting and analyzing data, most buyers will accommodate in terms of data requirements. They also tend to send more business to those suppliers.

The basic descriptive statistics that can be used on virtually any data are mean and standard deviation. Basically, the mean is a measure of location, and the standard deviation is a measure of the spread. There are times when the median may be preferred over the mean. This happens when there are some extreme points that will influence the mean. These extreme values are sometimes called outliers or "fliers." An easy way to identify possible outliers is by collecting data in groups of odd numbers (e.g., 3, 5, 7, 9). Most of the data will be around the "true" average, and the outliers will be in a distinct group apart from the main body (Figure 11.1).

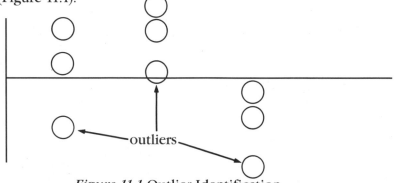

Figure 11.1 Outlier Identification

The mean is the sum of all values divided by the number of values going into it. The median is the centerpoint of all values in a group. So if there were seven values in a group of data , the median would be the fourth point when ranked from low to high. The mean would be the sum of all the points divided by seven. The numbers may not be the same.

The standard deviation is a measure of the spread of the data. If you have a calculator that does not calculate the standard deviation, the simplest way to do so is by using the information provided in Table 11.1

Another measure of the spread is the range. This is simply the difference between the highest and lowest values in a group of data. For the data in Table 11.1, the range is $90 - 70 = 20$.

So now any set of data can be looked at in terms of location (average or median) and the spread (standard deviation or range). Now we can estimate the percent conformance to a specification based on the sample. If for the data in Table 11.1, we have a specification of 80 ± 15, then the upper specification limit is 95 and the lower specification limit is 65:

$$Z_H = \frac{USL - \overline{X}}{S} = \frac{95 - 77.2}{12.1} = \frac{17.8}{12.1} = 1.47$$

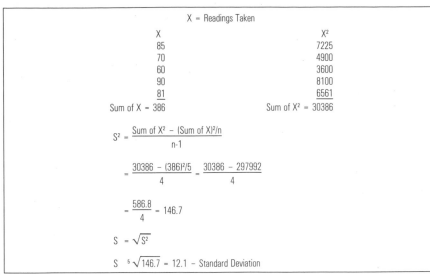

Table 11.1 Calculating Standard Deviation

$$Z_L = \frac{LSL - \overline{X}}{S} = \frac{65 - 77.2}{12.1} = \frac{12.2}{12.1} = 1.01$$

Using a normal probability table, we can estimate the area under the normal curve:

$$Z_H = .9292$$
$$Z_L = \underline{.1562}$$
$$.7730 = 77.3\% \text{ within } 80 \pm 15 \text{ specifications}$$
$$\text{or } 22.7\% \text{ outside specification}$$

(See Table 11.2.)

Given our sample of five parts, we estimate that these will be almost 23 percent nonconformance — much greater than most companies could tolerate!

Another way to use the data is to plot them. Plotting data enables the buyer to get a picture that can be very revealing. With supplier data, there are three types of plots that work well: histograms, control charts, and Bossert charts. A histogram is "a plot of a frequency distribution in the form of rectangles whose bases are equal to the cell interval and whose areas are proportional to the frequencies." The shape of any histogram can best be determined when there are between 30 to 50 data points. When there are less than 30 data points, it may not be obvious whether the data are normally distributed. How many cells is always a question. A popular rule of thumb is to take the square root of the number of data points as long as it is no less than five. There are many ways to

Proportion of total area under the curve that is under the portion of the curve from $-\infty$ to $\dfrac{Xi-\mu}{\sigma}$. (Xi represents any desired value of the variable X)

$\dfrac{Xi-\mu}{\sigma}$	0.00	0.01	0.02	0.03	0.04	0.05	0.06	0.07	0.08	0.09
-3.5	0.00023	0.00022	0.00022	0.00021	0.00020	0.00019	0.00019	0.00018	0.00017	0.00017
-3.4	0.00034	0.00033	0.00031	0.00030	0.00029	0.00028	0.00027	0.00026	0.00025	0.00024
-3.3	0.00048	0.00047	0.00045	0.00043	0.00042	0.00040	0.00039	0.00038	0.00036	0.00035
-3.2	0.00069	0.00066	0.00064	0.00062	0.00060	0.00058	0.00056	0.00054	0.00052	0.00050
-3.1	0.00097	0.00094	0.00090	0.00087	0.00085	0.00082	0.00079	0.00076	0.00074	0.00071
-3.0	0.00135	0.00131	0.00126	0.00122	0.00118	0.00114	0.00111	0.00107	0.00104	0.00100
-2.9	0.0019	0.0018	0.0017	0.0017	0.0016	0.0016	0.0015	0.0015	0.0014	0.0014
-2.8	0.0026	0.0025	0.0024	0.0023	0.0023	0.0022	0.0021	0.0021	0.0020	0.0019
-2.7	0.0035	0.0034	0.0033	0.0032	0.0031	0.0030	0.0029	0.0028	0.0027	0.0026
-2.6	0.0047	0.0045	0.0044	0.0043	0.0041	0.0040	0.0039	0.0038	0.0037	0.0036
-2.5	0.0062	0.0060	0.0059	0.0057	0.0055	0.0054	0.0052	0.0051	0.0049	0.0048
-2.4	0.0082	0.0080	0.0078	0.0075	0.0073	0.0071	0.0069	0.0068	0.0066	0.0064
-2.3	0.0107	0.0104	0.0102	0.0099	0.0096	0.0094	0.0091	0.0089	0.0087	0.0084
-2.2	0.0139	0.0136	0.0132	0.0129	0.0125	0.0122	0.0119	0.0116	0.0113	0.0110
-2.1	0.0179	0.0174	0.0170	0.0166	0.0162	0.0158	0.0154	0.0150	0.0146	0.0143
-2.0	0.0228	0.0222	0.0217	0.0212	0.0207	0.0202	0.0197	0.0192	0.0188	0.0183
-1.9	0.0287	0.0281	0.0274	0.0268	0.0262	0.0256	0.0250	0.0244	0.0239	0.0233
-1.8	0.0359	0.0351	0.0344	0.0336	0.0329	0.0322	0.0314	0.0307	0.0301	0.0294
-1.7	0.0446	0.0436	0.0427	0.0418	0.0409	0.0401	0.0392	0.0384	0.0375	0.0367
-1.6	0.0548	0.0537	0.0526	0.0516	0.0505	0.0495	0.0485	0.0475	0.0465	0.0455
-1.5	0.0668	0.0652	0.0643	0.0630	0.0618	0.0606	0.0594	0.0582	0.0571	0.0559
-1.4	0.0808	0.0793	0.0778	0.0764	0.0749	0.0735	0.0721	0.0708	0.0694	0.0681
-1.3	0.0968	0.0951	0.0934	0.0918	0.0901	0.0885	0.0869	0.0853	0.0838	0.0823
-1.2	0.1151	0.1131	0.1112	0.1093	0.1075	0.1057	0.1038	0.1020	0.1003	0.0985
-1.1	0.1357	0.1335	0.1314	0.1292	0.1271	0.1251	0.1230	0.1210	0.1190	0.1170
-1.0	0.1587	0.1562	0.1539	0.1515	0.1492	0.1469	0.1446	0.1423	0.1401	0.1379
-0.9	0.1814	0.1814	0.1788	0.1762	0.1736	0.1711	0.1685	0.1660	0.1635	0.1611
-0.8	0.2119	0.2090	0.2061	0.2033	0.2005	0.1977	0.1949	0.1922	0.1894	0.1867
-0.7	0.2420	0.2389	0.2358	0.2327	0.2297	0.2266	0.2236	0.2207	0.2177	0.2148
-0.6	0.2743	0.2709	0.2676	0.2643	0.2611	0.2578	0.2546	0.2514	0.2483	0.2451
-0.5	0.3085	0.3050	0.3015	0.2981	0.2946	0.2912	0.2877	0.2843	0.2810	0.2776
-0.4	0.3446	0.3409	0.3372	0.3336	0.3300	0.3264	0.3228	0.3192	0.3156	0.3121
-0.3	0.3821	0.3783	0.3745	0.3707	0.3669	0.3632	0.3594	0.3557	0.3520	0.3483
-0.2	0.4207	0.4168	0.4129	0.4090	0.4052	0.4013	0.3974	0.3936	0.3897	0.3859
-0.1	0.4602	0.4562	0.4522	0.4483	0.4443	0.4404	0.4364	0.4325	0.4286	0.4247
-0.0	0.5000	0.4960	0.4920	0.4880	0.4840	0.4801	0.4761	0.4721	0.4681	0.4641

Table 11.2   Areas Under Normal Curve

$\frac{Xi-\mu}{\sigma}$	0.00	0.01	0.02	0.03	0.04	0.05	0.06	0.07	0.08	0.09
+0.0	0.5000	0.5040	0.5080	0.5120	0.5160	0.5199	0.5239	0.5279	0.5319	0.5359
+0.1	0.5398	0.5438	0.5478	0.5517	0.5557	0.5596	0.5636	0.5675	0.5714	0.5753
+0.2	0.5793	0.5832	0.5871	0.5910	0.5948	0.5987	0.6026	0.6064	0.6103	0.6141
+0.3	0.6179	0.6217	0.6255	0.6293	0.6331	0.6368	0.6406	0.6443	0.6480	0.6517
+0.4	0.6554	0.6591	0.6628	0.6664	0.6700	0.6736	0.6772	0.6808	0.6844	0.6879
+0.5	0.6915	0.6950	0.6985	0.7019	0.7054	0.7088	0.7123	0.7157	0.7190	0.7224
+0.6	0.7257	0.7291	0.7324	0.7357	0.7389	0.7422	0.7454	0.7486	0.7517	0.7549
+0.7	0.7580	0.7611	0.7642	0.7673	0.7704	0.7734	0.7764	0.7794	0.7823	0.7852
+0.8	0.7881	0.7910	0.7939	0.7967	0.7995	0.8023	0.8051	0.8079	0.8106	0.8133
+0.9	0.8159	0.8186	0.8212	0.8238	0.8264	0.8289	0.8315	0.8340	0.8365	0.8389
+1.0	0.8413	0.8438	0.8461	0.8485	0.8508	0.8531	0.8554	0.8577	0.8599	0.8621
+1.1	0.8643	0.8665	0.8686	0.8708	0.8729	0.8749	0.8770	0.8790	0.8810	0.8830
+1.2	0.8849	0.8869	0.8888	0.8907	0.8925	0.8944	0.8962	0.8980	0.8997	0.9015
+1.3	0.9032	0.9049	0.9066	0.9082	0.9099	0.9115	0.9131	0.9147	0.9162	0.9177
+1.4	0.9192	0.9207	0.9222	0.9236	0.9251	0.9265	0.9279	0.9292	0.9306	0.9319
+1.5	0.9332	0.9345	0.9357	0.9370	0.9382	0.9394	0.9406	0.9418	0.9429	0.9441
+1.6	0.9452	0.9463	0.9474	0.9484	0.9495	0.9505	0.9515	0.9525	0.9535	0.9545
+1.7	0.9554	0.9564	0.9573	0.9582	0.9591	0.9599	0.9608	0.9616	0.9625	0.9633
+1.8	0.9641	0.9649	0.9656	0.9664	0.9671	0.9678	0.9686	0.9693	0.9699	0.9706
+1.9	0.9713	0.9719	0.9726	0.9732	0.9738	0.9744	0.9750	0.9756	0.9761	0.9767
+2.0	0.9773	0.9778	0.9783	0.9788	0.9798	0.9798	0.9803	0.9808	0.9812	0.9817
+2.1	0.9821	0.9826	0.9830	0.9834	0.9838	0.9842	0.9846	0.9850	0.9854	0.9857
+2.2	0.9861	0.9864	0.9868	0.9871	0.9875	0.9878	0.9881	0.9884	0.9887	0.9890
+2.3	0.9893	0.9896	0.9898	0.9901	0.9904	0.9906	0.9909	0.9911	0.9913	0.9916
+2.4	0.9918	0.9920	0.9922	0.9925	0.9927	0.9929	0.9931	0.9932	0.9934	0.9936
+2.5	0.9938	0.9940	0.9941	0.9943	0.9945	0.9946	0.9948	0.9949	0.9951	0.9952
+2.6	0.9953	0.9955	0.9956	0.9957	0.9959	0.9960	0.9961	0.9962	0.9963	0.9964
+2.7	0.9965	0.9966	0.9967	0.9968	0.9969	0.9970	0.9971	0.9972	0.9973	0.9974
+2.8	0.9974	0.9975	0.9976	0.9977	0.9977	0.9978	0.9979	0.9979	0.9980	0.9981
+2.9	0.9981	0.9982	0.9983	0.9983	0.9984	0.9984	0.9985	0.9985	0.9986	0.9986
+3.0	0.99865	0.99869	0.99874	0.99878	0.99882	0.99886	0.99889	0.99893	0.99896	0.99900
+3.1	0.99903	0.99906	0.99910	0.99913	0.99915	0.99918	0.99921	0.99924	0.99926	0.99929
+3.2	0.99931	0.99934	0.99936	0.99938	0.99940	0.99942	0.99944	0.99946	0.99948	0.99950
+3.3	0.99952	0.99953	0.99955	0.99957	0.99958	0.99960	0.99961	0.99962	0.99964	0.99965
+3.4	0.99966	0.99967	0.99969	0.99970	0.99971	0.99972	0.99973	0.99974	0.99975	0.99976
+3.5	0.99977	0.99978	0.99978	0.99979	0.99980	0.99981	0.99981	0.99982	0.99983	0.99983

(Source: Grant, E. L. and Leavenworth, R. S., *Statistical Control*, 4th Ed., McGraw-Hill, 1972.)

Table 11.2 (cont.)   Areas Under Normal Curve

calculate the cell intervals; the important thing is that you consistently calculate it the same way. Histograms can have three basic shapes: skewed left, normal, and skewed right (Figure 11.2).

| Symmetrical or bell-shaped | Skewed to the right (positive skewness) | Skewed to the left (negative skewness) |

Figure 11.2 Three Basic Shapes of Histograms

If the data are skewed, then there is reason to suspect that the underlying distribution is not normal. A nonnormal distribution can cause problems when determining specifications and the type of control charts to use. For example, defects are not normally distributed so that a "c" chart is the most appropriate control chart to use.

Control charts are simply charts of data graphed in a time sequence. This enables the receiver to see what is taking place over time. The most common charts are X-bar and range/standard deviation charts; chart of individuals with a moving range for variables (measured) data; and "p," "np," "c," and "u" charts for attribute (counting) data. There are others which are used for special cases such as cumulative sum, exponentially weighted moving average charts, acceptance control charts, adaptive control charts, and multivariate control charts. There are also various rules for determining whether a process is in a "state of control." The most common rules are 1, 2, 4, and 8 point rules where the control chart is divided into zones. The theory behind these rules is based on the probability of a particular number of points occurring in a normal population.

Another chart that can be used is called a Bossert chart. This chart plots the range or standard deviation of a grouping of data. If the buyer is purchasing the same material from three suppliers, the buyer can plot the characteristics of interest of all three suppliers and see how consistent the suppliers are. These charts are simple to make, and show a lot of information. For example, if we were looking at three suppliers of a chemical that had a pH specification of 5.5 to 6.0, the buyer could gather all the data from the past year on each supplier. The buyer then could obtain the range of pH for each and plot the range with a vertical bar for each supplier. The means are connected (Figures 11.3, 11.4, and 11.5). This plot shows how consistent the suppliers are to each other compared to the specification. When there are more than nine data points, a standard deviation can be used.

The bottom line on any plot is: Keep it simple (KIS). An effective plot is one that tells a story with little or no explanation. A busy person cannot afford a "busy" plot. A clean chart enables a decision to be made quickly. A busy chart requires time and explanation.

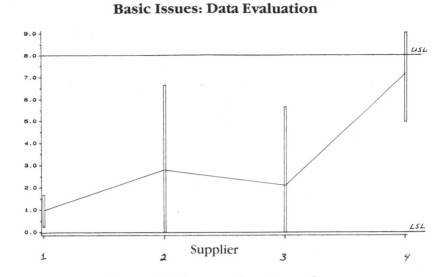

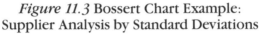

Figure 11.3 Bossert Chart Example:
Supplier Analysis by Standard Deviations

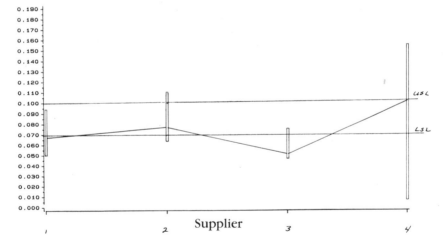

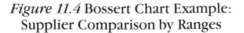

Figure 11.4 Bossert Chart Example:
Supplier Comparison by Ranges

CHAPTER 12

THE IDEAL SYSTEM

Key Words: Site Inspection, Certification, Control Charts, Follow-Up

Summary:
- **How a company works with its supplier**
- **How one supplier improved itself**

This book has been a discussion about many issues around the philosophy and strategy of buying high-quality products. It is appropriate to show two examples of systems that come close to the ideal. The first is the Supplier Quality Improvement Process at Cummins Engine Company, Inc. (Columbus, Indiana), and the second is what a supplier did to make its company a model to the Deming philosphy.

The Cummins Supplier Quality Improvement Process is a 20-step process that begins with a preliminary site inspection at a supplier's company and ends with supplier certification (Figure 12.1). The flow diagram shows the evolution of the partnership. Steps 1 to 4 are the dating phase, steps 5 to 15 are the engagement phase, step 16 is the marriage, step 17 the honeymoon, and steps 18 to 20 the long-term partnership.

Some suppliers have initiated their own programs to ensure quality. One supplier took four years to develop its program. It did not achieve instant success, but worked hard to establish the following system.

When raw material is received at the facility, the receiving personnel have a checklist that is followed for all incoming product. If any characteristic is not in conformance on the checklist, the material is returned immediately to the supplier. As the truck is pulling away, purchasing is calling to inform their supplier why this material is being returned.

If the material passes the receiving inspection, a copy of the checklist is attached to the material. This checklist will remain with the material until it is shipped out as the product. All employees who handle the material will stamp the checklist as it goes through the transformation from raw material to product. Each step of the operation has control charts in place. Even with the control charts, there are critical steps in the process where audits are made to ensure conformance. At each process step, the specifications are displayed where all personnel can see them. No deviations are allowed. Equipment and personnel are routinely recertified to ensure performance expectations. As the product leaves the plant, there is a control chart of the final process step which goes with it. This supplier maintains routine communication with all customers and has not had any product returned in two years. It also has all the original equipment still working and in a "state of control." The plant is 40 years old.

The Ideal System

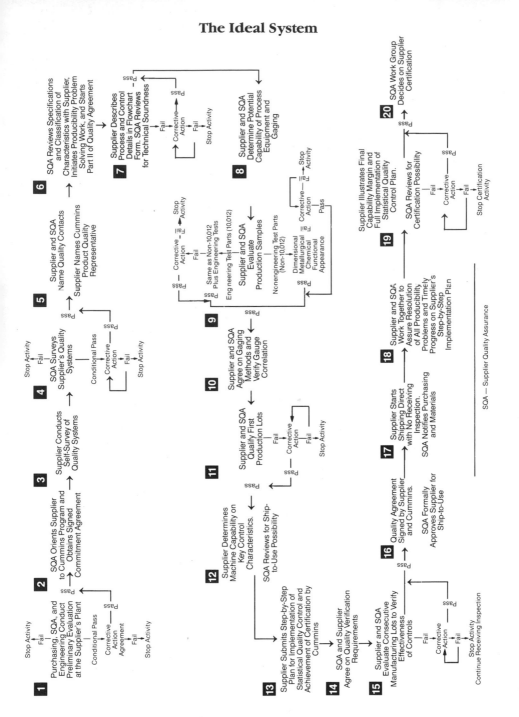

Figure 12.1 Cummins Supplier Quality Improvement Process
(Reprinted with permission by Cummins Engine Company, Inc., Columbus, Indiana)

123

The next three chapters are edited reprints of the "how to" series the Vendor-Vendee Technical Committee published from 1976 to 1985. These cover three areas that are critical in the establishment of a supplier quality program.

Procurement Quality Control

CHAPTER 13

HOW TO CONDUCT A SUPPLIER SURVEY

Key Words: Team, Preparation, Visit, Evaluation, Documentation, Corrective Action, Follow-Up

Summary:

- **Goals**
- **Team organization**
- **Visit**
- **Evaluation of a period system**
- **Final report**
- **Follow-up**

Introduction

In conducting a supplier survey, you, as a quality professional, will be performing one of the most critical jobs you can do for your company.

To the supplier, you will represent your company. Up to this time, perhaps only a single salesman from the supplier may have called on your organization. Now, virtually everyone in the supplier's plant will be watching you and judging your company by your acts and omissions. In fact, the quality surveyor may be the only person from your firm they ever see face-to-face.

This guide has one purpose — to help a professional in the field of quality do the best possible survey of a supplier. Some 20 of your fellow professionals have contributed toward this end. The guide begins from the point where your manager or supervisor assigns a survey task to you. It then follows through the preparation, the visit and tour, evaluation and judgment, report documentation, corrective action, and follow-up, ending when you sit back and review your activities, trying to decide whether you really conducted yourself as a quality professional.

Rather than presenting what to evaluate, we will stress the "how to" aspect of surveying. We would like to make you aware of the philosophies, techniques, and realities of performing successful surveys. The methods described are applicable in virtually every industry or service, in all kinds of companies, large and small, with new suppliers or old, and within your own organization.

The guidelines we present are not intended to stand alone. ANSI/ASQC Standard C1-1985, *General Requirements for a Quality Program,* forms the basis of these survey guidelines and should be used in conjunction with any survey performed. In specialized cases, other standards may also apply, and should be used. However, all the guidelines and standards are of little use without the alert, inquiring mind that should characterize the quality professional, along with experience, training, and knowledge. Basic to everything is the guidance and support of the quality professional's manager or supervisor.

Goals of a Survey

We pluralize "goals" to stress that the survey will almost always have more than one goal. Most basic to understanding how to conduct a supplier survey is the recognition that a survey involves interaction between two or more people.

Unlike writing reports, which may be a solitary activity, surveying always involves more than one person. At the very minimum, it would involve you for your company and someone representing the supplier. Most surveys will involve many more people from at least two organizations.

While you may be trying to learn what quality standards an organization has, or is capable of, always remember that the supplier you are evaluating also has at least one aim: to present its organization in the best light (sometimes by hiding one or more defects). In conducting a survey, be mindful of your company's goal(s), which may often be dependent on the type of supplier you are evaluating:

Circumstance	*Typical question to be answered by survey*
New Supplier	Can this operation provide the product quality we need?
Old Supplier	Can this operation continue giving the product quality we need?
Problem Supplier	What must be done so that this operation can give us the product quality we need?
Reformed Supplier	Has this supplier really made the improvements necessary to give us the product quality we need?
System Evaluation	Is this operation following all the procedures needed to give us the product quality we need?

128

Such listings could be extended greatly. Every new survey you conduct can have its own matrix of goals. Although it may seem hard enough to identify the proper goals of your company, this is much easier than trying to identify the goals of the organization you are surveying.

Not only may the supplier have a variety of goals, but the emotional interplay of the individuals must be considered. Imagine being told that *your* company will be surveyed by your customers — whether they are customers, government, wholesalers, etc. Further, try to imagine that how well you do on such a survey may determine if your company gets a large contract, or if your company will get further orders, or how your management may view your personal performance. Confidence, pride, anxiety, caution, worry, secretiveness, apprehension — just what kinds of emotions would the prospect of such a survey rouse in you?

If your counterparts in the company to be surveyed are good actors, you may never learn the supplier's real goals. Conversely, the supplier may never learn yours. If you're unsmiling by nature, you may give the impression that you're predisposed against the supplier. Then, the supplier may rush through the survey considering each moment spent as wasted. If you are too friendly and easygoing, the supplier may believe you're a pushover, inclined to approve, and thus may not go into great depth about the quality system.

Such influences must be anticipated, and allowed for whenever suspected. Otherwise, your company may pass by a capable source for needed materials, or may unwittingly downgrade a supplier who might be able to offer a better product.

Preparation for the Survey

When you are preparing for a supplier survey, you will naturally want to gather as many facts and figures about the supplier as you can. In doing this, it's important to keep in mind your company's goals, and any existing history of relationships between the supplier and your company.

If a current supplier is to be surveyed, available documentation in your company files should be reviewed. These could include receiving inspection reports, purchasing agent's periodic reports, records of corrective action, delivery records, outstanding contract quantities, product specifications, etc.

If your company has been experiencing problems with the supplier, you may want to contact the designers, purchasers, inspectors, and production people in your plant for their opinions. However, you must be careful and realize that some of these people may themselves be associated with the causes of the problems.

For new or potential suppliers, your purchasing agent's visit report (if the supplier has been visited) is essential. Don't ignore information you might get from the supplier's annual reports, from Dun & Bradstreet, or from your professional colleagues in other companies. If you know the names of the supplier's quality control personnel, glance at the author index of various quality and other technical journals. Any articles published over their names may give you an insight into the supplier's quality philosophy. Similar information on other companies in the same business is also helpful, particularly if data on the company to be surveyed are hard to find.

However, it must always be kept in mind that preliminary information should never be used to prejudge a supplier. The preliminary information is only a guide to what to look for in the survey.

When approaching an industry segment or supplier with whom you have never done business, be careful of the sophistication level you expect. Always keep in mind your company's needs and the supplier's ability to meet the particular needs. Someone in the drug industry evaluating a plastics company for its capability to produce trays might be horrified at not finding a quality control manager or department or inspector. But, the company may be fully capable of producing the right goods at the right price.

In such situations, the true quality professional will be armed with the knowledge of what is current practice in the strange industry, and to always keep in mind just what the company needs from that kind of supplier.

A final note on preparation: Try, whenever possible, to document both positive and negative information. Receiving inspection may claim that a supplier is unacceptable. Yet, a fuller examination of the records may show that internal problems are the real culprit.

On the other hand, an "A-OK" report may really mean that the supplier's shipments came in so late that incoming inspection was dropped in favor of on-line culling to keep production going. These are vendor problems induced by the vendees and capable of internal correction by the latter.

Team Organization

More often than not, the quality professional conducting the survey will have little to do with the makeup, selection, and organization of the team. The survey team may consist of only the quality professional who will visit the supplier for a few hours, or several professionals from varied disciplines who may stay a week. Whatever the scope of the survey, whether one person or several, remember that you're part of a team and that you represent the company.

Even one-person surveys by quality professionals may bear information on labor negotiations, procurement policy, new design concepts, process capabilities, or security for report to concerned departments, such as personnel, purchasing, development, engineering, or shipping. When favorable, such information is usually pointed out pridefully by the supplier, and the supplier would be surprised if your report did not mention them.

The effect on concerned departments in your company is reasonably predictable: Your personnel department is gratified that labor negotiations are progressing; development may want to follow up new design concepts; engineering may feel safer if it believes that production people are in charge of the process; and your shipping department may draw comfort from the impression that the safety of the product in transit is assured.

The moral is: Don't stick blindly to checklists. Keep your ears (and mind) open to receive useful information of any kind. This is easier with a team approach (because rarely are two people on a team specialists in the same field). A forewarned quality professional will approach the survey with a receptive attitude.

Often, on multimember teams, purchasing will participate. Sometimes, with purchasing present, the impression may arise that purchasing should head the team in the belief that it must control intimate vendor contracts. Heading the survey team by someone from purchasing is not essential, unless a considered company policy so dictates. Whoever heads the team must take into account findings of others who are usually more expert in areas other than the team leader's specialty.

An organization meeting must be held after the survey team is picked to set strategy and outline responsibilities. Such decisions should be made well in advance of the team's visit to the supplier. Do not schedule this important meeting for the airport waiting room, or enroute, or at the hotel the night before the meeting. Someone may miss the plane, you may not be seated together, and you may be able to meet at the suppliers only a few minutes before you begin. Meetings to organize the survey team should take place well in advance of the actual survey. Your company goals should be clearly recognized and openly discussed. Team members should be assigned their area of responsibilities and their particular objectives. Information about the supplier of potential interest should be made available.

If the team includes more than one member with a given specialty, specific responsibilities should be clearly assigned so that the team doesn't stumble over its own feet. It is also important at this time to agree on who will be the team leader responsible for the coordination and administration of the survey.

If the necessary preliminary meetings are held early enough, it is usually possible to identify the need, and supply extra personnel, information, or support by request to your management.

It may be decided that you need a facilities engineer, more product information, or a better analysis of the field complaints on the supplier's merchandise. If the upcoming survey is particularly important and the team roster is supposed to include an inexperienced person (and remember, everyone has to make a start sometime), it may be possible to put the learner on another team for training-by-doing or to otherwise give preliminary instruction.

Though it may seem perfectly obvious to you, many surveys run into problems for the lack of checking the following:

- The current address and phone number of the supplier.
- The name of the host individual you will contact.
- The correct date for the survey.
- The supplier's readiness for the survey.

The Use of Quantification in the Evaluation Format

The end result of all surveys should be a decision. Ideally, the decision should be a clean-cut acceptance or rejection. With complex undertakings such as a manufacturing process, this may not always be feasible. An area of indecision, large or small, may remain and must be taken into account in any final recommendation of the survey team.

To minimize such a gray area, a survey team must clarify and formalize its approach to information collection and quantification. Many different tactics can be adopted as long as "the major requirements for an adequate system" are evaluated equally in each facility you review.

Valid and acceptable measurements are any that are reproducible within limits which do not compromise the usefulness of the initial quantity evaluated. A vendor survey is one form of measurement. Thus, all methodology that ensures accuracy, impartiality, and repeatability of physical measurements applies to vendor surveys of performance measurements. Numerical, alphabetical, or other regularly sequenced scores must be used if you want to make valid judgments. The most direct way of checking repeatability of a survey is to quantify the measurements.

Mathematical tools are available to show the interrelationships between cause and effect in a random system of events. The fundamental model for any production process is just that, a process whose variability is determined by a system of events which occur at random. Some manufacturing processes do not conform exactly to this model, but the mathematics can still be adapted to draw useful conclusions.

The prime reason for a survey is to estimate or, preferably, *measure* the extent to which the supplier being surveyed operates under a planned quality system. Never forget that the reason you are there is that your company needs the kind of products the supplier can produce. If the supplier has carefully quantified his product mechanics, provided a quality measuring system, and an adequate control and corrective network, the survey will be significantly more accurate. If the survey team has to provide or extemporize means of such quantification, the results may not be as accurate or predictable, especially when they are reviewed by another individual remote from the site of the survey.

Get all the information you can to make decisions. Have your supplier's staff fill in a presurvey evaluation form before the visit. This evaluation form will tell the supplier what you want to know. Also, you will be able to judge how well your supplier reacts to communication from outside the company. The physical survey should follow soon after receiving the filled-in evaluation form from your supplier.

Your survey will be used by people who have not visited the plant under review or who may not know you personally. Be careful to describe all quantification methods and what rating scales are used, and see to it that the report is comprehensible without your personal explanation or amplification of the results.

Your survey will be used to compare competing sources of services or materials essential to your company's production. The award of contracts will likely depend on information contained in it. The survey must be straightforward and intelligible, and capable of supplying figures for cost and other computations which may have to be made during the selection process.

Lastly, everyone has a personal error level, though not everyone is normally aware of it. This is a product of previous activity, experience, and lifestyle. The format of any survey must seek to minimize variability from this cause.

Opening Conference

The first order of business when you arrive at the supplier's plant is the opening conference — it's get acquainted time! Explain exactly why you are there, what you are going to try to do, and, in a general way, the sort of results you expect.

If your purchasing agent is a member of your team and has met the people from the supplier, let him introduce you. Have the purchasing agent emphasize the importance of your evaluation and its effect on future business with the supplier.

For the supplier, the meeting should be attended by the representative's quality manager, sales manager, engineering department head, other operating managers, the executive(s) over all these groups, and the representative's boss — if possible. It is essential that all levels of supplier management understand the scope and purpose of the evaluation survey.

The explanation of your purpose should help calm the supplier's managers, especially if they have not been surveyed often or if — unhappily — they have recently been visited by an inept surveyor! It is unbelievable what some people imagine is going to happen, in spite of what they were told when you first arranged your visit. Reactions may range from, "They're just here to get out of their offices!", "This will be a military type white glove inspection!", "Heck, it's just another Mickey Mouse program!", to a defiant, "We can teach them a few things." Since the truth lies, as usual, somewhere in between, it is important that a correct perspective be established.

The opening conference is also the time to establish your credentials. False modesty is as out of place as a "snow job." Stick to the facts. It is not wrong to impress the supply of management with what you know.

Avoid bragging or exaggeration, because you'll surely come out looking like a fool. Explain firmly that you are a professional in the field of quality, and that you have had training and experience in evaluation (if such is really the case). If you are entitled to some special distinction or designation, such as "ASQC Certified Quality Engineer," tell them — this is not just name-dropping. The surveyor should briefly discuss his role in his own company, his expertise in the supplier's field if he has any (but no lame excuses if he lacks such expertise), and his understanding of component(s), material(s), or service(s) for which the supplier is being considered.

Handle the establishment of credentials in a calm, confident way. If you have any fears about this part of your visit, try a bit of role-playing with your peer group before the trip — rehearse your act! And, above all, be honest and friendly!

Everything said up to now about the opening conference is to assure that the supplier is comfortable with you. If he is at ease — if he knows that you are knowledgeable enough to give him a fair and sound evaluation — he is likely to be open, cooperative, and not at all defensive. But, if he does not know where you stand, he will ponder the meaning of every question.

Of course, if the supplier has shaky quality, explanation of your credentials may tend to make him apprehensive. If you sense this, remind him that your team has come only to see the present situation in his plant. Tell him you are eager to try to indicate what kind of changes may put him in the ranks of a potential supplier. Your sincere reassurance may well convince him that he stands to benefit from your survey, and you may gain cooperation.

The next step is to ask one of the executives present for a general description of the company, when founded, how many plants, people, etc. — more or less to update/verify your previous research on the company. Ask the quality manager to describe the quality system and the reporting level of the personnel with whom he works. The quality manager should briefly discuss the handling of design information, the manufacturing and test equipment, the nature of the inspections and tests, and the documentation that supports the whole program.

How to Conduct a Supplier Survey

At this point, the survey team is trying to get a general feel for the quality program — how it works, how it fits together, what are the check-points — in brief, trying to understand what they will be viewing shortly on the plant tour. This is not yet the time to ask for detailed explanations, and certainly not the place to try and make a judgment of the workability of any facet of the quality program.

The opening conference is, however, a good time to make at least a preliminary judgment on management attitude toward quality. If the supplier's personnel are serious, yet excited, about their efforts to achieve high quality, you can do a lot with that vendor, even if he hasn't got it all together at the moment. If the company executives appear to look on their quality system as a necessary evil, a required but unwelcome overhead, then tread most carefully and alertly.

A mention of the most significant features or critical characteristics of the component, material, or service to be provided should have a part in the opening conference. This will give the supplier's quality manager a chance to explain in fuller detail and depth how his system seeks to control such particular facets of requirements.

What if, at the opening conference, the company president quietly admits that he lacks a formal quality control organization? This takes careful thought and handling. The evaluator must ferret out who controls the quality of the product — no matter what actual titles may be. The evaluator must unravel the quality responsibilities granted to each part of the manufacturing and engineering functions. The surveyor must see the operation in action. Then, and only then, can he judge if the lack of a formal quality organization so weakens the assurance of quality as to disqualify the company. It is a fact that some (though few) companies that have no quality control group have as good a quality system as could be expected in their particular industry. Sometimes, especially in smaller companies, the top boss is very quality conscious and exacts a high quality product.

What else can you do at an opening conference? At some time during the opening conference the survey team should ask about significant problems the supplier has identified and is in the process of correcting. The opening conference is also a good time for the survey team to brief the supplier on the intended use of the product and to discuss design adequacy, limitations, etc. The good evaluator takes plentiful notes — better to put down more than you need than miss important tidbits. Most of the time, there will be so many facts fired at you that it will be impossible to evaluate their significance at the moment. Often, such evaluation must wait until you are writing your report. If the supplier's group is not inhibited by one, a tape recorder may be helpful. However, there is a fringe benefit from trying to take written notes. The obvious effort of trying to keep up in writing with the spoken words tends to keep the pace more manageable. Both sides have more time to formulate questions and to reflect a bit on their responses.

And, after you have enough notes, it's time for the next step in the survey: the plant tour.

Handle the opening conference very carefully. If it is mismanaged, it can spoil the whole evaluation. Carried off skillfully, it can make a valid and accurate survey much easier.

What to Look for in the Quality Program

A major concern of your survey team is how to look at the quality program. This is important since few quality programs are exactly alike. Programs differ and each must be considered in the context of its environment, top management policies, and employee personalities.

The objective of your survey is to see if the combination of quality system and plant facility can consistently assure that the purchased product meets specification requirements. Your prime task in the survey is to conduct an evaluation of the quality program, not to dictate specific system changes.

To be effective, a quality program must be supported by top management, even though it is carried out on lower levels. There must be a top management quality policy statement for guidance and as authority to initiate and operate the quality plan. The quality statement reflects a company's dedication to supply a product or service as stated. Because of its implications to quality, you need to become familiar with the policy.

It is important that the quality function be separated from the manufacturing function, and either report to top management, or to a level that has direct access to top management.

The combination of the quality system and plant facility may be viewed from the aspect of the system or the aspect of the process. One or the other, or both, may be evaluated on the same visit, but not necessarily by the same member of the survey team.

Several basic considerations should be noted as the survey team considers the quality system. The plan should concentrate on defect prevention. The plan should try to provide best control where personnel capabilities are weakest or lacking. The plan must define responsibility for each of its elements. The plan should provide for planning and documentation of information feedback to measure the plan's effectiveness adequately. This should include a breakdown of quality costs in the broad sense.

When you evaluate process controls, you should become aware whether control elements are included in the operator's written process instructions. Are the customer's minimum requirements for specification conformance a part of process control? Assuming you observe a satisfactory control that identifies, evaluates, and segregates nonconforming products, does the plan provide for action to prevent recurrence of the defects? You should end your process evaluation by assuring yourself that sufficient documentation is kept to verify the effectiveness of the program.

How to Gain the Most from a Plant Tour

The decision to visit a plant usually results from the realization that required information or assurance of compliance with contractual agreements can only be obtained that way. As suggested previously, you will have outlined an agenda or plan well before your visit to make a plant tour as helpful as possible.

As your tour progresses, look into the corners of various rooms and areas to see if the floor has been recently swept or washed. If cleaning or washing of such areas looks like a sometime thing, beware! Your hosts may consider your visit *very* special, and may be taking extraordinary steps to try to impress you.

Check all instrumentation and/or testing equipment for noticeable patterns of dust marks, particularly in areas where there should be minimal dust if the instruments/equipment are used regularly. If any of the instruments/equipment have covers, check to see if they are dirty all over. This too may indicate that the instruments/equipment are not used very much.

Try to look at some or all of the quality control procedure manuals, such as would be used by plant inspectors/monitors/auditors. Fingerprints, smudges, stains, frayed edges, and turned pages might mean that the procedures were in use at the plant. On the other hand, it may mean that the procedures were not updated very often. Look for dates of revision, particularly if given in open figures. You might casually inquire from plant personnel who should be using procedures if they have ever seen or heard of the quality control manual.

Try to determine how samples are chosen for inspection, where they are taken, and at what intervals. What you observe in this respect will tell you if quality inspection is well planned and executed, or whether it is haphazard afterthought. With many plants and products, look for retained samples and how they are managed. Systematic operation of a retained sample library will tell you that top management is really quality conscious or that, having had a bad quality experience in the past, they are hoping to learn from problems and want to try to avoid them.

If you're going to discuss proprietary information, or visit areas where proprietary products or processes are open to your view, your team should get competent legal instruction BEFORE your visit. Determine with your host which specific areas are considered proprietary, trying to distinguish between those which are truly proprietary and those which represent novel company practices that cannot be legally protected.

Don't sign secrecy agreements until your attorney has scrutinized their contents, has discussed the extent of your obligations under them, and has approved them. Hold to the essential few the members of your team who may involve themselves with access to proprietary data.

Naturally, under no conditions disclose proprietary data in violation of a signed agreement. Your team should interest itself only in those areas or processes that can truly affect your product of interest.

Evaluation of a Record System

Before you can evaluate a record system, you must define management and contractual requirements. In most procurements, the latter demand that the vendor establish an inspection system. A valid inspection system requires not only documentary evidence of the quality status of the product, but must also include all facets that contribute to quality, such as inspection records, test data sheets, raw material certification, heat treating records, calibration data, plating records, X-rays, etc.

Perhaps the most effective way to evaluate a record system at the inspection level is to select a lot/part/assembly and trace it back to the "raw material" state. Choose a specimen that is not too old, so the vendor can't duck behind, "This is before my time," or so new that, "It isn't completed." Pick a sample within the oldest time frame acceptable to the vendor, in which time frame excuses for nonconformance cannot be supported. This will also check the accuracy of the data retrieval system. In the event of a failure, ability to retrieve relevant information is important when traceability, assignment of cause, and identification of similar potential time bombs already in the possession of customers may become vital. The degree to which you check your supplier's records should only be enough to make you feel confident of his record keeping.

Let's clarify this. If you pick a complex assembly, ask for records of only one leg of the assembly. If, in your opinion, there are too many anomalies, reject the system. If there are no anomalies, accept the system. If you are not convinced one way or another, pick another leg to trace.

Do not try to trace every single step. You are trying to evaluate the working effectiveness of the data-keeping system, not the acceptability of a single piece of hardware. To sum up this phase: Choose a significant number of observations so that you may make a judgment as to the acceptability of the vendor's record system. If you need to take too many samples before you can decide, this indicates a weak or indifferent record system.

Avoid the type of surveys in which you, as the potential vendee, examine in minute detail all records so as to identify each and every discrepancy that has existed. The vendor may correct everything you identify but assume no responsibility for the correction of defects that may have been missed by your evaluation. Keep in mind that you are trying to identify actual and potential problem areas. It is up to the vendor to correct these and all similar areas in which there may be similar conditions.

How to Conduct a Supplier Survey

Up to this point, we have been philosophizing about the conduct of a survey of a record system. Now, let's consider the specifics of actually looking at the records and how we should evaluate after the examination of the records.

Are the records neat? Scribbled records, if legible, are not cause for rejection; illegible records are cause for rejection.

Are changes to records made properly? If a single line crosses out original data but does not obliterate it, and the change is initialed by a responsible person, such changes may be acceptable. Other ways suggest sloppy practices and hint of "cooking the books."

Are all blocks filled in on printed forms? Dashes or n/a (not applicable) are acceptable. Ignoring the blanks consistently may indicate failure to comply with requirements. Dashes or n/a suggest that the inspector has considered the requirements and acted accordingly.

Is the retrieval system timely and adequate? Unavailability or lost records may point to an inadequate system. Speedy retrieval indicates an accurate filing system run by competent personnel.

Are variable data being recorded? Lack of variable data is not in itself cause for rejection unless it is in violation of the specific contractual requirements. However, its presence is usually a sign of a professional quality system, and should be noted favorably by the auditor.

What is the "quality" of the data? If the exact value is being recorded conspicuously often for a given parameter (particularly if it just within an agreed limit), the data should be questioned. Perhaps it's the case of inspectors "flinching"; perhaps the measuring equipment is calibrated too coarsely. You would normally expect most data to show some kind of unbiased distribution curve. Often, you can picture the distribution mentally as you're reviewing the data.

Refer back to original data. Reproduction can hide many sins.

Are the files current? A large backlog of unfiled data may include a lack of personnel, concern, or genuine quality activity. Just collecting data is not quality control.

Most important — is the data used to influence product quality? Most contracts with vendors from prime contractors will not normally call for detailed variables data, quality cost trend analysis, control charts, etc. However, much of this will appear in plants that have an underlying commitment to quality. Maintenance of data to verify inspection status is required to protect hardware integrity. The use of data to adjust the quality plan to achieve the most economical cost balance identifies a true professional system. Serious consideration should be given to the effective use of quality data in a vendor's record system.

Closing Conference

The closing conference is your final contact with the supplier's management group before you leave the plant after the survey. Take time to prepare your presentation before the conference. Be specific on discrepancies you found during your survey. Write them down in descending order of importance. Be prepared to explain each one in terms of deficiencies and discrepancies. Be quick to point out good points of your potential supplier's quality system so that you keep his confidence. If there is anything particularly laudable, begin your presentation with it.

If the supplier cannot be made to understand a discrepancy, be fully prepared to go with him to the area in question to show him. If the supplier fails to understand what is wrong, he may make a futile attempt at correction, perhaps resulting in another discrepancy, which might trigger another, perhaps unwarranted survey.

Do not try to lay the blame for discrepancies you find on the supplier group you are meeting with. It is most probable that the group will have to secure higher management approval to make changes in its quality system.

After discussion, each discrepancy should be noted in writing at the closing conference. Your supplier should give an estimated date for completion of corrective action for each discrepancy. If possible, the discrepancy list should be signed by a representative from the supplier and from the survey group to indicate that there is full understanding.

Final Report

The end product of your survey or quality program evaluation should be an understandable final report. A good one effectively communicates the findings using the original observations to support the conclusions. The report must be an honest, objective summation of your efforts. Even when conveying results that are not always favorable, a properly written professional report should be of potential benefit to its recipients. The report should portray the situation dispassionately and give directions for suggested corrective action. And, when things are better than you had expected them to be, don't forget to give full credit. However, take some care: Unwarranted accolades, as well as improper criticism, destroy the credibility of any report.

An improper report destroys relationships, breeds dissension, and creates mistrust. Such a report may deal with personalities, avoid understanding, and overlook facts.

Know your audience. The report must always be in a format and language to suit those for whom it is written. Don't forget that even a formal report can be in narrative style. Unless you're quite sure that most of those who may read your report will understand them, use an absolute minimum of charts, tables, and ratings. If you do use them, keep them as simple as possible, stressing only the important points. Another way of handling such graphic or tabular material is to refer to them in the body of the report, but transmit them as attachments or appendices to the report itself. Remember the KIS principle in report writing: Keep it simple.

List all individuals on both teams — don't overlook anyone. Make sure that names and positions are spelled correctly. A seeming lack of concern here might annoy someone needlessly and make the corrective task much more difficult.

Unlike older, more formal reports, the best modern reports open with a capsule summary of the work carried out and salient recommendations. This lets the busy executive gain an immediate overview of the basic facts. After this the observations, supporting discussions and, where necessary, detailed recommendations are added. Recommendations should also be given when a specification, procedure, or process is violated. An opinion for a better way to do something may be given as a suggestion or a comment.

Your report should be sent to the management team with whom you met. Copies should also be sent to the quality control manager and the sales department, if they were not represented. In your own company, copies should be distributed through the quality control manager.

The vendor survey will usually indicate an acceptable vendor, a limited vendor, a potentially acceptable vendor, or an unacceptable one. Naturally, a report about an acceptable vendor is more pleasant to write than the others. However, a report about an unacceptable vendor need not be marred by unpleasantness. Unless you shouldn't have been there to begin with, most of the negative surveys will suggest how to rise into at least the potential or limited vendor category. In such cases, handling the report with finesse makes all the difference. It can lead the potential vendor to want to take suitable corrective action. Grace makes it easier for the limited vendor to accept his limitations, and may even bring the unacceptable vendor to understand his problems and work toward future acceptability.

Don't forget to close your report with expressions of appreciation for the vendor's time, assistance, and cooperation.

Follow-Up to Vendor Qualification Surveys

Survey follow-up is carried out to ensure that satisfactory corrective action has been taken by a vendor who did not qualify at the time of your previous survey visit. You may have to judge if a follow-up visit is warranted, balancing the nature of the findings against the costs of travel and manpower involved. Accompanied by suitable documentation, a report from the supplier of corrective action may be enough.

Keep a genuinely helpful and constructive attitude at all times, and show it by timely support when you deal with all levels of the supplier's personnel. Doing this consistently may be difficult, but as a quality professional, you must do it.

The supplier and your company, as potential vendor and vendee, should have reached agreement during the closing conference on the timetable for corrective action. Documentation of the corrective action schedule should be included in the survey report and the formal vendor response. You must thoroughly review the survey report and the formal vendor response before a follow-up visit.

Contact the vendor and arrange a mutually agreeable date for the follow-up visit. Schedule a date for the follow-up visit as soon as possible after the execution and reported completion of required corrective action. Make sure that all required corrective action has been completed. If corrective action has not been effected within the required time, your management's policy should provide directions for suitable alternative action.

Show a positive attitude during the follow-up visit. Your vendor has told you that the corrective actions you agreed on have been carried out. You are there to verify that the corrective actions have been taken satisfactorily. If all corrective actions are acceptable and no additional problems become known, the vendor should qualify as an approved supplier.

If you cannot verify adequate corrective actions, consider the following:

1. If the vendor has made an effort to comply but has not met your requirements, you may have a communications problem. Review the survey report and reported corrective action with the responsible vendor personnel.
2. If requirements have not been satisfactorily fulfilled, the vendor should be advised that he has failed an approved supplier status. Mutually agreeable alternatives should be arranged before a visit and the supplier advised accordingly.

You may encounter a situation where the vendor has unique capabilities important to your company, but does not have the resources to invest to provide the quality assurance specified. If possible, the follow-up report should include suggestion(s) for alternative controls, or for direct assistance to the vendor to overcome certain conditions. Competent, understanding assistance in critical situations can be a rewarding investment in securing a satisfactory supplier base.

Post-Survey Team Critique

So you've finished another survey. Congratulations are in order... or are they? More than one team has faced that question after a survey. How can you answer it? One of the best ways is to do a team critique.

How to Conduct a Supplier Survey

You carry out a critique to increase the professional competence of the surveyors. It may be tough to face, but the recognition of individual or team shortcomings is the first necessary step in correcting them. Hopefully, individual or team improvement may get noticed by management and by the individuals and groups your surveyors contact in your company.

Remind yourself that vendors about to be surveyed by vendees are never happy with what is about to happen. A survey takes time and time means money. A survey improperly handled opens the vendee to criticism by the vendor. In a vendor's plant, each department is expected either to put on a good show or to mislead the evaluators. Such efforts make good surveys difficult. A critique undertaken on the same basis is absolutely worthless.

A proper critique must be realistic. It should consider all the items normally encountered in a vendor or corporate quality survey. The headings of this chapter are an excellent list of subjects to consider in your team critique:

- Goals of a Survey
- Preparation for the Survey
- Team Organization
- Use of Quantification in the Evaluation Format
- Opening Conference
- What to Look for in the Quality Program
- How to Gain the Most from a Plant Tour
- Evaluation of a Record System
- Closing Conference
- Final Report
- Follow-Up to Vendor Qualification Surveys
- Post-Survey Team Critique
- International Suppliers
- Vendor Information and Reassurance

A critique by an individual or a team can be a highly emotional activity, so conduct it in a professional manner to reduce emotion and increase effectiveness. Just as in all quality control operations, you must identify nonconformities and weaknesses rather than blame individuals for weaknesses and inadequacies. Timing of the critique can help set the proper frame of mind. A critique cannot be effective as a crash program or after some disaster. One good time is shortly after completing a survey when details are still fresh in mind and before the next one may be scheduled.

It is probably true there is no perfect product, drawing, or specification. Likewise, there is no perfect survey, vendor, nor vendee, and there really can be no perfect evaluators. The critique is a search for self-improvement. Any individual or team that believes operations cannot be improved is probably very poor rather than very good.

Therefore, as individuals we must expect that a critique is going to point out areas for improvement and change. Such is the purpose of a critique. What was good yesterday may not be good enough tomorrow. All surveys look for improvements and ways of making them.

In a critique it is important that unsatisfactory results be identified, but equally important that areas where improvement can be achieved are also identified. The one often means the other! Identification of areas that can be improved is the purpose of the critique. They are not the causes. It is necessary that the methods for improvement also be identified so that individuals can improve their performance and increase their efficiency and effectiveness.

As an example, the critique may disclose that in a recent survey the reliability tests and results were not properly evaluated. Why did this happen? Were the individuals or perhaps the whole team inattentive? Did they have insufficient training in reliability methods, procedures, and statistics? Another question might well be: Why were the records not completely and properly evaluated? Were they available to the members of the team or the individual doing the survey — the same people now doing a critique? Was it carelessness or failure to realize the importance of this area? Was this poor planning?

In conducting a critique it is essential that the problem and not the people be evaluated. This is a self-searching process to find a way to improve the operation.

To be worthwhile, a critique requires honesty and integrity. Just like other data analysis situations, it is not a procedure aimed at finding excuses, but rather at finding areas of the program where major improvements can be effected. This may point to a study course in some particular area. Perhaps just a review with someone at the plant as to what is needed can provide insight that can be developed by home study material. An evaluator cannot be an expert in every field, nor necessarily as expert as someone who is conducting a particular kind of operation. However, the evaluator must have sufficient insight to recognize when things are patently wrong, or when things appear to be done properly.

At the end of the critique, a list of areas needing improvement should emerge. The next is deciding how to obtain improvement in each named area. In some areas, provision of training and a program of study, counseling, or management consultation may be in order. In other instances, it may become obvious that the next survey team should include a specialist if specific areas are likely to arise. In any event, plans must be formalized and a commitment made to carry them through and improve the quality of performance of surveys.

As an alternative to the team critique, a peer review similar to those used for design reviews should be considered. In a supplier survey, communication is of prime importance; therefore, the form of the critique should be a confrontation situation in which the survey team defends its report and survey action to a peer group in the team's own company. The peer group should be drawn from the purchasing and production staff who would deal with the new supplier. They should have access to the history of the survey and copies of the proposed final report prior to the meeting.

The survey team must present its report and support its conclusions to this group plus a review chairman supported by two observers. The plant team is then free to question the survey team or each member on specific recommendations or conclusions from the report. The in-house staff will have to finally accept or reject the report as a useful addition to its working information.

The chairman and observers record significant points presented by both teams and produce an analysis of the proceedings after review. This method of in-house evaluation and improvement has proved most useful in many design fields, in value engineering, and in other situations where communication and action resulting from communication is vital.

The in-plant team gains from its exposure to the group that actually visited and measured the capabilities of the potential supplier. The review makes contact a little easier and the people in the supply source a little more three-dimensional.

Finally, the survey team sees the impact of its report on the other half of its own operation. The survey team members have to reason out why things were done and why conclusions were drawn. It is a satisfactory method of learning provided the chairman and observers ensure that the confrontation is properly conducted and does not degenerate to personalities.

International Suppliers

What has been discussed to this point has been how to deal with the survey of a potential supplier in your own country. The situation may well arise where you may have to consider a supplier abroad. Here are a few tips on how to proceed.

Quality assurance has developed rapidly in Europe and Japan, where it is recognized as a very important part of export or international sales. When your company has commitments involving evaluation of international sources of production, be very careful to check what information may be available to you from official or quasi-official bodies.

Most developed countries have state-sponsored organizations responsible for interfacing with foreign business interests, and, in this sense, *you* are the foreign interest. These organizations can usually supply product and manufacturing quality references and approvals to expedite sales and maintain their national image.

In Eastern Europe, this organization is sure to be an arm of the state. It may be necessary to invoke the assistance of your government representative in a particular country to make initial contact to get product or manufacturing system verification of quality assurance procedures or practices. Your contact person may be a commercial or industrial attaché or representative in the country with which you have to deal.

Where the prospective supplier is located in a NATO or western-oriented country, contacts should be established with trade ministries, standards institutions, or professional organizations in quality work to get information on local quality practices (which are sometimes surprisingly good). Most countries have both certification and accreditation procedures that are applied to local quality assurance or testing organizations, usually backed by a national surveillance program to make valid evaluation data available to you. Use such sources whenever possible. In most cases, your professional affiliations will be able to give you information on how to go about contacting indigenous groups in whichever country your company plans to do business at a given time.

Quality assurance is much more formalized outside of continental North America than it is within. Be sure to benefit from any bona fide source of evaluation data available to your organization from such national bodies. Although it may be a very costly mistake to assume that some given quality information from abroad is fully equivalent to one you are used to, it is by no means rare to discover that in certain fields of quality accreditation, suppliers abroad may have to regularly meet standards that would strain some of your domestic suppliers to their very limits.

Just as with a quality survey of a domestic supplier, treat quality accreditation information abroad with the same open attitude. It may save you from accepting as qualified a supplier who is not, and it may also save you from rejecting a supplier who is more qualified than any you might find at home.

Vendor Information and Reassurance

So you're going to take part in a supplier survey — but it's *your* plant that is being surveyed. You may wonder how to get ready for the survey. First of all, relax and remember that tens of thousands of vendor surveys take place every year. You are not alone.

You may be surveyed by competent quality professionals, perhaps someone who has read this book. Since you're reading it too, you have an idea of how to get ready. It would also be useful for you to review any specific standards that might apply. In short, start by arming yourself with knowledge. Know what the surveyor may be looking for.

The next step is to make a realistic appraisal of your plant's quality situation. Do you have a good quality system, or don't you?

If the answer is "no," it's practically certain that it's too late to build one before the survey date. Your best bet is to tell your own management clearly of existing deficiencies. Try to sell management on support of a quality control program. Then when a survey team shows up, learn as much as you can and take your lumps. Point out that your management has (hopefully) given the support for necessary corrective action. It's foolish to try to hide true facts from a competent evaluator. He'll almost surely find out, and you'll look even worse.

If you have a good system, stand firmly. It may not be perfect — nothing ever is. Doubtless the evaluator will find deficiencies somewhere, and you may end up debating necessary corrective action. But don't make the mistake of trying to dress up the operation with a lot of "spit and polish." Such effort is sure to make your operation look artificial. A competent evaluator knows what a working facility looks like. He'll rarely be impressed by a "snow job," but he may become suspicious and wonder what and how much you are trying to cover up.

Make sure that the key people have been thoroughly briefed and that their schedules will permit them to be available at the time of the survey for introductions and to answer questions pertaining to their functions. Have an organization chart available (most quality control manuals have charts you can use for models) that can be presented to the survey team and indicate who carries out what function in your plant. Also make sure that the documentation that should be available is available.

Recognize that no two systems are alike. Know your own system and how it works. Don't be afraid to defend your system if it really does work. A competent evaluator is interested in new techniques and new ideas. But don't be so defensive that you are unwilling to learn from him if he lets you know of a better idea!

It is not out of place to extend a modest show of professional courtesy to the survey team. The team represents a potential purchaser, which means sales and income for your firm. The survey team will almost surely appreciate the availability of a little office space. Some hospitality — lunch, for example — is not out of line.

Perhaps your evaluators may need overnight accomodations. Since you are at the site, you are in the best position to arrange this. The same goes for transportation to visit your facility. You don't have to be pushy, but your offer of help may be really appreciated. Eventually, when you are an approved supplier, and the same evaluators return on regular check-up visits, you may even develop a warm personal relationship. But don't rely on charm to hide deficiencies — it can only delay the ugly discovery of shortcomings.

If it is the evaluator's first trip to your plant, he will probably expect you to take him on a tour. Plan such a tour in advance and estimate the timing. Make sure that the plant personnel has been informed of who the evaluators are, what their purpose is, and how your personnel can help by giving straight replies to the evaluators' questions. After the evaluators have seen your plant as a whole, they may ask to revisit specific stations for in-depth study. Don't be alarmed: Perhaps they've found something unusually good. If it isn't, they may be in a position to suggest to you how those sections of your plant could be improved. You'll usually win if you deal fairly with the survey team.

CHAPTER 14

HOW TO EVALUATE
A SUPPLIER'S PRODUCT

Key Words: Design Control, Tolerances, Product Qualification, Process Audit, Certification Program, Purchase Orders, Drawings

Summary:

- **Preaward conference**
- **Initial production**
- **Source inspection**
- **Utilizing vendor data**
- **Nonconforming product**
- **Performance evaluation**

Introduction

Evaluating a vendor's product is an important element of a company quality control program. This chapter describes some of the more commonly used methods of evaluating purchased products. Obviously, a cookbook approach to evaluation is not practical as each product requires specific decisions; however, the methods discussed here have proven effective. Using these concepts, the vendee can develop operating procedures that will maintain an ongoing program for evaluating vendor products.

Each aspect of the program will be important but higher priorities must be assigned those areas that offer the vendee the greatest payback. Considerations also must be given to the types of products and processes especially when new procedures are being established.

Product evaluation procedures can range from simple to complex, and the degree of formality in any program depends on product and vendee requirements. Individual ingenuity and integrity on the part of both vendee and vendor quality control personnel are essential to optimize operating procedures and to provide maximum effectiveness to the program.

This chapter describes successful methods of vendor product evaluation. These are not the only ways to evaluate a vendor's product, but they are the most important for developing a purchased material quality control program.

Preaward Conference

Prior to evaluation of a vendor's product, contractual requirements applying to that specific product must be established. Both the vendor and the vendee must have a clear understanding of the basic product requirements as well as any special quality requirements. A most effective way to accomplish this understanding is to hold a preaward conference.

Need for a preaward conference is usually determined by discussion between the vendor's purchasing and quality assurance departments. A conference should be called where high cost or special circumstances are involved in the contract. Often a preaward conference is considered when the job is new to the vendor. The conference provides an opportunity to finalize product or process requirements.

The preaward conference brings together technical and management personnel representing both the vendor and vendee. The departments generally involved are product design/development, manufacturing, testing, purchasing/sales, and quality assurance. Depending on the type of product, representatives from service, financial, legal, marketing, and other functions may also be involved. Attendance could be governed by the requirements of the contract.

Once the need for a conference is established, it is generally the responsibility of the vendor quality assurance department to develop an agenda that ensures all applicable product quality requirements will be covered. Normally, the vendee's purchasing department schedules and chairs the initial meeting. The vendee's quality representative serves as secretary and coordinator to see that product requirements are understood and accepted, responsibilities are assigned, and agreements made at the meeting are documented.

The agenda is used by both vendor and vendee staffs to prepare for the meeting as a guide in conducting the meeting. A typical agenda could include the following items:

- Design acceptance
- Production facilities
- First article inspection
- Process requirements
- Production quality control
- Packaging
- Records

How to Evaluate a Supplier's Product

- Quality audits and past performance
- Warranty provisions
- Communications
- Schedules

The preaward conference should be as extensive as necessary to cover all subjects pertinent to satisfactory completion of the contract. A successful meeting virtually eliminates the "I didn't know we had to do that" or "That's going to cost more" response when the product goes into production. The importance of the preaward conference becomes clear as the various agenda items are discussed.

Design acceptance is perhaps the most critical factor since it is difficult to evaluate a product that is not clearly defined. Questions that must be answered include:

- Who is responsible for design control?
- Are tolerances and specifications realistic and within the capability of the vendor?
- Are test requirements adequate to assure fit and function?

These important questions must be discussed at the preaward conference and it is essential that clear agreements be reached prior to release of the contract.

Once product requirements and specifications are agreed to, consideration must be given to the facilities and equipment necessary to produce and check the product. In many cases, the vendee may furnish tools or equipment. Yet without mutual agreement as to the design and use of this equipment, the vendor may be unable or unwilling to use it. Possibly the vendor may have a better or more economical method of production. The point is that production and test methods must be clearly agreed on prior to release of the contract or purchase order.

First article complete inspection is the first real product evaluation. Product requirements must be defined in detail to allow the vendor to understand what is expected. The "first article" may be a sample, a dozen items, or any specified quantity or volume. The conditions of first article inspection must be understood, accepted, and documented. Requirements for inspections, tests, reports, etc., must be defined and responsibilities established for future implementation.

Many jobs, particularly in the chemical field, are controlled through specific process requirements. An understanding, therefore, should be reached as to responsibility for authorizing process control changes. Communication channels must be defined. Both the vendor and vendee must understand and agree on specific areas of responsibility for approving product or process deviation.

Production quality controls planned by the vendor are yet another major topic of the preaward conference. For instance, some jobs require special operator skills or qualifications; therefore, details of these requirements must be discussed. All significant elements of the vendor's quality plan should be reviewed and agreement reached regarding methods of inspection, sampling plans, acceptance standards, etc.

Manufacture of a product in conformance with vendee specifications is not the only important subject discussed at the preaward conference. Special attention also should be given to packing, protection, and shipping. If the product is damaged or deteriorates during shipment and storage, all the efforts to assure conformance are wasted. For many products, the loading, handling, and packaging requirements are as tightly controlled as the product itself. Again, the requirements of the specific product must be clearly defined and a mutual understanding between the vendor and vendee achieved.

Some products require special records so that traceability may be maintained in reference to applicable inspection and test reports. All aspects of this identification, inspection, and reporting must be discussed and agreements documented so that they become an integral portion of the purchase contract.

Information gained while reviewing the vendor's quality proposal often can be used to plan subsequent audits of the vendor's production operation. Once agreements are reached, it is relatively easy to plan objective audits to determine if the conference agreements are being fulfilled.

The preaward conference also provides an opportunity to review prior problems and plan for prevention. When the potential vendor is to furnish an existing product with which the vendee has had extensive experience, the vendee can provide information that will help reduce future problems and defect costs.

The conference's discussion of warranty should cover a multitude of activities ranging from vendee complaints to responsibility for returned product. In many instances, special warranty coverage may have to be negotiated. A factor that should not be overlooked is handling and evaluating returned goods to ensure that the vendor can plan and implement corrective action. Guidelines for cost recovery on warranty returns as well as an agreement on product improvement costs should be established at this time.

Finally, a preaward conference should include an open session where all parties may submit relevant subjects for discussion. In this manner, anything of importance not previously discussed may be covered. Everyone involved with the conference has an opportunity to contribute and all viewpoints are considered.

After a preaward conference has been completed, it is customary to include all agreements as a part of the purchase contract. This is done by amendment of the purchase order to require conformance to the agreements of the conference. A copy of the conference report accompanies the purchase documents.

Some conferences recommend the proposed contract be revised or cancelled. It is best to prevent an unsatisfactory project from starting if agreements cannot be reached. One of the prime reasons for a contract being revised or cancelled is the vendor's inability to comply with the vendee requirements.

The preaward conference is one of the most productive prevention-oriented quality functions performed as an element of purchased material control. It is often the initial step in evaluation of the vendor's product. Each company must develop its own preaward conference program. The information presented here simply highlights some significant factors of such a program. The preaward conference alone cannot assure freedom from problems, but combined with sound planning and implementation of the product evaluation techniques discussed in this chapter, it can significantly minimize the potential for problems involved with purchased products.

Initial Production

The first evaluation of a product or a process is the most critical stage in establishing a good working relationship with a vendor and in assuring that the product to be received on a production basis conforms to the desired characteristics. Assurance that the received product is correct begins on the initial purchase order with appropriate performance requirements. First article or process evaluation is done not only to ensure that drawing and specification requirements are met, but to ensure that the product is consistent with contractual requirements.

Product Qualification

Prior to receiving the initial product, a checklist of evaluation characteristics should be established. The list should consider all significant elements of the product and its performance. Inputs from each design/development group that will be involved with the product should be obtained and added to the checklist.

Upon receipt, the product should be checked for problems incurred in shipping. Once this is done, the evaluation procedure already developed should begin. At each step, both acceptable and unacceptable test results should be documented. For uncomplicated products, a standard form for documenting results is helpful. It ensures that all steps are adequately and consistently evaluated. The results of each step should be considered while the product is being processed so that any additional evaluation parameters may be included in the tests.

The documented test results should then be reviewed with engineering, manufacturing, and other concerned groups, and compared with the vendor's results to identify problems. After the evaluation, the package should be sent to the vendor either to request corrective action in areas where discrepancies exist, or to provide documented acceptance of the product. If the product is complex, a joint review of the results may be necessary to ensure measurement correlations between vendor and vendee.

Methods for accomplishing this correlation are negotiable. The negotiations should be handled by the purchasing department and, once the methods of corrective action are finalized, they should be transmitted by purchasing to the vendor.

Prior to receipt of the corrected product, a new checklist should reidentify the characteristics to be evaluated. Close scrutiny should ensure that the corrections do not affect original product characteristics. The vendor should be requested to provide a written description of the process or procedural changes necessary to correct the product. This description provides verification of correction. The procedures should be included in future evaluation requirements.

Upon receipt, the corrected product should be checked again for packing and handling discrepancies and then evaluated according to the new checklist. If the product still does not meet required performance characteristics, the same review and negotiations for correction may be required as when the product was first received. If the product is acceptable, recognition by design/development, manufacturing, and quality control should be transmitted to the vendor through the purchasing department.

Process Identification

Prior to a process evaluation, a checklist should identify characteristics to be evaluated. A flow chart, as part of the checklist, should point out the step-by-step characteristics and the controlling parameters of the process. The checklist also should identify manufacturing system control parameters. These parameters include material routing procedures, change control, defect identification, isolation, evaluation and disposition, production capabilities, calibration capabilities, process documentation, system audit, and tool control procedures.

A description of the production facility, its management, and quality policy is helpful before any evaluation. These can and should be obtained through the vendee purchasing department.

Process Audit

Once the checklist is developed, arrangements for process audit can be made through the purchasing department. If possible, the timing of the audit should coincide with the movement of preproduction or acutal production parts through the process. This allows the evaluation team to review the product characteristics as described in the original design parameters under working conditions.

After visit arrangements are made, the vendor should have a chance to review the scope of the evaluation plan to ensure that none of the processing activities are proprietary and to determine if any special activity will be required.

Auditors should arrive promptly to conduct the audit. They must evaluate the details of the process and system control as part of the supplier's manufacturing cycle. Records on process parameters must be checked for out-of-control conditions and evidence of corrective action. Where practical, process parameters should be compared with daily records. Each operation must be checked to assure that enough safeguards are in place to maintain the process in control or to identify an impending out-of-control condition. Weakness or deviations from the expected results should be recorded. Most processes are likely to maintain the desired output if normal controls will prevent deviation; however, special controls established specifically for the product should be emphasized as they are likely to be overlooked in routine operation.

When the audit is complete, a summary of findings should be reviewed with the vendor. If needed, a plan for corrective action with implementation dates should be developed. Methods for demonstrating corrective action should also be developed and accepted. A complete, documented report including the agreed upon corrective action should be sent to the supplier by the purchasing department. A follow-up by telephone should assure that the vendor has received and understood the report. Additional telephone contacts can follow the progress of the corrective action although additional visits to the vendor's facility may be required to evaluate implementation of corrective action.

Qualification by Suppliers

Product, process, and article requirements developed for first article inspection and process evaluation should again be reviewed before establishing characteristics of vendor qualifications. Once these requirements are determined, the records can be developed to achieve the desired evaluation results.

These requirements should be documented and transmitted through the purchasing department to the vendor. The vendor should be contacted to assure that the requirements are understood and to establish timing for completion of the evaluation. An on-site inspector can help ensure that the evaluation is carried out accurately and completely.

The evaluated product and the results of this evaluation, both provided by the vendor, must be audited for accuracy and completeness. This audit can include evaluation of critical characteristics and parameters. If the audit procedures show results different than those shown in the vendor evaluation tests, additional parameters should be measured or additional information requested from the supplier. The review and audit results should be documented and transmitted by the purchasing department to the supplier. Discrepancies should be followed up and corrective action obtained.

Qualification by Independent Laboratory

Qualification of an article or process by an independent laboratory is essentially the same as qualification by the vendor. However, the capability of the independent laboratory must be determined prior to any tests.

The scope of the desired task, cost, expected reports, and outputs should be established and agreed on by the contracting parties. When the results are received they should be reviewed, audited, and transmitted to the supplier for his information. Any questionable areas should be clarified with the laboratory or the supplier with appropriate corrective action and follow-up evaluations performed until an acceptable correlation or product can be demonstrated. Several independent laboratories' analyses may be needed, depending on the complexity and diversity of the evaluation.

Certification Program

An alternative to the quality control methods described above is a ship-to-stock or certified product program. As the name implies, the product essentially is treated as a "free" lot in skip lot inspection and is released without being subjected to the conventional receiving inspection.

This alternate method depends on a strong vendor-vendee relationship that emphasizes preventive planning, detailed product and process audits by the vendee, and a high degree of integrity on the part of the vendor. Extensive planning liaison is required and agreements generally are reached prior to release of the purchase contract.

As with all sound quality planning, the job requirements must be defined and documented. Specific audit guidelines must be developed and a schedule established for periodic evaluation during the production schedule. The supplier's plan for control of the process and product must be documented carefully and included as an integral part of the purchase agreement. This plan becomes the benchmark for planning and auditing throughout the life of the contract.

The certification program normally is not used with a new vendor since a history of demonstrated ability by the vendor to control operations is essential. New products may be considered for this plan when a good vendor-vendee relationship exists, but again extensive planning must be done and detailed agreements reached prior to production.

When the vendor has a strong operational quality program and the vendee maintains timely and effective audits of the specific job, this program can be an alternate to receiving inspection.

Incoming Inspection

Incoming inspection is one of the most important functions in the overall quality assurance program. In simple terms, incoming inspection reveals whether the vendor can produce and deliver what he said he could like he said he would! The following is a sequence of events that can be used as a guide in formulating specific flowcharts and procedures for use in the incoming inspection area of any specific plant or operation.

Purchase Orders and Drawings

Access to copies of every purchase order and drawings/specifications is necessary. The receiving copy of the purchase order can save duplicate files, etc.

Upon receipt of the parts from the vendor, the receiving department normally will pull the purchase order, count the parts, and check for damage. If the cartons and/or parts show physical damage, the receiving department should immediately process a shipping damage claim to the carrier and/or the insurance company with whose procedures they should be familiar. If everything is in order the receiving department will put the purchase order with the items and forward the order to incoming inspection for the required inspection and test.

In a small company, it may be advantageous to have the vendor of metal work, printed wiring boards, or similar items return with the shipment the original drawings/specifications used to produce the part or finished item. In many cases, receipt of all the drawings/specifications will prevent future vendor problems related to design changes. This method provides some confidence that the vendor cannot build more parts without new or updated drawings/specifications. Receiving the drawings/specifications with the parts also saves the cost of maintaining a drawing file in receiving inspection.

The incoming inspector with the purchase order, the drawings/specifications, and the parts, now can begin to ensure the following:

1. The purchase order is accurate and calls for the specific item(s), part number and revision, test data (if required), etc.
2. Parts are not damaged due to defective packing and packaging.
3. Parts are as called for on the purchase order with drawing/specification by part number, color code, etc.

Inspection, Test Records

Under normal circumstances, the quality system or program will require the incoming inspector to select a sample per an approved sampling plan if quantities will allow. If not, all parts should be inspected and/or tested to ensure conformance to the drawings/specifications or inspection instructions.

The inspector must have the necessary tools, gages, and equipment to inspect and/or test the items properly. All inspection tools, gages, and equipment must be calibrated to ensure accuracy. Either the sample or the total quantity should conform in order to be accepted and released to stock. The incoming inspector should complete the incoming inspection record in detail and process the items to stock if they are accepted.

Rejected Material and Records

If for any reason the items do not conform to the drawings, specifications, standards, or inspection instructions, the items should be rejected. A rejection report should be completed and placed with the items for review and disposition by quality management. Under normal circumstances, the defective item(s) would be processed through purchasing for return to the vendor for corrective action or replacement. Under special conditions — if they were required because of time and if they could be corrected/or used within the facilities — the items might be presented for material review board action. Material review procedures would control these activities.

The intent of incoming inspection is to assure that the item(s) received are as stated on the purchase order and that the item(s) conform to specifications and drawings. The intent of incoming inspection records is to document the facts with regard to the performance of vendors and to provide purchasing and quality management with data from which decisions can be made.

Source Inspection

Successful source inspection begins with the first vendor contact, whether it occurs during a preaward conference or during evaluation of the vendor's facilities. It is of utmost importance that source inspection effort be regarded, by the vendor and the vendee, as a desirable method of proving the vendor's production to the purchaser's satisfaction.

For a good working relationship, the vendee quality personnel must maintain direct contact with the vendor quality personnel. Their first such contact should be made through the purchasing department, whether at a preaward conference or by telephone. Subsequent contacts could be made directly between the quality personnel of the two companies. Of course, the purchasing department should be informed of any substantive conversations. This interchange of intercompany quality data is vital to a good working relationship.

Good source inspection depends on a thorough understanding of the product. Thus, careful review of the drawings, specifications, and purchase order is necessary for the quality professional who will conduct the inspection. Source inspection criteria, whether developed by design or quality, should be selected carefully and reviewed by design, purchasing, production control, manufacturing, and quality. All concerned parties should agree that the salient points have been covered. At this point, agreements also should be reached concerning assistance, by any of the aforementioned functions, for the quality professional assigned the source inspection.

With the vendee quality team in agreement as to what will be done and who will do it, the quality professional is ready for his first survey trip to the vendor's plant. The trip should have three purposes: (1) establishment of good working relations, (2) evaluation of the vendor's quality system, and (3) discussion of the areas to be inspected during source inspection. If first article inspection is planned, changes in the source inspection as a result of that inspection should be discussed and agreement reached on how and when such changes should be implemented.

An estimated production schedule should be provided by the vendor during this plant visit. That schedule should be updated as necessary by the vendor's quality personnel to ensure timely response by the vendee when the "hold points" for the source inspection are reached. The vendee's quality professional, in turn, should notify those who are to assist him regarding any schedule changes.

Actual source inspection could include detailed inspection of dimensions, visual examination of parts, functional testing, review of records, and any other aspect of the product. It is important that the vendee representative create minimum disturbance in the vendor's manufacturing process. Proper communication will ensure the availability of the source inspector(s) when the product has reached inspection "hold points." Thorough preparation will ensure familiarity with the product and reduce the time required for the source inspection. Proper attitude will result in a good relationship with the vendor and prevent needless conflict. Source control should be implemented only after the supplier has validated product acceptability; this may also be done concurrently by joint agreement.

Once source inspection is completed for the first item/lot, the results must be evaluated carefully. Most likely the initial quality plan will need changes, reducing some requirements and strengthening others. It is important that the source inspection requirement be flexible enough to allow the vendee's quality professional to reduce inspection of subsequent lots if the initial ones prove satisfactory, or to increase control if production proves to be out of control. Whether or not a reduction takes place, the quality professional should monitor any defects found during his company's receiving inspection and/or during his company's production cycle. Defects found are justification for increased or modified source inspection criteria during the supplier's production cycle.

Once the vendor's production line is running and actual source inspection has been reduced, the vendee's quality professional might consider surveying the product by random audits or visits to ensure that all continues to go well. Such surveillance would take up little time and could be conducted in conjunction with trips to other plants. Additionally, it would maintain the good working relationship between partners which is necessary in a source inspection program.

Utilizing Vendor Data

Vendor data includes product, process, or equipment information obtained from a vendor. This may be a description of the equipment and/or process, process/product yields, product input/output variable or attribute measurements, X-ray films, laboratory analysis, or other related sampling or 100 percent measurement. Data should be required contractually by drawings and specifications described in the purchase order. Acquiring and processing data costs money, thus, the necessity for contractual understanding.

Vendor data are used primarily to ascertain compliance to specifications. Data also are used to evaluate process capabilities, equipment correlations, trend information, and product-related factors. Data from more than one vendor may be combined for performance comparisons in one of the many vendor rating schemes, but that is a separate subject. This section is limited primarily to the use of vendor data to verify conformance for acceptance of purchased material. References here to the *inspection* include test activities, where applicable. Similarly, references to *equipment* and *process* encompass those required by manufacturing as well as quality.

Optimum benefits are derived when data are reviewed in a timely manner. Depending on the phase of development or production, review may take place at the vendor's or vendee's facility. Many mathematical models exist for data analysis at various stages of production. During the preproduction or development phase, data may be used to review available process capabilities, including manufacturing and inspection measuring equipment. Assessments of product and equipment design and the adequacy of quality assurance functions often are made through data review in the early stages of production.

Experienced quality management will arrange for the analysis of specific vendor data from the first production units. Timely review of first-lot data is essential when the production situation dictates limited expenditures. This investment in vendor quality assurance often becomes critical in terms of quality and schedule assurance. First production unit data review will highlight any corrections that may be necessary before full production.

How to Evaluate a Supplier's Product

Depending upon the type of material and its end use, vendor data may be used in lieu of vendee inspection and tests. One such alternative involves calculating the degree of correlation between vendor and vendee testing. Normally, the vendee must perform comprehensive testing on initial receipt to determine if the material conforms to contractual specifications. It should be understood that inspection costs are included in product prices so the vendee already is paying for material in the vendor's inspection. Therefore, a purchase order requirement for the vendor to furnish specified inspection data should not be a significant additional cost. With the vendor's data in hand, plus his own inspection information, the vendee can perform a correlation analysis to determine the relation between in-house tests and the vendor's plant inspection. If the correlation is satisfactory, subsequent receipts may be accepted upon a verification type review of the vendor's inspection data. This plan may be augmented by testing selected parameters on each receipt. Other modifications may require complete vendee testing periodically to assure a continuing correlation. The correlation study method can be readily applied to metals, raw material, and mechanical piecepart-type products.

Another alternative is to arrange for evaluation and approval of the vendor's inspection equipment and associated calibration controls. This method is particularly appropriate for control and acceptance of electronic/electrical components. Approval of the vendor's equipment is given on a specific basis defined in vendee standards. As with all methods using vendor data, adequate measures must be applied contractually to control any changes or modifications affecting equipment, standards, or processes after they have been approved. Additionally, all or selected parameters may be verified on the initial receipt, usually as part of the vendee's formal qualification approval. Selected parameters may be tested periodically by the vendee to maintain a satisfactory confidence level of the continuing verification. Again, depending on the degree of the high reliability requirements, correlation studies can be included in this alternative.

For purchased material not requiring critical high reliability, vendor data may be used without performing correlation studies, equipment approvals, or verification testing. The basis for this judgment may be the quality history of previous receipts, the quality of similar material, and the vendor's established reputation within the industry or a cost-type measure of next assembly failures.

The bottom line on controlled use of vendor data is to be cost effective, primarily by eliminating redundant inspection equipment and associated receiving inspection operations.

Nonconforming Product

After inspection, a vendor product may be reported as nonconforming to one or more of the established standards: form and appearance, material, fit and dimensional characteristics, or function. The inspection report must then be reviewed to determine if the product can be used and what corrective actions are required. Acceptance will depend on whether the product can be modified to perform its intended function without risk to user and whether the added cost of the modifications or corrections is acceptable. Other questions will need answers: Will the corrective actions be carried out at the vendor plant or possibly in the vendee's operation? Does the variation appear to be repetitive or an isolated case?

Key aids in this analysis are inspection history sheets, the latest vendor survey, the histogram of the defect, the repeatability of the inspection or testing method, the type and completeness of the qualification test or proof sample, and knowledge of the specific process that created the discrepancy. An excellent vehicle for carrying out the analysis is a materials review board (MRB) with representatives from the functions responsible for the item. This review, however, is effective only if a complete history can be presented to the board by the inspection supervisor or the quality engineer.

If it is determined that the vendor is at fault, the purchasing department should arrange a meeting with the vendor, or relay the information via a cover letter plus a copy of the report and corrective action request. A decision on the most effective method of repair is usually made by the materials review board.

Visits to the vendor in connection with the MRB action may be made by purchasing, the quality engineer and, if necessary, other engineering functions (product design, tool design, manufacturing engineering, etc.). If the problem is recurrent and/or very serious, plant management or a higher representative should also be invited.

Before visiting the vendor's plant, the adequacy of in-house inspection procedures and the way they are being carried out should be checked and verified. When visiting the vendor's plant, the vendee should take along all current data, prior history, and if applicable, analysis of the most likely cause of the problem. Concluding the fixed tooling needs repair or that a design change is required will have different backup than a recommendation to increase or improve detectability.

Supplier Total Performance Evaluation

The purpose of performance evaluation is to permit both the vendor and vendee to react quickly to unfavorable trends affecting product quality, product availability, and mutual profitability. A vendor's performance can be evaluated in many ways, but quality, delivery, and cost must all be considered if the measure of vendor performance is to be comprehensive. It is important to measure the conformance of a specific part or lot, but the vendor's past performance must also be measured so that special action may be taken if problems are repetitive.

With increased emphasis on quality cost, both the vendor and vendee must be aware of the economic consequences of a nonconforming product. To maintain an effective quality program, even a small company must recognize its quality costs. The emphasis in today's quality program is prevention.Effective quality planning must be done to optimize quality costs. It has often been said that "Hindsight has 20/20 vision whereas foresight is very seldom good." Taking advantage of all available information can help identify potential problems.

Measuring the elements of quality, delivery, and cost constitute a form of vendor rating based on objective information. Since no one single guideline can define a workable system for everyone, a rating program must be developed and implemented by each individual organization.

All companies, regardless of size, accumulate much of the information required to perform a complete vendor analysis. A major problem, however, is retrieval. Having records in a computer is an advantage if the information is accessible in a usable format. For discussion purposes here, the quality factor will be considered as the percent defective. The most readily available information is based on the relation of rejections to receipts. If actual usage quantities are available for this factor, all the better.

The units of measure must be consistent with those received whether they are in pieces, pounds, gallons, meters, etc. No considerations are given for theoretical percent defective based on a sample, since a lot rejected is unavailable to production and generally would be returned to the vendor, reworked, repaired, or used as is. In another sense, this is comparing the quantity of product requiring special action to that which was accepted or processed through normal procedures.

In the quest for simplicity, no attempt is made to weigh or adjust the numbers based on formulas or computations since percent defective is more a measure of nuisance than anything else. As an example, a vendor may have a 40 percent reject rate, but if the total value of the product rejected is only $20, no one gets excited and little if any action can be economically justified.

The most universally understood unit of measure is the dollar and the cost factor of vendor performance evaluation is by far the most effective measure of vendor performance. When purchasing advises a vendor that $1,500 worth of a product has been rejected, it has far greater impact than saying a lot is seven percent defective.

All manufcturing operations work to a budget and quality costs such as scrap and rework generally are budget items closely monitored by management. Where purchased material is involved, the purchasing department usually is charged for the rejected material and it is that department's responsibility to see that nonconforming product is repaired or replaced, and that the defect costs are recovered.

Ideally, the vendee should be able to collect and report all defect costs, such as rework and repair, and establish the cost of a product at the time of rejection. It is conceivable to include also costs of extra inspection, testing, engineering, etc. Many companies operate on a standard cost system and have values assigned for the various stages of product completion. Rework or repair costs usually are accumulated through a shop labor reporting system.

Using total defect cost data, the vendee can evaluate the distribution and rank vendors in terms of defect cost contribution. In this way, the reasons for the defect costs can be determined and the responsible vendors directed toward corrective action. The information gained through this program also helps in quality planning so that preventive measures may be incorporated in future quality requirements.

Again, this means dealing with factual values — dollars charged to a rejection. This can be especially meaningful when dealing with a relatively inexpensive product that can create defect costs far in excess of its purchase price. It is not uncommon in some industries to find costs of several hundred dollars to remove and replace a part that may only cost a dollar or two. In this situation, a five percent reject rate of some $2 parts could cost the customer over $1,000 in labor to remove and replace five pieces from a 100-piece lot. When only $10 is involved, few persons become interested, but increase the cost to the actual $1,000 and management of both companies undoubtedly will seek immediate corrective action.

It doesn't take many such illustrations to point out problem areas where substantial savings can be made for both the vendee and vendor. If neither the vendor nor the vendee has an effective form of quality cost tracking, it is doubtful that the impact created by defective product will be realized until the year end financial statement is reviewed. Then profits will be far less than anticipated.

When defect cost information is available, perhaps the most significant indicator of vendor performance is the relationship of defect cost to the purchase cost of the product. Depending on the complexity of the vendee's defect cost reporting system, the evaluation may be summarized as comparison within commodity, by part number, total by vendor, etc. Again, it must be stressed that objective data are recommended without resort to formulas, weighing, or other mathematical manipulations.

When objective quality cost information is available to the vendee's purchasing department, it can effectively use the information when analyzing jobs for potential resourcing and for placement of new jobs. A vendor with the lowest quoted price may not present lowest overall cost to the vendee when defect costs are considered. The vendee's purchasing department can improve its source selection by combining the defect cost potential with the quoted price. Paying more than the lowest bid may be jsutified to achieve a lower total cost.

The last element of vendor performance evaluation is delivery, or a measure of the vendor's ability to react to schedules. This aids a purchasing department in reviewing past performance. Although expeditors may be aware of specific jobs, it is important to follow the overall trend of a vendor's delivery performance so that special action may be initiated for unsatisfactory performance.

In summary, vendor performance evaluation is essential to measure the effectiveness of the vendor's quality program. Analyzing data obtained from a review of the vendor's past performance identifies problem areas and permits planning action to prevent recurrence of the reported problems.

Procurement Quality Control

CHAPTER 15

HOW TO ESTABLISH EFFECTIVE QUALITY CONTROL FOR THE SMALL SUPPLIER

Key Words: Interpreting Product Requirements, In-Process Inspection, Measurement Assurance, Quality Procedures, Independent Laboratories, Source Inspection, Planning

Summary:

- **Organization**
- **Planning**
- **Certification of personnel and equipment**
- **Testing, inspection, and measurement**
- **Handling nonconforming material**

Introduction

In today's world of consumer affairs, with product liability and an endless listing of government and industry regulations, the small business must develop a quality control system that satisfies customer requirements and remains cost effective. To this end the small business manager must rely heavily on customer requirements. Initial contacts with potential customers should aim at understanding these requirements and regulations.

For the small business, the basic understanding of quality control has been less critical than in major industry. However, the division between commercial and military procurement that historically dictated separate control by product line has changed rapidly. Consumer actions in the private sector now require quality system control equal to, if not exceeding, military procurement.

The small business is therefore faced with required product controls that demand additional expenditures. To keep these expenditures in check, the small business manager must develop a quality program that meets customer requirements while controlling and maintaining product conformance. Certain assumptions have been made in this chapter. With due respect to the reader, it is assumed that the reader is primarily concerned with the technical and financial aspects of the business and has little knowledge of the quality control function. To this end the quality professional's jargon has been reduced to a bare necessity. It has also been assumed that there is a business in place, producing a product which a quality organization can support. This chapter, which has been authored by experienced quality professionals, is intended to serve as a useful guide in establishing an effective quality control system. However, it has not been designed as a do-it-yourself guide as it does not contain the scope or depth required to formulate a professional quality organization.

Organization

An owner of a small business stated, "I would like to establish a quality control organization, but where do I start?" That's a reasonable and not profound question, but extremely difficult to answer because there are no concise answers.

First, the owner must understand the primary objective of quality control. Many volumes have been written on this subject and to reduce it to a single statement may seem presumptuous, but here is an attempt:

Quality control is that effort applied to assure the end product/service meets its intended requirements and achieves consumer's satisfaction.

In a well-designed product, requirements and customer satisfaction should be synonymous. As products and requirements have many variations, so must quality control. Each organization must meet the requirements of the customer and the business. The objective is to apply only the required effort to economically control the end product or service. To illustrate this point let's take an authentic situation involving a Chicago plastic manufacturer. His primary business was that of producing containers for major pharmaceutical firms under the rigid requirements of the Federal Drug Administration. Taking advantage of his expertise, he also manufactured plastic flower pots. This was done on an automatic molding machine that ran 24 hours a day. The only attendance given the machine was to fill the hopper periodically with raw material. On the container line he employed a complement of trained quality personnel. Why?

In the first situation, rejection would impose severe dollar losses, invoke the customer's displeasure due to production line delays, and result in probable loss of future business. On the flower pot line, his quality control consisted of a visual check by the employee who filled the hopper to see that the pots were whole and free of cracks. Why? A malfunction of the machine could be easily detected visually and the parts not shipped. He did not have a customer dependent on his product and furthermore unacceptable material could be ground up and recycled. He would be hard pressed to justify more than a few dollars a day devoted to quality control on the flower pot line. This may be a unique situation that covers the extreme ends of the spectrum, but it does illustrate the need for examining the requirements and evaluating the penalties of failure. Most applications are not as simple as the preceding example and require knowledgeable management decisions.

Quality control has developed in a pattern because of the requirements imposed at the various stages of industrial growth of an individual organization. If quality control grew in this pattern, then quality organizations should perhaps grow in the same progression.

In the days of a single-person shop with apprentices, inspection was nonexistent, except for a cursory review by the master journeyman. Inspection came into being with the multiperson shop and was intensified with the high volume production line when operators performed a single operation. The first addition to inspection came during World War I. The U.S. Navy found that shells from one manufacturer would fit a gun breach and shells from another would not fit. Exhaustive investigation revealed that the equipment used by the gun manufacturer and both shell manufacturers did not give the same results. It was only by luck that one shell fit. From this came the requirement for calibration.

Between World War I and World War II the significant change was the introduction of statistical sampling and statistical process controls. These were necessitated by high volume production making 100 percent inspection costly, if not impossible. During World War II and into the 1960s the industrial/military complex came into existence. Many small businesses found themselves facing a myriad of complex requirements, some of which were unnecessary and they passed on these rigid requirements to vendors' plants. Quality organization in prime contractors flourished. As in any expanding market many nonprofessionals did a great deal to tarnish the quality control image. The saving grace was the recognition that quality control be structured to be a contributing member of the management team.

One measure of success or failure of a quality system is quality costs. In simple terms, it recognized inspection as the backbone of quality. The cost of scrap, rework, reinspection, and customer rejections are accumulated and analyzed as to the cause. By taking corrective action to determine cause and eliminate this cost these dollars can be saved. Additionally, by careful preplanning as to complete understanding requirements, these rejections can be minimized and productivity will increase as cost decreases.

Today's high technology products often make it impossible to detect failures until the final test. The cost at this stage of manufacture is probibitive and the replacement cycle unacceptable. Quality has again adapted to the changing environment with a trend toward controlling the process. Process control — be it tooling, pressure, temperature, speed, feed, fixtures, process, chemical solutions, etc. — needs to be maintained at optimum values to significantly improve the chances of final acceptance. Inspection and calibration are essential elements of a system that generates information that is fed back and used to maintain a process that yields good products. This is quality control. From this point the small business must make its own decisions. What is the extra cost of rejected material including rework, reinspection, scrap, and cost of customer complaints? Can the business come out ahead by saving more money than is spent on an effective quality control system? Other considerations are customer satisfaction, degree of technology, company image, program delays, and their impact on future business. Only an astute manager can make this evaluation as these have nebulous values. It is incumbent for the manager to make a flowchart of his business, identify the strong and weak areas, place inspection in the most critical areas, assign responsibilities, and rearrange or hire personnel as required.

The small business must make a total commitment to quality. It must guard against the natural impulse to favor shipments and monthly billing at the expense of a quality product. Quality must be given management support to accomplish its objectives.

On the other side of the fence, quality cannot be dictatorial with arbitrary rejections. Its basic function is to protect the engineer's design. It should be responsible to convincingly communicate its acceptance or rejection posture.

Above all, the small business should be aware that a properly managed quality control organization will contribute to the company's profits and project a favorable quality image to the customer.

Interpreting and Reviewing Product Requirements

Interpreting and reviewing product requirements when accepting a purchase order is primarily the responsibility of sales and marketing. Product requirements can be explicit, implicit, or both. Explicit requirements are readily apparent in customer drawings, specifications, inspection procedures, technically descriptive letters, and requests for quotations. Implicit requirements are in undefined areas and, usually, are very difficult to ferret out.

Review of explicit requirements starts with information supplied with the quotation request which generally supplies either a number or a description as a cornerstone for building details of the requirements. The most important blocks in constructing the total requirements picture are the customer's drawings and specifications for products to be supplied. Similarly, technical descriptions and/or specifications are keys to the services to be performed.

The vendor must review the drawing for tolerance limits, conflicts, and buildups that might affect assembly. He should examine requirements and see whether the dimensional reference surfaces or baselines are clearly defined and adaptable to his processes. Wherever necessary, he should prepare recommendations for changing the dimensioning methods and tolerances, and for improving clarity. The vendor must make sure that material requirements are fully defined, as well as physical conditions, such as hardness, finish, conductivity, etc. Information might be contained in references such as specifications, other drawings, gages, etc. The vendor must determine the type of verification or certification required for completed work.

The vendor should analyze the specifications to see whether the item is to be built to a performance specification with dimensions and materials as a reference, or to the dimensions and materials with performance as a reference. One possible combination is to supply the item within several material and dimensional constraints and to a set of performance requirements.

In addition, the vendor has to determine what type of testing is required by the customer to prove conformance with the specification. Is the testing both design qualification and production lot-by-lot testing? He must know how to carry out the tests and have the appropriate equipment and people or the ability to use a qualified outside laboratory. If the customer is supplying test equipment or gages, the vendor should review the operating procedure as well as calibration methods and the potential drifts or wear.

The customer's inspection procedure is a guide to the significant dimensions and performance requirements. This may lead the vendor, for example, to assure that the method of manufacture and drawing dimensions are compatible. If not, the vendor must be sure that there won't be a conflict or recommend a change in inspection methods.

The request for quotation should be read carefully for such items as marking, packaging, shipping instructions, special quality requirements, and delivery schedules. At this point the vendor should be able to determine if he is capable of handling the contract. If he is supplying a service, he should review the request for conflicting or incomplete requirements, and for the method of determining satisfactory fulfillment of the requirements. This is his opportunity to recommend standard procedures, materials, and packaging.

Quality Manual

A quality manual is a compilation of the company policies and procedures that implement the quality policy established by the senior company executive. It is the documented statement of the quality standards the company has established for its product and employees. The quality manual is a companion document to similar manuals published by engineering, manufacturing, or procurement and, as such, should be comparable in structure and depth. The manual must be a living document. It is the guide to day-to-day practices.

The quality manual should be prefaced with a written statement by the chief executive establishing the company's quality policy and philosophies. The statement should be explicit about how the company will guarantee and support the integrity of its product or services. This statement by the chief executive is essential and establishes the quality program and a system to monitor the achievement of the stated goals.

The quality manual provides several important elements for the conduct of business:

- Makes both the customer and employee aware of the company's quality philosophy, standards, and goals.
- Provides a documented baseline for measuring the effectiveness of the quality programs.
- Serves as the basis from which audits are performed to assure compliance to the company's quality objectives and methods.
- Provides written instructions and guidance to assure repeatability, uniformity, and consistency in application of work elements and process standards.
- Establishes the responsibilities of each department.

The size and complexity of the manual is dependent upon the operational needs of the organization. Several factors must be considered:

- Number of employees and their skill levels.
- Complexity of the manufacturing processes required to produce the product or service.
- End use of the product and the extent of internal controls necessary to assure customer satisfaction.
- Requirements of any regulatory agency involved with the particular industry.

The quality manual should provide the policy statement, procedures, work instructions, and process specifications as applicable. In small, less complex operations, these elements may be contained in a single document. In larger, more complex organizations, it may be necessary to divide the elements into separate documents or manuals for effective use.

Quality Policy. Here the company's quality policy and objectives are described narratively. It may be necessary to describe operating policy in several functional areas, such as warranty claims, correction action, design review, subcontracting, process control, etc. It may also describe how decisions are to be made regarding conformance and suitability of product or services.

Quality Procedures. These documents define responsibility and authority for implementing the quality program. They outline the information and work flow and provide a generalized "how to" series of instructions.

Work Instructions. In some cases, it is necessary to provide step-by-step instructions for specific activities such as plating, heat treating, wire bonding, completing test reports, etc. It is beneficial to separate this type of instruction from the more generalized procedures described above. In this case, a separate package of detailed work instructions can be made available to the work force.

Process Specifications. These technical documents provide for control of operations where verification of the end result is not practical under ordinary inspection techniques. Some examples are heat treating, chemical formulation, aging/curing, plating, impregnation, nondestructive examination, etc.

The format of the quality procedures and work instructions can be shaped to the desires and needs of the company. The documents, however, should identify the subject, purpose, scope, method or procedure and responsibilities. The quality manual should be divided into sections based either on functional or organizational areas. Dividing the manual according to function permits compiling all directives pertaining to a particular operation into a single section. Dividing the manual on an organizational basis permits compiling all directives pertaining to a specific department into a single section. In either method, all organizations responsible for achieving the objectives of the directive must be identified and their participation clearly outlined. The contents of the manual should be coordinated with all departments to assure agreement and understanding.

The procedures, work instructions, etc., should be numbered to assure control and identification. In a typical industrial application, a quality manual's table of contents may include the following:

- Preface
- Introduction
- Company Quality Policy
  - -Statement of quality objectives
  - -Organizational chart
  - -Description of manual or instructions for use
- Index or Table of Contents

Procurement Quality Control

- Section 1 Configuration Control
    - -1.01 Product configuration control
    - -1.02 Documentation control
    - -1.03 Service bulletins
    - -1.04 Government conformity inspection
- Section 2 Receiving Inspection
    - -2.01 Receiving inspection — raw material
    - -2.02 Receiving inspection — high value material
    - -2.03 Receiving inspection — hazardous/toxic material
    - -2.04 Identification of incoming material
- Section 3 Material Storage and Release
- Section 4 Inspection Marking
- Section 5 (etc.)

Additional subjects to be considered include:

- Purchase order review
- Control of suppliers and subcontractors
- In-process inspection
- Assembly inspection
- Final inspection and test
- Control of nonconforming material
- Tool and gage control
- Packaging and shipping
- Control of special processes
- Training and skill certification
- Sampling inspection
- Quality system audits

The quality manager should establish a cycle periodically reviewing the manual to ensure its applicability and to purge unnecessary or obsolete instructions. The table of contents should carry the date of the latest revision. Copies of the manual should be distributed to everyone who needs it to perform their duties and to those who should be aware of its contents. A distribution list should record the copy number of the manual provided to each person. This way changes, revisions, and new publications can be sent periodically to all appropriate individuals. The manual holder will be responsible for updating his manual. Unused manuals should be returned to the quality assurance organization.

Under some conditions, a customer or regulatory agency may request a copy of the manual. A determination must be made whether the issue is on a one-time, uncontrolled basis whereby no updating material will be furnished, or on a controlled basis that requires forwarding new releases and modifications. In the latter instance, the manual holder is responsible for keeping his manual up-to-date.

The quality manual serves as the baseline for the audit, both internally and by customers and regulatory agencies. It must reflect the methods actually being used. Either the methods conform to the manual or changes are made to make them conform.

Overall, a quality manual is an instruction to company personnel on how to perform in a uniform and consistent manner. This avoids confusion and mistakes. To achieve this objective a quality manual should be as simple as possible.

Inspection

Major purchase orders may require a plan for quality control that begins with preproduction activities and extends through full production. A quality plan should include measures for defect prevention and provide controls for processes and product.

Inspection instructions must outline, in general sequence, the process to be followed and the minimum inspection requirements. The instructions provide a uniform method for performing inspection and tests, and reporting results. Drawings, specifications, and related manufacturing instructions must be reviewed to prepare inspection instructions. Therefore, an ongoing evaluation for clarity, completeness, and accuracy should be made for all documentation. Potential manufacturing and inspection problems must be identified at the preproduction stage. This includes equipment, personnel capability, and any special requirements or controls.

The instructions must define, by part number, the characteristics to be inspected and the sampling plan, equipment, and method to be applied. The basic information can be found in drawings and specifications, manufacturing instructions, equipment operating instructions, and schedules. Considerations must include functional requirements, reliability, quality history of this or similar products, and quality costs.

The quality plan must also consider the supplier's requirements: test data, material analysis, certifications, and special process approvals. These requirements must be included in the purchase order so that necessary documentation of inspections and tests may be obtained contractually and used as objective evidence for acceptance.

Inspection instructions require a review of the referenced drawings, specifications, and other documents to verify that the instructions are compatible with the authorized product definition.

Sampling plans provide for effective and economical inspection. Although economical, sampling does provide a degree of risk to both the producer and consumer. A commonly used reference, complete with sampling tables, is MIL-STD-105D issued by the Department of Defense. MIL-STD-105D provides sampling plans for various levels of protection depending on the criticalness of the dimension. In addition, many companies define critical, major, and minor defects on their drawings using symbols. Many impose quality requirements for critical defects such as 100 percent inspection for conformance to specification, adequate documentation, and part identification that is traceable to inspection reports. Often, the customer will dictate the sampling level or require approval of the plan selected by the supplier. Use of statistical or plotted sampling can reduce expenses. Inspection results can be tabulated or plotted in a manner that allows periodic reviews to identify trends and problem areas.

Consideration should be given to the use of inspection stamps to identify final acceptance, in-process acceptance, and defective material. Obviously, the issuance and use of inspection stamps must be formally controlled. In some cases, signatures, dates, and the use of specific inks are required on final inspection documents.

Receiving Inspection

For manufacturing operations, the inspection function is normally divided into receiving inspection, in-process inspection, and final inspection. Receiving inspection requirements are determined by functional considerations, operating costs, and applicable specifications. The requirements are interrelated and may be affected by inventory, flow time, and seller warranties.

Functional considerations include the need to verify selected measurements and tests prior to assembly operations: for example, to assure that bar stock is a specified stainless steel prior to investing costly machining operations, to assure that an inexpensive component is performing within specified limits before installing into a costly assembly, or to assure that a costly purchased product conforms to specified requirements within warranty limitations. In short, ordinary good judgment should determine the amount of receiving inspection required for functional considerations. Good judgment, however, must be based on facts.

Operating costs determine whether to verify the conformance of purchased material by performing receiving inspection or by applying "next assembly measurements." For example, when there is little or no flow time through an inventory, incoming material may be checked initially only for count, shipping damage, and identification. Controls then can be applied to measure the product for conformance in conjunction with next assembly inspection and/or test. The decision to perform receiving inspection at next assembly must be weighed against the potential cost of processing rejected materials at that stage as well as warranty time limitations. This alternative normally would be advisable when historical data indicate that the supplier can be relied on to provide acceptable material with a minimum of rejections.

Customers may specify the degree of receiving inspection to be applied. This is common practice among large prime contractors in government procurement. These requirements should be analyzed for abnormal costs prior to submitting a price quotation. For example, requirements to test all raw and fabricated material and to verify raw material certifications periodically by independent testing laboratories can significantly affect flow times and operating expenses.

The receiving function should have a system for checking in materials on receipt. This should include examining the material for shipping damage, verifying the count, and checking for the presence of certification or test data, shipping document identification, and lot control information.

The writing and issuance of inspection instructions should be controlled sufficiently to define purchase order requirements including applicable specifications, inspection equipment, sampling plans (if applicable), and material control requirements.

Receiving inspection must be able to withhold acceptance of material until it verifies that required certifications, specifications, and specified parameters are conforming. Inspection results should be documented; made available to appropriate purchasing, engineering, and quality personnel; and maintained in a retrievable file.

Source inspection may be substituted for receiving inspection by the customer when it is economical: (1) where duplication of costly inspection or test fixtures or equipment can be eliminated, (2) where direct shipment to field site is advisable, or (3) where shipping costs would make the return of large and bulky items expensive.

Nonconforming material must be identified, segregated, and held for disposition. The buyer should advise the supplier of rejected material and be responsible for obtaining corrective actions. Follow-up measures should be applied by the quality control function.

In-Process Inspection

In-process inspection can be used in certain operations to provide early detection of processes producing nonconforming products. Like receiving inspection, the requirements for in-process inspection are determined by the interrelations of functional considerations, operating costs, and customer specifications. Functional considerations primarily involve parameters that must conform to specification before they are sealed or otherwise covered up by a subsequent operation. Failure costs (in-house and customer) must be weighed against the cost of in-process inspection. Reliability, consumer acceptance (reputation), truth in advertising, and the potential for liability suits resulting from latent defects must be included in the determinations.

In-process inspection frequently involves a first article inspection before a production run is approved. This verifies that the operator, machine, and associated setup are capable of producing acceptable products. As with other specified inspection, documentation should be available for review when required.

Final Inspection

Final inspection is the last opportunity before shipment to assure that the product conforms to customer requirements. The extent of inspection should depend on the amount of receiving and in-process inspection already applied, complexity, shop defect levels, customer use information, and the potential for liability suits.

Some customers specify the level of inspection and test required, ranging from sampling to 100 percent. Test results and record maintenance may also be specified. Inspection records should include the quantity received, lot and/or serial number, number accepted, number defective, nature of defects, date, and inspector identification. Records should be maintained in such a manner that retrieval and review can be performed readily upon receipt of any authorized request. Such records, reflecting reasonable quality control practices, can be extremely important in cases of a product failure causing an accident or otherwise involving large sums of money.

It is good practice to identify and segregate nonconforming material. Nonconforming material subjected to repair or rework must be resubmitted to inspection for acceptance. Authorizations for shipping nonconforming material must be well documented and controlled. When possible, units accepted at final inspection should bear an inspection stamp (or marking) denoting acceptance and identifying the inspector.

Management should provide procedures that describe receiving, in-process, and final inspection requirements, including the assignment of specific responsibilities. All functions should be audited periodically by a representative of quality management for conformance to policies and procedures. This can be performed in a constructive manner, and the results can be of mutual benefit to the company, customers, suppliers, and the profit margin.

The following is a checklist of items to be considered for all inspection operations:

- Product definition (adequately specified and control assured for making changes)
- Inspection instructions
- Adequate (size and segregation) area for products in work, to be worked, accepted, rejected, and hold
- Adequate work benches [lighting, environmental controls, Occupational Safety and Health Administration (OSHA) requirements]
- Current calibration of acceptance equipment
- Adequate handling equipment

- Clean work area
- Adequate supervision (with identified authority and responsibilities)
- Trained inspection personnel
- Flow time controls through inspection
- Current product status (in work, to be worked, and hold)
- Record of inspection results
- Timely measurements
- Identification of accepted material
- Identification and segregation of nonconforming material
- Material certifications (as required)
- Identification of inspector (and qualification, as required)

Independent Laboratories for Testing and Evaluation

Many small business firms require, on an occasional or continuous basis, the services of a laboratory for testing purposes. The cost of a test laboratory, in terms of capital cost for facilities and equipment plus operating costs, may be prohibitive. Therefore, a business logically might choose to purchase testing services from an indepenent laboratory.

Once a business has determined the type and frequency of the testing services it requires, it should find sources capable of fulfilling the requirements. As in any subcontract activity, a small business should attempt to locate two or more qualified sources. Adequate timely test or evaluation reports may be critical to a company meeting commitments to its own customers; consequently, reliance on only one source of testing services may, in some cases, be inadequate.

An initial list of firms having the required capability may be obtained by:

- Reviewing trade indexes or trade journals.
- Discussing with colleagues in industry, government, or academia.
- Contacting trade associations such as the American Council of Independent Laboratories, Inc., 1725 K Street NW, Washington, DC 20006; or the Canadian Testing Association, Box 13033, Kanata Postal Station, Ottawa, Ontario K2K 1X3.
- Reviewing telephone directories.
- Contacting sources already approved by the customer.

Once the potential source list is prepared, some laboratories may be eliminated because of geographic location or other reasons. All remaining firms should then be contacted to determine if they are interested in providing the needed service. At this time the vendee should make it clearly understood that he intends to evaluate their facilities from a technical and managerial viewpoint.

The next step is to evaluate the selected laboratories. The following items aid in performing a meaningful evaluation:

- A checklist of equipment required to conduct the tests.
- Copies of applicable standards and methods.
- A list of additional requirements for review and/or observation:
    - -Sample identification and control/disposal
    - -Test reports, format
    - -Qualifications of testing personnel
    - -Security of samples and/or test reports
    - -Ownership of firm
    - -Receiving and shipping
    - -Laboratory capacity (where timeliness of tests is critical)
    - -Laboratory quality control procedures
    - -Test equipment calibration procedures and records
    - -Traceability to national standards

(Evaluating a testing laboratory is similar to evaluating suppliers. See Chapter 13, *How to Conduct a Supplier Survey.*)

Upon completion of the evaluation, the contractor may wish to invite the firms to visit his business location. This will help laboratory personnel understand the requirements from both a technical and business viewpoint.

Two of the standard methods of billing used by testing laboratories are flat rate for standard tests and hourly rate for equipment and personnel. Both methods normally are negotiable subject to volume, etc. Once a laboratory has conducted the required tests a number of times at an hourly rate, they may be willing to negotiate a standard cost per test.

Since critical decisions will be based on the laboratory test results, confidence in a laboratory's capability to provide accurate test results is imperative. This may be achieved by:

- Periodic visits and/or reviews of test results with laboratory personnel.
- Use of an audit sample. This is a sample wherein one portion is sent to another qualified test laboratory and one portion to the laboratory being audited. There will be some variation in test results from laboratory to laboratory or sample to sample; however, if the results from two laboratories are widely divergent, the problem may be resolved by:
    - -Reviewing test methods with both firms,
    - -Discussing test results with both firms, independently, or together, or
    - -Using a third laboratory as a referee.

-Where feasible, it is advisable to retain an archive sample that is fully representative of the sample submitted for tests.

Inspection, Measurement, and Test Equipment

Accurate inspections and tests are dependent on the calibration and control of all inspection and test equipment, and on the proper maintenance of all measuring instruments, tools, fixtures, gages, and measurement standards. A calibration and control program should provide for:

- Selection of appropriate standards and measuring equipment.
- Periodic calibration.
- Identification of equipment.
- Training and qualifications of personnel.
- Documented calibration procedures.
- Records of calibration and historical data.
- Tool and gage control.
- Maintenance, modification, storage, and handling of equipment.

Equipment selected for inspection and measurement should have adequate accuracy, stability, and range for the intended use. When several different types of equipment can perform a specific measuring function adequately, selection should be based on availability, equipment history (including repair work), initial cost, maintenance costs, and the manufacturer's service.

Whenever practical, equipment should have a rated accuracy of about 10 percent of the tolerance being measured. Similarly, standards used to calibrate measuring equipment and instruments should have appropriate capability. As a general rule, and within state-of-the-art or economic limitations, the standards of measurement system used should have a tolerance no greater than 10 percent of the allowable tolerance of the equipment being calibrated.

Through the proper selection of standards of appropriately higher accuracy levels, the equipment should be maintained in a state of calibration with the measurement of parameters traceable to the U.S. National Bureau of Standards or other acceptable levels of reference.

Equipment should be calibrated at regular intervals on the basis of stability, purpose, degree of usage, accuracy requirements, standard practices, and operating history. There can be no rigid formula for the frequency of calibration because so many factors come into play; however, the following partial list of basic inspection instruments and test equipment, initially, may have the calibration intervals shown:

Procurement Quality Control

Equipment	Calibration Frequency
Digital indicators	Quarterly
Digital voltmeters	Monthly
Micrometer	Quarterly (plus each time before use)
Optical comparators	Annually
Pressure gages	Semiannually
Scales	Semiannually
Torque wrenches	Quarterly
Voltmeters	Quarterly

To assure required accuracy, calibration intervals should be monitored continuously and lengthened or shortened according to the results of preceding calibrations recorded by the calibration agency. If a gage is not used for an extended period, the calibration cost could be avoided by placing it out of service in a controlled access area. The gage then needs to be calibrated only when it is returned to service.

Records on all equipment should denote location and calibration status. The records should contain identification information, calibration maintenance history, calibration status, calibration interval, and repair history. The records and historic information are useful in determining future recall requirements of the equipment.

All equipment should carry labels, seals, or tags identifying its serviceability and calibration status. When equipment use is meant to be limited, it should be identified accordingly. Seals should be used, when necessary, to assure that instrument calibration will not be disturbed. When an instrument is too small to be tagged or labeled, its container or storage box should be appropriately identified.

Tools, gages, jigs and fixtures, and production tooling that control or measure dimensions, contours, or locations affecting quality characteristics should be checked for accuracy prior to use. Periodic check and recalibration should be made at predetermined intervals to ensure continued accuracy.

Periodic audits should assure compliance with, and effective implementation of, procedures established for calibration and control of equipment. The surveillance should verify that:

- Applicable procedures are available and being used.
- Calibration personnel are qualified.
- Records and data are being maintained.
- Proper equipment is being used.
- Appropriate labels, seals, and tags are attached to equipment.
- Calibration dates are being adhered to in a timely manner.

Additional information on calibration program implementation appears in military standard MIL-STD-45662, *Calibration System Requirements.*

Frequently Used Calibration Terms and Definitions

Accuracy. The degree of agreement of the measurement with the true value of that parameter. The difference between measured and true value is defined as error.

Calibration. The comparison of an instrument or equipment to a measurement standard of known accuracy, to detect, correlate, report, and adjust, as required, any deviation from the standard.

Precision. The ability of an instrument to repeat the same reading when making the same measurement in the same manner and under identical conditions.

Prevention Maintenance. The service, cleaning, lubrication of parts, alignment, adjustment, functional test, repair, modification, and over-haul, as required, to ensure there is no deterioration of eqiupment per-formance.

Reliability. The susceptibility of a measuring device with a visual display to having its indications converted to a meaningful number, also expressed as the legibility of a visual display, normally expressed as the minimum measure and increment that can be discriminated in the terms of the display.

Resolution. The smallest change in input necessary to produce the smallest detectable change in output of the instrument under test.

Sensitivity. The ability of a measuring device to detect small differences in a quantity being measured.

Standard. An item designated as an authorized measurement reference and used to calibrate other standards or measuring and test equipment.

Documentation and Traceability

A manufacturer is accountable for the product quality of items delivered to his distributor and, ultimately, to the end user. Consequently, he also is responsible for the quality of materials and components procured from vendors and subcontractors, and incorporated into his product. Increasing emphasis on product liability and growing public pressure is forcing manufacturers to recall and correct defective products that could endanger consumers.

Customers are requiring assurance that the products they buy are safe to use and will perform to expectations. Various regulatory commissions are directing that critical components* have documented certifications that are traceable from inception through all fabrication phases to ultimate distribution. Products that require certifications cross almost every industry: metals, chemicals, petroleums, food and drugs, textiles, lumber, rubber compounds, etc. The list is endless.

For quality assurance purposes, a certification of compliance is, "A document signed by an authorized party affirming that the supplier of a product or service has met the requirements of the relevant specifications, contract, or regulation. (Comment: Compliance can pertain to a broad spectrum of requirements which may include procedural, conformance, timely delivery, reliability, or other elements" [ANSI/ASQC Standard A3-1978 p. 4]).

For effective supplier control, the definition can be expanded to:

> A statement of fact pertaining to the quality of products or services, that is based on observations, measurements, or tests which can be fully verified. It is evidence that is expressed in terms of specific quality requirements or characteristics, which are identified in drawings, specifications, and other documents which describe the item process or procedure.

Certification or objective quality evidence (OQE) can be looked upon as protection. OQE is proof to the customer that the product has been manufactured and tested to specifications. In some instances, OQE is the basis on which regulatory agencies issue a license for the product's sale and use. In the event of product liability claims, OQE may be the basis for substantiating that the product met all the material and design criteria.

Purchase orders for critical items usually specify objective data to be furnished with the product. In many instances, the documents and data are as essential as the hardware itself. Without the documentation, materials and hardware components cannot be incorporated into assemblies or placed into service. Many operating activities will not accept materials or authorize payment when documentation is missing, incomplete, or in error. Incoming materials usually are rejected or held until documentation problems are resolved.

In many instances, a simple part is the same or similar to a component used in a critical application. Often times, these similar or look-a-like parts are fabricated in the same shop using identical product lines. The difference is the additional testing imposed to certify that the item meets the needs of a critical application. Adequate controls are required to prevent similar components from being mixed in the manufacturing process or at the supplier's location.

Certifications that are merely statements of compliance to specifica-

---

*Critical components are items (metals, chemicals, finished assemblies, etc.) whose defect or failure would likely result in hazardous or unsafe conditions for individuals using, maintaining, or depending upon the product, or whose defect is likely to prevent performance of a major end item, such as a ship, aircraft, safety equipment, hospital unit, etc.

tion or phrases, such as "equal to" or "is similar to," are usually not reliable, and generally worthless and unacceptable to user activities. Some companies will forward, along with their purchase orders, specific instructions for data format and preparation. Other companies are much less explicit and must be contacted for their requirements.

In order to satisfy the minimum requirements of most activities, certification data should contain:

1. The original or exact copies of the quantitative test reports. It should indicate the specification to which the tests were performed, the methods used, and the actual test results obtained.
2. Identification of the activity or laboratory where the tests were performed, date, and laboratory control numbers. Test reports must be signed by an appropriate official of the testing organization.
3. Documentation traceable to purchase order numbers, lots, heat, batch, or traceability code numbers marked on the materials. Normally, original analysis and test reports furnished by material producers are accepted as verification of furnished materials; however, if any subsequent processes are performed (e.g., heat treating, forging, cold working, aging, etc.) that could change the characteristics of the materials, additional tests will be required that are representative of the finished state.

Traceability and Marking

The best certifications are of little value without traceability to the material. Anyone must be able to look at a part and, using the identifying code numbers, be able to find documentation verifying that the part has been tested and conforms with specifications/performance requirements. This must be accomplished using objective data.

Traceability is best accomplished by permanent codes marked directly on the material. Some buying activities will issue specific instructions as to type, depth of marking, location, etc. Normally, component manufacturers are allowed to use their own code numbers provided they are traceable to the original heat, lot, batch, laboratory analysis, and performance test reports.

In practice, parts, containers, or tags should be marked permanently with unique code numbers and any other identification required by the purchase document/specification plan. Markings should be located so as not to affect form, fit, or function and preferably so they will be visible after assembly. Critical items installed internally in an assembly by a prime or subcontractor should carry a certified document listing each item in the assembly and its associated identity code numbers and data. Items too small to mark, should be packaged and labeled, or tagged as required for permanent markings.

Procurement Quality Control

Traceability begins with a review of all incoming purchase orders to determine customer requirements. All outgoing orders also must be reviewed and quality requirements transmitted to vendors or subcontractors.

Written instructions should go to receiving personnel to review all test reports and certifications, ensuring conformance to the drawing specifications. All certified materials must be marked and identified with the same unique, traceable numbers recorded on the certificate. Items such as chemicals and rubber products should be checked to determine that shelf life and cure dates have not been exceeded.

A certification from the supplier does not itself always assure compliance with the purchase order requirements. As a safeguard against breakdowns in a supplier's quality system, the vendor's data should be checked routinely by having a sample of the material verified by in-house or independent testing. This often can be accomplished by testing only a few of the more critical elements.

Every business handling certified materials must keep incoming logs and materials segregated. This requires a formal procedure for permanently marking materials and finished parts with heat, lot, batch, or code numbers that are traceable directly to the test reports and laboratory analyses covering them. These requirements should be demanded of the vendor (subcontractor). There must also be strictly enforced procedures requiring identity markings obliterated during manufacture to be reapplied immediately after the operation during which they were removed.

Permanently documented and maintained records must be kept on all contractually specified tests and special processes performed. This includes operational and/or reliability testing, nondestructive tests, chemical analysis, physical properties, pressure tests, welding, heat treating, plating, etc. In order for the tests and special processes to be valid, they must be performed by a certified employee and accomplished according to procedures for which the license was granted. Records must verify that personnel qualifications and process approvals were valid at the time the tests or special processes were performed.

In most instances, documented data for the product itself must be retained for its operating life. The average record retention period is seven years, but may extend indefinitely for certain specialized industries. Many companies reduce these records to microfilm after several years.

The traceability story is an example of total quality assurance from planning, procuring, manufacturing, handling, inspecting, and more. It could fill a complete volume in itself. It is hoped that this brief discussion will provide a reference point for establishing document control.

Personal Skills and Equipment Certification

During development of a business plan to produce and market a product, company management determines the types of equipment and facilities needed. Management also determines what employee skills are necessary. These employee skills cover a spectrum from engineering to fabrication through inspection to packaging for shipment. Manufacturing skills can include special methods of joining or bonding machining of exotic materials, handling of hazardous materials, performing chemical processes, soldering, performing nondestructive testing/inspection, etc.

It is not unusual for management to find that the inventory of personal skills available is not adequate and must be acquired or developed. Depending on their size, companies conduct training programs ranging from simple on-the-job training to sophisticated classroom and bench-type programs which may extend for several months. Training also is available at educational institutions as short courses or extended programs leading to a degree. Some professional societies, such as the ASQC, the American Society for Nondestructive Testing, and others, have developed training material and assist local groups and educational institutions in conducting training and certification programs.

Once acquired, some skills need no further on-the-job or classroom training, since expertise is added and maintained by continued use. Other skills require occasional upgrading due to advances in technology. Still other skills require periodic demonstration of operator proficiency due to the nature of the operation or product itself. In these cases, success depends on the aptitude of the operator since final determination of adherence to the process usually requires subjective evaluation or destructive testing of the product.

For some operations, fabrication or assembly tools are certified periodically, in addition to their regular calibration, to assure repeatability of the process and to reduce the variables resulting from operator techniques. Certification of equipment and processes will be discussed later.

In discussing personal skills, two terms should be defined: *qualification* and *certification*. Qualification is the skill, training, and/or work experience required for a person to properly perform assigned duties. Certification is a written document indicating that the holder has demonstrated, through written or oral questioning or examination of work samples, his knowledge and ability to perform specialized duties.

The customer may determine which skills need certification. A Department of Defense contract may cite one or more of the following specifications, each of which requires periodic skill demonstration:

- MIL-STD-1537, *Military Standard Electrical Conductivity Test for Measurement of Heat Treatment of Aluminum Alloys, Eddy Current Methods*

- MIL-STD-410, *Military Standard Nondestructive Testing Personnel Qualification and Certification (Eddy Current, Liquid Penetrant, Magnetic Particle, Radiographic and Ultrasonic)*
- MIL-STD-5021, *Military Specification Tests; Aircraft and Missile Welding Operators' Qualification*

Prime contractors or manufacturers may require additional certification and periodic validation of skills they believe are necessary to ensure quality and reliability. Beyond the mandatory certifications established in the contract, a manufacturer must examine his own requirements. Professional or trade associations can offer further assistance and guidance.

The differences between training and certification must be examined in light of the operation's complexity and the ability to verify the end result. A machinist may require only initial training to operate a numerical controlled machine. Similarly, because of the dimensions of an end product are easily validated by standard measuring instruments, a machined parts inspector usually needs one-time training in basic mathematics and the functions of micrometers, calipers, parallel bars, and other standard measuring instruments. However, skill in interpreting X-ray film requires extended periods of training since the interpretation, due to the medium itself, is subjective. Company management must carefully determine which skills require one-time training and which require certification.

Another factor to be considered is the cost of periodic certification. Continuation of certification requires a periodic evaluation of the individual by obtaining special work samples, requiring a written or oral examination, or by keeping a record of work results to establish error patterns. A combination of testing and an actual demonstration of skill is required by some military specifications. If the skill is not defined in a military specification or in a trade standard, a testing program should be developed and enforced. Test results should be kept for an appropriate length of time.

Training and skill certification programs are best administered by designated centers. If the certification is prescribed by a military specification or trade association, the requirements are documented and available. If the skill or process, or the need for such is unique to the manufacturer, the requirements should be documented and made part of the company's manufacturing or quality records.

Some skills, such as nondestructive testing, require that the person who certifies others must have special education and work experience. Program surveillance normally is assigned to the product assurance organization. A number of methods can help verify that currently certified employees are performing work predetermined to require a certified operator:

1. Issuing each operator a card indicating his name, employee number, the skill for which he is certified, and the period of

certification. The card should be in his possession whenever he performs that operation so that his current qualification can be checked at any time.

2. Posting the names of certified operators at the work station so that management or inspection can match the operator to the name on the list.

3. Certifying all operators in a work area (cost center, etc.) so that work assignments can be made without fear of using a noncertified operator.

4. Issuing an identification stamp to the employee so the product and/or documentation can be traced to him. This also will indicate that the process has been accomplished by a certified person.

The product assurance manager must decide whether his inspectors require training similar to that of operators so that they can more objectively determine product acceptability. For example, should an inspector of welds be qualified to weld if the weld inspection is accomplished using nondestructive test methods? Whatever approach the product assurance manager finds appropriate, he must establish a program for monitoring the skills of his own employees. The specification (drawing, work instruction, procedure, contact, etc.) must identify where a certified skill, process, or operation is required.

Manufacturing and the product assurance managers must determine whether the shop paper (assembly instructions) should identify operations requiring a certified skill. Verifying the performance of an operation by a certified operator is easier for management when the shop paper is annotated. Whatever method is used, manufacturing and product assurance must agree on the identification of skills, the period that certification is valid (when not controlled by military or customer specification), and the method of confirming use of skilled operators.

The product assurance manager further enforces the skill certification program when, through failure reports or observation, he determines that the quality of work performed by a certified operator falls below an acceptable level. At this point, the product assurance manager should initiate action to suspend the certified status of the operator and require retraining or other action as necessary to restore the skill level.

Some manufacturing operations require similar certification consideration due to the process itself. Some examples are bonding leads on micro devices, crimping or insulation stripping, or a spot welding operation where the inspection or test of each weld is not feasible due to cost or the destructive nature of validation. In these instances, it is customary to initiate a two-step program:

Step 1
The machine, instrument, or process is tested to the appropriate

specification or manufacturer's instruction. When the operation is performed within acceptable limits, all adjusting features (screws, slides, power settings, etc.) are "sealed" to prevent unauthorized or inadvertent adjustments. These "seals" should remain undisturbed until maintenance or recalibration is required.
Step 2
A schedule is developed to produce an adequate number of test specimens at the beginning of each work shift or other predetermined cycle. These specimens are verified through destructive or nondestructive means prior to production.

Verifying the repeatability of equipment or process is a certification action. A log maintained at the equipment or process area records the original proofing and certification. It may be necessary to repeat this step several times during the work shift if the process is time- or quantity-oriented, or at the beginning of each shift if the process is operator-oriented. In any case, work specimens should be retained long enough to permit examination during failure analysis or post audit.

Certification does not guarantee product quality. It is a program to reduce or eliminate process and operator variables.

Handling Nonconforming Material

Since most production processes inevitably yield some defective products, every production facility must establish methods to prevent further processing, completion, or delivery of defective products. The products must be segregated as soon as the nonconformance is recognized to ensure that appropriate action is taken to control or localize the defective items. The defective material must be marked clearly and removed from the normal work flow to a special holding area. Once nonconforming material is isolated, someone must decide what needs to be done before the material can either be returned to production or scrapped. Evaluating nonconforming material is an important quality control activity between the vendor and the vendee. Excessive nonconforming material usually occurs because of a breakdown of the producer's operations.

Many things produce nonconformance. It may be caused by chance alone. The design may be so advanced that no means yet exists for eliminating the causes. The cost of elimination may not be economically possible, i.e., it may be cheaper to scrap items. The design criteria may be too severe. The process capability may be wider than the tolerance. In any case, the parties involved should be concerned because of its effect on the operation's efficiency and the potential for hidden costs in the production process or end product.

190

Prompt, effective corrective action essentially is good business. Non-conforming items cost money because scrap, repairs, or rework mean additional operations. The producer should find and correct the causes of nonconformance wherever economically feasible. He should use both his own expertise and that of his customers through informal consultation or, if warranted, a formal review board appointed by top management.

The decision-making group, formal or informal, should review all aspects of the process and material used to produce the nonconforming item. The investigation should continue until proper disposition of the material can be made. The group must find the causes of nonconformance, individually or collectively, and see that appropriate corrective action is taken. A summary of the group's findings should include product identification, the stage in production under review, nature and extent of nonconformance, technical assessment and decision, disposition action to be taken by the producer, and advice of corrective action to all concerned.

Methods of disposing of nonconforming material include scrap, rework or repair, and use "as is" under concession from the proper authority for return to the supplier. All material to be used in production either "as is" or after repair or rework must remain segregated until it is cleared up by inspection or test for production use. Records of nonconformance, corrective action, and disposition should be saved for comparison in future reviews.

When parts fail to meet the customer's requirements, the producer is obligated to notify him and come to a decision as to acceptability or possible repair. It is not ethical to knowingly ship out-of-specification material.

Planning for Customer Quality Survey

The primary purpose of a customer quality survey is to find out whether the supplier has a quality system capable of measuring and controlling contract requirements. Obviously, the customer's procurement organization believes the supplier has something to offer them or the survey would not be performed. The supplier must present himself honestly. If a supplier convinces a customer that he can do something and subsequently fails to perform as contracted, both customer and supplier lose, but the supplier loses on future contracts as well.

A survey has three basic parts: opening conference, plant tour, and closing conference. The opening conference is a key part of the survey. At this time, the customer's survey personnel will present their credentials and explain their function. They will briefly define the products, intended use, and design requirements. At this time, they also should briefly outline the quality controls that will be required. It is important for the supplier to have manufacturing and quality personnel who are thoroughly familiar with the operations at this conference. They should give the survey team a brief accurate overview of their quality system however detailed or informal it may be. Overstatements at this time will be negated during the detail survey. This is the time to describe the quality controls as they exist. This allows the survey team to determine whether the controls are adequate for the product or process under consideration.

Evaluation of the supplier's quality system begins with a review of the quality manual. In the small company it may be only a few typewritten pages, but it must accurately represent the quality controls being used. A major problem can occur if a manual promises more than actual procedures deliver. When this happens, the evaluator can only assume that the supplier is trying to falsely impress him.

Basic survey categories include.

- Drawing and specification control.
- Purchased material control/receiving inspection.
- Manufacturing control/in-process inspection/final inspection.
- Gage calibration and test equipment control.
- Storage, packaging, and shipment control.
- Nonconforming material control.
- Quality program management.

During the plant tour, the supplier should demonstrate the procedures in each of these areas. Since the survey is a classic "show and tell" situation and, since all things will not be immediately visible to the surveyor, the supplier should provide information in any area that an evaluator surveys. If the evaluator does not see the controls in action, he cannot grant credit for them. On the other hand, the supplier should not babble endlessly about how good his control is. He should understand what the evaluator is seeking and openly demonstrate the quality system.

When evaluating drawing and specifications control, the surveyor wants to see if the supplier has a method of assuring that requirements, including changes, are transmitted to manufacturing and verified by quality.

Many surveyors like to start with the incoming rough product and follow it through to completion and shipping. So that important procedures are visible and operational, it is best that the presentation be made by persons knowledgeable in the operation rather than by an executive who may be more concerned with making an impression. Beginning in receiving inspection, the supplier must be able to document that requirements have been communicated to the vendors and that the incoming product has been inspected and appropriate records maintained. This is the first area where the importance of visibility becomes evident.

Being able to randomly check a lot of material that is properly identified and that carries evidence of inspection helps demonstrate control of operations. Identification alone, however, is not going to satisfy the surveyor. It is important to show evidence of planning for the characteristics to be checked and to specify sampling frequency. Demonstrataing the use of a recognized sampling plan, such as MIL-STD-105D, is far more meaningful than claiming that everything is checked "real heavy," or 10 percent, etc.

Many small companies depend on outside laboratories for testing or evaluating material. Here, again, it is important to have this information available, as well as examples of current reports for review. It is embarrassing to say, "We have stuff checked all the time," but not be able to remember the laboratory's name or find any reports for the last 18 months. If laboratory work is required for the product, it is essential to demonstrate a good working relationship with the laboratory.

In the area of in-process operations, several important items need to be checked. These deal with the importance of written work instructions in the shop. Documentation of controls follows the fundamental steps of telling the worker and inspector what to do, and giving them the tools to measure their work and the means to record the results. In some small operations, an operation sheet can be combined with an inspection plan and inspection record. It is difficult to fault objective plans and data. A sound, handwritten instruction performed by qualified persons who use calibrated equipment and record the results of their checks is far more meaningful than fancy printed forms that are incomplete or improperly used.

If the surveyor can stop at a work station and find that the operator has the applicable drawings, specifications, work instructions, inspection equipment, and record sheets, the supplier is on the right track. Having only one "complete" work station is not going to impress a surveyor because control should be evident throughout the shop. Furthermore, it is quite obvious when a supplier has made a quick tour through the shop, hanging tags on everything and getting all the right forms on the job the day before a survey; it is best to be honest and demonstrate something that can be substantiated. After all, the objective is to evaluate the quality program. Surveyors generally expect to see documentation of inspection instructions and to find the use of sampling plans in receiving inspection. The response that "Charlie has checked them for years and knows all about it" will only draw the counter "What do you do if Charlie isn't here?" There is no substitute for being able to show: "These are the characteristics that we check; this is our inspection frequency. These are our criteria for acceptance and here are our records of inspection."

Also regarding inspection or testing, surveyors will notice the presence of equipment required to check the parts being reviewed. It is not wise to make claims for doing things without having the equipment or capability to perform. Rusty "JO" blocks, damaged gages, lack of standards, etc., will not establish confidence in the supplier's calibration and maintenance of inspection tools. If inspection tools or gages cannot be found, it is difficult to convince the surveyor that the items are calibrated and in use. Again, the supplier who can demonstrate well-maintained equipment, records of calibration, and traceability to known standards is on the right track to a satisfactory survey evaluation.

The show and tell concept continues and the importance of the tour guide's knowledge of the quality program becomes more evident. The survey really is nothing more than a review of operating methods to determine the capability to produce in conformance with specifications and requirements.

Inspection is not the final element since the survey is a comprehensive evaluation of operations. The supplier will have to demonstrate controls in warehousing, packing, and shipping. If a part of product is not packaged or identified properly, it may present more problems than if it were nonconforming to some other requirements. In numerous instances, product may be damaged during handling and shipment. Therefore, it is important to show that customer requirement information is available to shipping personnel.

Thus far, the survey has revolved around positive preplanned elements. However, control of nonconforming material must be evaluated too. It is essential to be able to show the surveyor positive identification and, in the case of some contracts, segregation from production. As with the other elements, this mean s the ability to control operations. Information feedback on the evaluation of rejected material and corrective action is often covered. Therefore, it is necessary to be prepared to explain what is done in response to customer complaints. A system should be operational for evaluating the returns and documenting the findings and action taken.

The survey category dealing with quality program management includes not only the quality manual mentioned previously, but also management's philosophy toward the growth and development of people responsible for quality. This is the time to demonstrate whether one person can take over if another is out. Is there an automatic stand-in for key quality persons? Are the inspectors taking or have they taken any courses in quality control? Are they members of a professional society such as the ASQC?

Other elements are covered in some surveys and a standard recipe cannot be provided for receiving an outstanding rating every time. The supplier will do best if he is honest with the surveyor and presents his system as it is operating and in effect. If he follows sound, accepted principles and can demonstrate control of operations for the type of product or process being considered, he should receive an acceptable rating. The key to a successful survey is planning and demonstrating control of operations.

At the closing conference, the survey team can summarize for the supplier which areas were good and which had discrepancies. It is important for the supplier to understand each discrepancy. Possibly the surveyor did not see a particular control or procedure and, at this time, the supplier can clarify a misunderstanding. If, on the other hand, the discrepancy is valid, the supplier can find out what the customer is looking for so that appropriate corrective action can be taken. The supplier gets a written report detailing discrepant areas. Upon its receipt the supplier should respond in writing, designating any improvements made or planned and their estimated dates of completion. If the price of the order does not justify the changes required to upgrade the system, the supplier should indicate his point of view at this time. (The supplier should provide an adequate meeting place to hold both the opening and closing conferences.)

In conclusion, when the customer defines what is needed and the supplier successfully demonstrates what he actually can do, the result could be receipt of orders with the supplier's capabilities, benefiting both the customer and supplier. Generally, customers are willing to assist a supplier who is candid, open to suggestion, and who honestly strives to maintain an effective quality program to produce products meeting contractual requirements.

Planning for Source Inspection

Source inspection is a process wherein the customer, or an agency representing the customer, inspects the supplier's product at his facility prior to shipment. Source inspection has the following advantages over normal incoming inspection:

1. It avoids duplication of costly specialized inspection or test equipment at the customer's plant.
2. It expedites the flow of needed items to the production line by eliminating or reducing the need for incoming inspection.
3. Material needing rework can be corrected while the product is in the supplier's plant thus avoiding time lost in returning defective material.
4. When certain parameters cannot be fully tested after assembly, source inspection allows verification while the product is being manufactured.
5. Awareness of the supplier's processes, systems, and people allow for better control by the source inspector.
6. The presence of a source inspector allows the supplier to discuss and seek advice about customer specifications and requirements.
7. Source inspection allows closer relations between the customer and supplier.
8. It permits direct shipment to locations other than the customer's plant.

Procurement Quality Control

During contract negotiations and purchase order review, the supplier should inquire whether in-process and final source inspection requirements exist.

The supplier should notify the customer's purchasing agent at least three days prior to the date when source inspection is needed. (Every supplier cannot get source inspection coverage the last day of the month.) When notifying the customer, it is best to provide the name of the person whom the source inspector should contact and the specific plant location.

When the source inspector arrives, plant personnel should be courteous and brief. The source inspector has a busy schedule and does not have time for idle chatter. More importantly, inspection records and any certification of outside testing, such as nondestructive testing or laboratory analysis, should be ready and available for the source inspector.

Since the product already has passed for the supplier's final inspection, source inspection is basically an audit to verify that the supplier has completed the appropriate contractual requirement. Source inspection is not intended to replace the supplier's quality responsibility.

The product should be ready and in an appropriate area for the source inspector to work. Nothing is more upsetting to a source inspector, than to wait for the supplier to locate the product, find the gages, and set them up. Someone should be assigned to escort and assist the source inspector. If he is familiar with the inspection of the product, this person often can demonstrate a complicated inspection setup or test for the source inspector.

It is good practice for the supplier's management to arrange a brief closing interview during which the source inspector can explain his observations. Often he can provide valuable information. Supplier management also should be available to make decisions if rework, repair, or correction is required. Follow-up activities should assure that appropriate releases, acceptance paperwork certifications, etc., are included in the shipment.

On the question of hospitality, an occasional lunch may be in order, as this gives supplier management and the source inspector an opportunity to recap earlier events. Local use of the supplier's phone is normal as most calls are related to the product. It is customary for the supplier's secretary to assist in travel reservations.

Most source inspectors want to accept the supplier's product. If a discrepancy is found and corrected, the source inspector may have prevented the supplier's product from causing a failure in the customer's assembly that could have become costly for the supplier as well as the customer.

When the product has been made to specifications and has been controlled and inspected properly, the supplier has nothing to fear from the source inspector. The supplier's openness and willingness to demonstrate that he complies with the customer's requirements will help create positive relations with the source inspector and, thus, with the customer.

Finding and Hiring a Consultant

Industrial corporations hire lawyers and accountants as consultants on a regular basis. Few manage without these outside aides, yet many overlook the advantage of consultants. The professional engineering consultant can be an invaluable aid to profit. In the use of outside advisors, the key is the proper identification of the problems and the correct combination of attitudes on the part of corporate management, engineering advisor, and staff. The manager who has not used consultants probably is not aware of how to choose or where to find a consultant.

The relationship's success depends both on the client and consultant. The client should select his consultant only after carefully considering what he wishes to accomplish. The consultant — at least the ethical consultant — will have no qualms in refusing an assignment outside his field or one he considers impossible. The consultant is an extra hand. He has skills and special competence. When these skills are combined with client needs, success can be achieved.

There has to be a specific need for hiring a consultant. He should not be employed to manage a department. A consultant is most effective solving specific problems, analyzing problem areas, suggesting methods of finding solutions, writing manuals and reports, training, advising, and assisting a staff to develop required skills and procedures. The consultant also may provide management with systems and procedures that improve product, processes, and operations.

The organization looking for special assistance can use one or more of the following methods:

- Advertise for a consultant (this method is least recommended).
- Ask the quality control or reliability engineer to search for one.
- Consult the business card index (advertisements) of organizations that provide consulting services in journals such as *Quality Progress* (published by the ASQC).
- Call the ASQC office and request the names of one or more quality control or reliability engineering consultants in the client's area.
- Call friends or acquaintances for similar suggestions.

If the firm's quality manager or others in its quality department are members of the ASQC, they may know of appropriate consultants. Because the quality manager will have a good deal of contact with the consultant and must develop a good working relationship with him, having the quality manager in on the selection will be an advantage. Choosing a consultant in this manner is less likely to cause friction or create the false impression that the quality manager may lose his job to the consultant. Competent people can be trusted to hire competent help.

Procurement Quality Control

Once the manager (executive) has found one or more consultants, he must decide whether the consultant is suitable, competent, and will be valuable to the organization. He should inteview the consultant but, even before that, he will be interested in the consultant's background, training and experience, the cost of his services, and whether he can devote sufficient time to the task. In the initial contact the need for a quality control consultant is explained. Is he able to help? When can he meet to view operations and discuss problems? At that time he can determine what he believes can be done and how he proposes to work in the particular situation.

The consulting engineer will indicate whether he can undertake the task on the basis of his experience, competence, availability, and familiarity with the field. The consultant will want to discuss any possible conflict of interest with present clients. Sometimes clients will not object to an arrangement where the consultant services two or more organizations in the same business.

Fees

Many consultants will make an initial visit without charge if the client is local and the potential assignment lengthy. Others may want to be reimbursed for transportation costs. Trips can sometimes run into substantial costs. If the interview precedes a task or contract of short duration, the travel expense and fee are more usual.

How much do consulting engineers charge? Most fees are quoted on a per diem basis. They may run from $200 to more than $800 per day. To this is added travel expense, food, and lodging, if necessary. The usual work day is approximately eight hours. In some instances the eight hours are on site; in others, time is based on portal-to-portal pay scale. The consultant is an expert available at a fraction of what it would cost to have a full-time employee. Extremely competent engineers are available on this basis. To the small firm that does not need full-time services, this can be a bargain provided the job is accomplished properly. Even for large firms it is a distinct advantage.

How much time should the professional engineering consultant devote to the task? This is part of the negotiation. To complete a quality manual will take days — anywhere from four to 40 or more, depending on the complexity of the problem and the extent of existing material.

To install an operation and train the company in the proper use of the manual and its procedures is even more time consuming. It can be done slowly or on a crash basis over a shorter period. The consultant and company will have to agree on a schedule, the amount of time to be devoted to the task, and on the fees and when they become payable. Some contracts between company and consultant last for days, others for years, depending on what is needed. Most consultants bill on a monthly basis.

Time and Availability of Services

How can a consultant devote a great amount of time to one organization, particularly when it may need many weeks of continued effort? This depends on whether the consultant is:

- A large consulting company — more than 50 people.
- A medium-size consulting company — five to 50 people.
- A small group — two to five people who operate cooperatively.
- The one-man consultant — a full-time professional or a moonlighter such as a university professor.

The size of the consulting group is no indication of its competence, although a small group obviously cannot provide as many people as a much larger group. A good rule, whether dealing with a large or small firm, is to be sure the responsible executive meets and knows the actual consultants assigned to the task.

There are two ways to use a consultant. Let him do the work or have him help train employees. The latter is usually cheaper. Furthermore, control is in the hands of management, where it belongs.

One item most consultants cannot estimate with precision is how much time it will take to accomplish a task in a given company. They can come in, survey the plant, and write a report within specific time limits, but to tell management that tasks will take specific periods of time when the organization's staff is involved, means that they, and not the staff, are doing the work. Though estimates are possible, few consultants will do more than estimate, since corporate management and manpower can work with or against a consultant's recommendation.

If the corporate staff and the consultant cannot work together effectively, the program should be halted. It won't work. For this reason alone, most arrangements with consultants are agreements and not line-time contracts. If it isn't working, it isn't worthwhile to either party. Both parties should exercise this responsibility. Furthermore, when the job is finished, it is time to call a halt.

Reference

ANSI/ASQC Standard A3-1978. *American National Standard Quality Systems Terminology.* Milwaukee: American Society for Quality Control.

ς

APPENDIX A

PROCUREMENT QUALITY DEFINITIONS

Acceptance Sampling. Sampling inspection in which decisions are made to accept or not accept product or service; the methodology that deals with procedures by which decisions to accept or not accept are based on the results of the inspection of samples.

Appraisal Cost. Cost associated with measuring, evaluating, or auditing products, components, and purchased material to assure conformance with quality standards and performance requirements.

Attribute Measurement. Qualitative measurement that typically shows only the number of parts or the number of defects per part failing to conform to specified criteria.

Audits. Systematic examination of the acts and decisions with respect to quality to verify or evaluate compliance to the operational requirements of the quality program or the specifications or contract requirements of the product or service. Audits of a supplier's quality system or process must be performed at the supplier's facility. Audits of a supplier's product may be performed either at the supplier's facility or in-house.

Bilateral Tolerance. Splitting of a tolerance by a median axis so that each side is identical.

Calibration. Standardization by determining the deviation from a standard to ascertain the proper correction factors.

Capability Ratio (CR). Measurement of the proportion of specification width which is consumed by process variation.

Common Cause. Source of variation that is random and affects all the individual values of the process output being studied.

Continuous Improvement. Operational philosophy that produces products of increasing quality for customers in an increasingly efficient way and improves the return on investment on an ongoing basis.

Control Chart. Graphic method for evaluating whether a process is or is not in a state of statistical control.

Control Plan. Plan that establishes and maintains adequate written procedures covering all critical characteristics and key processes to ensure a consistent and acceptable quality product.

Corrective Action. Resolution of problems between user and producer arising due to product nonconformance.

Customer Complaint. Formal or informal allegation by the customer due to failure in meeting previously agreed on requirements by the supplier.

Design of Experiments. Planned test that is used to determine whether there is a statistical relationship between variables.

Deviation. Process through which a producer is authorized to ship nonconforming products to the user with the user's concurrence.

Disposition. Final arrangement or settlement of nonconforming product in an orderly way.

Distributor. Nonmanufacturing source of product. Usual where no transformation of product takes place.

Drawing (Blueprint). Sketch of the product being produced with specified tolerances of each characteristic.

Engineering Support. Essential part of a good quality system that encompasses product design and development, as well as reliability testing of new or revised products.

External Failure Cost. Cost generated by defective products in the field after having been shipped to customers.

Final Inspection. Examination of a product to ensure that it conforms to all applicable specifications and requirements before it is packaged and shipped to the customer.

Flowchart. Diagram that shows step-by-step progression of a product through a manufacturing system showing all factors that could adversely affect quality at the point where they occur.

Procurement Quality Definitions

Frequency Distribution. Tabulation of the number of times a given outcome has occurred within the sample of products being checked.

Gage Repeatability. Measurement of the consistency obtained with one gage when used several times by one operator while measuring the identical characteristic on the same parts.

Gage Reproducibility. Measurement of the consistency of different operators using the same gage while measuring the identical characteristic on the same parts.

Gage Variability. Measurement of the consistency of at least two sets of measurements obtained with a gage on the same parts as a result of time.

Incoming Inspection. Inspection of purchased parts at the customer's facility after the shipment of parts from the supplier to ensure supplier compliance with specifications and contractual agreements.

Inspection. Process of measuring, examining, testing, gaging, or otherwise comparing the unit with the applicable requirements.

Inspection (100 Percent). The inspection of all parts in a lot for all characteristics to ensure compliance to specifications.

Internal Failure Costs. Costs generated by a producer in making defective and nonconforming materials and products that do not meet company quality specifications.

Key Process Characteristics. Manufacturing processes deemed crucial in producing a product to its design intent.

Key Product Characteristics. Properties deemed crucial by the user to satisfy the design intent.

Lot Control. System that provides the means to trace pertinent information about the materials and/or components comprising a given product.

Material Certification. Process through which documented evidence establishes that a product is in compliance with designated specifications.

Measuring and Testing Devices. Equipment used to evaluate a product's conformance to its specifications.

Nonconforming Material. Material that is not in compliance with specifications.

Procurement Quality Control

Normal (Gaussian) Distribution. Condition where measured variation is symmetric about a central value and has a bell-shaped form.

Prevention Cost. Cost of strategies directing actions and analysis toward continuous improvement of process management.

Process. Combination of people, equipment, materials, methods, and environment that produce output to a planned effect.

Process Audit. Analysis of elements of a process and appraisal of completeness, correctness, or conditions.

Process Capability. Limits within which a tool or process operates based on minimum variability as governed by the prevailing circumstances.

Process Capability Index (PCI). Ratio that measures the inherent variability of a process in relation to specification limits.

Process Capability Ratio (CPK). Ratio that measures the centering and variability of a process in relation to specific limits.

Process Survey. Survey used to evaluate whether a supplier has process controls in place to ensure that the supplier's process will manufacture quality products. Process controls include proper tooling, equipment, inspection, etc.

Procurement Quality. Any and all aspects dealing with the purchasing of products.

Product Audit. Quantitative assessment of conformance to required product characteristics.

Product/Process Characteristic. Any given attribute of a product or process.

Rating Method. Quantitative method of evaluating systems and performance.

Ship-to-Stock (STS). Program in which the supplier and customer work together for improved quality and conformance of manufctured parts to eliminate the need for incoming or source inspection of purchased parts or products. Under this program, individual products or processes are qualified as opposed to an overall supplier certification. Also, maintenance of this program is provided through audits.

Procurement Quality Definitions

Skip-Lot. Plan in acceptance sampling in which some lots in a series are accepted without inspection when the sampling results for a stated number of immediately preceding lots meet stated criteria.

Special Cause. Source of variation that is not inherent in the system and can be prevented.

Source Inspection. Inspection of purchased parts at the supplier's facility by a customer representative to ensure supplier compliance with specifications and contractual agreements.

Specification. Specific limits or parameters that are required to assure the success of a product to perform as designed.

Standard Deviation/Sigma. Measurement of the spread of dispersion of a set or values about their average value.

Statistical Control. Process considered to be in a "state of statistical control" if variations among the observed sampling results can be attributed to a constant system of chance causes.

Statistical Process Control (SPC). Use of statistical techniques to analyze a process or its output to take required actions to achieve and maintain a state of statistical control and to improve the process capability.

Supplier Certification. Program aimed at qualifying suppliers already on an approved status to a higher level of approval called certification. This usually encompasses review of the supplier's past delivered product history, and an in-depth quality system survey. Certification of a supplier is usually all-encompassing and covers all products. Once certification is granted to a supplier, the customer institutes a reduced sampling at incoming inspection.

Survey. Broad overview of a supplier's system or process used to evaluate the adequacy of that system or process to produce quality products.

System Audit. Documented activity performed to verify, by examination and evaluation of objective evidence, that applicable elements of the quality system are suitable and have been developed, documented, and effectively implemented in accordance with specified requirements.

System Survey. Survey conducted to assess whether the supplier has appropriately controlled systems that will adequately prevent the manufacture of nonconforming products.

Variable Measurement. Quantitative data in which physical properties are measured, such as hole diameters or coating thickness.

Variation. Inevitable differences among individual outputs of a process that are grouped into common causes and special causes.

Vendor Rating. System of measurement of vendor or supplier performance against set goals or standards.

Verification. Physical confirmation of a stated condition.

See also:

1. ANSI/ASQC Standard A1-1978. *Definitions, Symbols, Formulas and Tables for Control Charts.* Milwaukee: American Society for Quality Control.

2. ANSI/ASQC Standard A2-1978. *Terms, Symbols and Definitions for Acceptance Sampling.* Milwaukee: American Society for Quality Control.

3. ANSI/ASQC Standard A3-1978. *Quality Systems Terminology.* Milwaukee: American Society for Quality Control.

4. ANSI/ASQC Standard C1-1968 (ANSI 21.8-1971). *Specifications of General Requirements for a Quality Program.* Milwaukee: American Society for Quality Control.

5. American Society for Quality Control Statistics Division. *Glossary and Tables for Statistical Quality Control,* 2nd ed. Milwaukee: American Society for Quality Control, 1983.

6. American Society for Testing Materials Committee on Terminology. *Compilation of ASTM Standard Definitions,* 6th ed. Philadelphia: American Society for Testing Materials, 1986.

APPENDIX B

Procurement Quality Control

AMERICAN NATIONAL STANDARD

ANSI/ASQC Q90-1987, *Quality Management and Quality Assurance Standards — Guidelines for Selection and Use*

Abstract

Quality Management and Quality Assurance Standards — Guidelines for Selection and Use provides guidelines for the selection and use of Standards Q91, Q92, Q93, and Q94.

AMERICAN NATIONAL STANDARD: An American National Standard implies a consensus of those substantially concerned with its scope and provisions. An American National Standard is intended as a guide to aid the manufacturer, the consumer, and the general public. The existence of an American National Standard does not in any respect preclude anyone, whether he has approved the standard or not, from manufacturing, marketing, purchasing, or using products, processes, or procedures not conforming to the standard. American National Standards are subject to periodic review, and users are cautioned to obtain the latest editions.

CAUTION NOTICE: This American National Standard may be revised or withdrawn at any time. The procedures of the American National Standards Institute require that action be taken to reaffirm, revise, or withdraw this standard no later than five years from the date of approval. Purchasers of American National Standards may receive current information on all standards by calling or writing the American National Standards Institute.

Approved June 8, 1987
American National Standards Institute, Inc.

Foreword

(This Foreword is not a part of American National Standard Quality Management and Quality Assurance Standards — Guidelines for Selection and Use.)

This standard, the first of five in the ANSI/ASQC Q90-94 series, provides guidance for the selection and use of other standards (Q91-94) in the series.

Rather than independently revising and extending its current *Generic Guidelines for Quality Systems* (ANSI/ASQC Z1.15-1979) the Standards Committee has elected to join other nations in adopting standards fully consistent with the ''ISO 9000-9004 Series'' of Quality Management and Quality Assurance Standards, since the latter were in agreement with the efforts of the ANSI/ASQC Z1.15 revision team .

These five ISO standards (ISO 9000-9004) were prepared by Technical Committee ISO/TC 176 on Quality Assurance in the interest of harmonizing the large number of national and international standards in this field. In addition to input from other countries, such U.S. standards as ANSI/ASQC Z1.15 and ANSI/ASQC Z1.8 were considered in the source material used in developing these ISO standards. The ANSI/ASQC Q90 through Q94 standards are *technically equivalent* to the ISO 9000-9004 series, but incorporate customary American language usage and spelling.

Users should note that all ANSI/ASQC standards undergo revision from time to time, and that any reference herein to any other standard implies the latest revision, unless otherwise stated.

Comments concerning this standard will be welcome. They should be sent to the standard's sponsor, American Society for Quality Control, 310 West Wisconsin Avenue, Milwaukee, Wisconsin 53203.

0.0 INTRODUCTION

A principal factor in the performance of an organization is the quality of its products or services. There is a world-wide trend towards more stringent customer expectations with regard to quality. Accompanying this trend has been a growing realization that continual improvements in quality are often necessary to achieve and sustain good economic performance.

Most organizations — industrial, commercial, or governmental — produce a product or service intended to satisfy a user's needs or requirements. Such requirements are often incorporated in "specifications." However, technical specifications may not in themselves guarantee that a customer's requirements will be consistently met, if there happen to be any deficiencies in the specifications or in the organizational system to design and produce the product or service. Consequently, this has led to the development of quality system standards and guidelines that complement relevant product or service requirements given in the technical specifications. The series of Standards (ANSI/ASQC Q90-Q94) embodies a rationalization of the many and various national approaches in this sphere and is technically equivalent to the International Standards ISO 9000-9004.

The quality system of an organization is influenced by the objectives of the organization, by the product or service, and by the practices specific to the organization, and therefore, the quality system varies from one organization to another.

A cross-reference list of quality system elements is given in the annex for information.

1.0 SCOPE AND FIELD OF APPLICATION

The purposes of this American National Standard are:

a) To clarify the distinctions and interrelationships among the principal quality concepts (see 4).

b) To provide guidelines for the selection and use of a series of Standards on quality systems that can be used for internal quality management purposes (Q94) and for external quality assurance purposes (Q91, Q92, and Q93) (see 5 to 8 inclusive).

NOTE: It is not the purpose of this series of American National Standards (Q90 to Q94 inclusive) to standardize quality systems implemented by organizations.

2.0 REFERENCES

ANSI/ASQC A3, *Quality Systems Terminology.*

ISO 8402-1986, *Quality — Vocabulary.*

ANSI/ASQC Q91-1987, *Quality Systems — Model for Quality Assurance in Design/Development, Production, Installation, and Servicing.*[1]

ANSI/ASQC Q92-1987, *Quality Systems — Model for Quality Assurance in Production and Installation.*[1]

ANSI/ASQC Q93-1987, *Quality Systems — Model for Quality Assurance in Final Inspection and Test.*[1]

ANSI/ASQC Q94-1987, *Quality Management and Quality System Elements — Guidelines.*[1]

ISO 9001-1987, *Quality Systems — Model for Quality Assurance in Design/Development, Production, Installation and Servicing.*

ISO 9002-1987, *Quality Systems — Model for Quality Assurance in Production and Installation.*

ISO 9003-1987, *Quality Systems — Model for Quality Assurance in Final Inspection and Test.*

ISO 9004-1987, *Quality Management and Quality System Elements — Guidelines.*

3.0 DEFINITIONS

For the purposes of this Standard, the definitions given in ANSI/ASQC A3 apply. Five key terms and definitions have been taken from ANSI/ASQC A3 and are included in this Standard because of their importance in the proper use of this Standard.

3.1 Quality Policy

The overall quality intentions and direction of an organization as regards quality, as formally expressed by top management.

NOTE: The quality policy forms one element of the corporate policy and is authorized by top management.

3.2 Quality Management

That aspect of the overall management function that determines and implements the quality policy.

---

[1]The cross-references in the annex to specific paragraphs and subsections in this series of ANSI/ASQC Standards apply to the first editions published in 1987.

NOTES:

1. The attainment of desired quality requires the commitment and participation of all members of the organization whereas the responsibility for quality management belongs to top management.
2. Quality management includes strategic planning, allocation of resources, and other systematic activities for quality, such as quality planning, operations, and evaluations.

3.3 Quality System

The organizational structure, responsibilities, procedures, processes, and resources for implementing quality management.

NOTES:

1. The quality system should only be as comprehensive as needed to meet the quality objectives.
2. For contractual, mandatory, and assessment purposes, demonstration of the implementation of identified elements in the system may be required.

3.4 Quality Control

The operational techniques and activities that are used to fulfill requirements for quality.

NOTES:

1. In order to avoid confusion, care should be taken to include a modifying term when referring to a sub-set of quality control, such as "manufacturing quality control," or when referring to a broader concept, such as "company-wide quality control."
2. Quality control involves operational techniques and activities aimed both at monitoring a process and at eliminating causes of unsatisfactory performance at relevant stages of the quality loop (quality spiral) in order to result in economic effectiveness.

3.5 Quality Assurance

All those planned and systematic actions necessary to provide adequate confidence that a product or service will satisfy given requirements for quality.

NOTES:

1. Unless given requirements fully reflect the needs of the user, quality assurance will not be complete.
2. For effectiveness, quality assurance usually requires a continuing evaluation of factors that affect the adequacy of the design or specification for intended applications as well as verifications

and audits of production, installation, and inspection operations. Providing confidence may involve producing evidence.

3. Within an organization, quality assurance serves as a management tool. In contractual situations, quality assurance also serves to provide confidence in the supplier.

4.0 PRINCIPAL CONCEPTS

An organization should seek to accomplish the following three objectives with regard to quality:

a) The organization should achieve and sustain the quality of the product or service produced so as to meet continually the purchaser's stated or implied needs.
b) The organization should provide confidence to its own management that the intended quality is being achieved and sustained.
c) The organization should provide confidence to the purchaser that the intended quality is being, or will be, achieved in the delivered product or service provided. When contractually required, this provision of confidence may involve agreed demonstration requirements.

The relationship of the concepts, the definitions of which are quoted in 3, is illustrated in the figure (page 216); this figure should not, however, be interpreted as a rigid model.

5.0 CHARACTERISTICS OF QUALITY SYSTEM SITUATIONS

This series of Standards on quality systems is intended to be used in two different situations: contractual and noncontractual.

In both these situations, the supplier's organization wants to install and maintain a quality system that will strengthen its own competitiveness and achieve the needed product quality in a cost-effective way.

In addition, in the contractual situation, the purchaser is interested in certain elements of the supplier's quality system which affect the supplier's ability to produce consistently the product or service to its requirements, and the associated risks. The purchaser therefore contractually requires that certain quality system elements be part of the supplier's quality system.

A single supplier will often be involved in situations of both types. The supplier may purchase some materials or components from standard inventory without contractual quality assurance requirements, and purhase others with contractual quality assurance requirements. The same supplier may sell some products in noncontractual situations and others in contractual situations.

6.0 TYPES OF STANDARDS ON QUALITY SYSTEMS

As indicated in 1, the following two types of standards, which embody the needs of the different situations classified in 5, are presented in this series of Standards on quality systems:

a) Q94 (together with this Standard) gives guidance to all organizations for quality management purposes.
b) Q91, Q92, and Q93 are used for external quality assurance purposes in contractual situations.

7.0 USE OF STANDARDS ON QUALITY SYSTEMS FOR QUALITY MANAGEMENT PURPOSES

After this Standard has been consulted, reference should be made to Q94 in order to develop and implement a quality system and to determine the extent to which each quality system element is applicable.

Q94 provides guidance on the technical, administrative, and human factors affecting the quality of products or services, at all stages of the quality loop from detection of need to customer satisfaction. Throughout Q94 emphasis is placed on the satisfaction of the customer's need, the establishment of functional responsibilities, and the importance of assessing (as far as possible) the potential risks and benefits. All these aspects should be considered in establishing and maintaining an effective quality system.

NOTES:
1. The elements that comprise a quality system are listed in the annex.
2. Activities aimed at providing confidence to the management of an organization that the intended quality is being achieved are often called *"internal quality assurance."*
3. Activities aimed at providing confidence to the purchaser that the supplier's quality system will provide a product or service that will satisfy the purchaser's stated quality requirements are often called *"external quality assurance."*

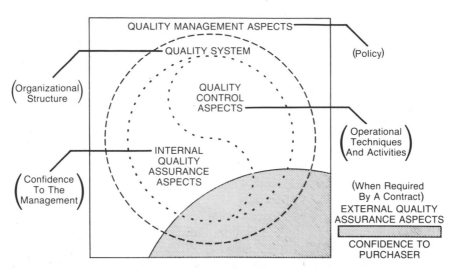

Figure Relationship of Concepts

8.0 USE OF STANDARDS ON QUALITY SYSTEMS FOR CONTRACTUAL PURPOSES

8.1 General

After this Standard has been consulted, the purchaser and supplier should refer to Q91, Q92, and Q93 to determine which of these Standards is most relevant to the contract, and what specific adaptations, if any, have to be made.

The selection and application of a model for quality assurance appropriate to a given situation should provide benefits to both purchaser and supplier. Examining the risks, costs, and benefits for both parties will determine the extent and nature of reciprocal information and the measures each party must take to provide adequate confidence that the intended quality will be achieved.

8.2 Selection of Model for Quality Assurance

8.2.1 General

As indicated in the introduction to each of these three Standards, certain quality system elements have been grouped into each of three distinct models based on the "functional or organizational capability" required of a supplier for the product or service:

a) Q91: for use when conformance to specified requirements is to be assured by the supplier during several stages which may include design/development, production, installation, and servicing.

216

b) Q92: for use when conformance to specified requirements is to be assured by the supplier during production and installation.

c) Q93: for use when conformance to specified requirements is to be assured by the supplier solely at final inspection and test.

8.2.2 Selection Procedure

The model should be selected by systematic consideration of the factors described in 8.2.3 with due attention to the economic factor.

8.2.3 Selection Factors

In addition to the functional criteria detailed in 8.2.1 a) to 8.2.1 c), the following six factors are considered to be fundamental for selecting the appropriate model for a product or service:

a) Design-process complexity.

   This factor deals with difficulty of designing the product or service if such product or service has yet to be designed.

b) Design maturity.

   This factor deals with the extent to which the total design is known and proven, either by performance testing or field experience.

c) Production-process complexity.

   This factor deals with:

   1) The availability of proven production processes.
   2) The need for development of new processes.
   3) The number and variety of processes required.
   4) The impact of the process(es) on the performance of the product or service.

d) Product or service characteristics.

   This factor deals with the complexity of the product or service, the number of interrelated characteristics, and the criticality of each characteristic for performance.

e) Product or service safety.

   This factor deals with the risk of the occurrence of failure and the consequences of such failure.

f) Economics.

   This factor deals with the economic costs, to both supplier and purchaser, of the preceding factors weighed against costs due to nonconformities in the product or service.

8.3 Demonstration and Documentation

The quality system elements should be documented and demonstrable in a manner consistent with the requirements of the selected model.

Demonstration of the quality system elements refers to:

a) Adequacy of the quality system (e.g. in design, production, installation, and servicing).
b) Capability to achieve product or service conformity with the specified requirements.

The nature and degree of demonstration may vary from one situation to another in accordance with such criteria as:

a) The economics, uses, and conditions of use of the product or service.
b) The complexity and innovation required to design the product or service.
c) The complexity and difficulty of producing the product or service.
d) The ability to judge product quality and fitness for use on the basis of final product test alone.
e) The safety requirements of the product or service.
f) The past performance of the supplier.

Documentation may include quality manuals, descriptions of quality-related procedures, quality system auditing reports, and other quality records.

8.4 Pre-Contract Assessment

Assessments of a supplier's quality system are utilized prior to a contract to determine the supplier's ability to satisfy the requirements of Q91, Q92, and Q93 and, when appropriate, supplementary requirements. In many cases, assessments are performed directly by the purchaser.

By agreement between purchaser and supplier, pre-contract assessment may be delegated to an organization independent of both contracting parties. The number or the extent of assessments can be minimized by using Q91, Q92, or Q93 and by recognizing previous assessments carried out in accordance with these Standards by the purchaser or by an agreed independent assessing organization.

8.5 Contract Preparation Aspects

8.5.1 Tailoring

Experience has shown that with a small fixed number of Standards available, one of the Standards can be selected that will meet needs adequately for almost any situation. However, on occasions, certain quality system elements called for in the selected Standard may be deleted and, on other occasions, elements may be added. If this should prove necessary, it should be agreed between the purchaser and the supplier, and should be specified in the contract.

8.5.2 Review of Contractual Quality System Elements

Both parties should review the proposed contract to be sure that they understand the quality system requirements and that the requirements are mutually acceptable considering the economics and risks in their respective situations.

8.5.3 Supplementary Quality Assurance or Quality System Requirements

There may be a need to specify supplementary requirements in the contract, such as quality plans, quality programs, quality audit plans, etc.

8.5.4 Technical Requirements

The technical requirements of the product or service are defined in the technical specifications of the contract.

Annex
Cross-Reference List of Quality System Elements

(This annex is given for information purposes and does not form an integral part of the standard.)

Paragraph (or subsection) No. in Q94	Title	Corresponding Paragraph (or subsection) Nos. in		
		Q91	Q92	Q93
4	Management Responsibility	4.1 ●	4.1 ◖	4.1 ○
5	Quality System Principles	4.2 ●	4.2 ●	4.2 ◖
5.4	Auditing The Quality System (Internal)	4.17 ●	4.16 ◖	—
6	Economics — Quality-Related Cost Considerations	—	─	—
7	Quality In Marketing (Contract Review)	4.3 ●	4.3 ●	—
8	Quality In Specification and Design (Design Control)	4.4 ●	—	—
9	Quality In Procurement (Purchasing)	4.6 ●	4.5 ●	—
10	Quality In Production (Process Control)	4.9 ●	4.8 ●	—
11	Control Of Production	4.9 ●	4.8 ●	—
11.2	Material Control and Traceability (Product Identification and Traceability)	4.8 ●	4.7 ●	4.4 ◖
11.7	Control of Verification Status (Inspection and Test Status)	4.12 ●	4.11 ●	4.7 ◖
12	Product Verification (Inspection and Testing)	4.10 ●	4.9 ●	4.5 ◖
13	Control of Measuring and Test Equipment (Inspection, Measuring, and Test Equipment)	4.11 ●	4.10 ●	4.6 ◖
14	Nonconformity (Control of Nonconforming Product)	4.13 ●	4.12 ●	4.8 ◖
15	Corrective Action	4.14 ●	4.13 ●	—
16	Handling and Post-Production Functions (Handling, Storage, Packaging, and Delivery)	4.15 ●	4.14 ●	4.9 ◖
16.2	After-sales Servicing	4.19 ●	—	—
17	Quality Documentation and Records (Document Control)	4.5 ●	4.4 ●	4.3 ◖
17.3	Quality Records	4.16 ●	4.15 ●	4.10 ◖
18	Personnel (Training)	4.18 ●	4.17 ◖	4.11 ○
19	Product Safety and Liability	—	—	—
20	Use of Statistical Methods (Statistical Techniques)	4.20 ●	4.18 ●	4.12 ◖
—	Purchaser Supplied Product	4.7 ●	4.6 ●	—

Key

● Full requirement
◖ Less stringent than ANSI/ASQC Q91
○ Less stringent than ANSI/ASQC Q92
— Element not present

NOTES:
1. The paragraph (or subsection) titles quoted in the table above have been taken from Q94; the titles given in parentheses have been taken from the corresponding paragraphs and subsections in Q91, Q92, and Q93.
2. Attention is drawn to the fact that the quality system element requirements in Q91, Q92, and Q93 are in many cases, but not in every case, identical.

AMERICAN NATIONAL STANDARD

ANSI/ASQC Q91-1987, *Quality Systems — Model for Quality Assurance in Design/Development, Production, Installation, and Servicing*

Abstract

Quality Systems — Model for Quality Assurance in Design/Development, Production, Installation, and Servicing specifies quality system requirements for use where a contract between two parties requires the demonstration of a supplier's capability to design and supply product.

AMERICAN NATIONAL STANDARD: An American National Standard implies a consensus of those substantially concerned with its scope and provisions. An American National Standard is intended as a guide to aid the manufacturer, the consumer, and the general public. The existence of an American National Standard does not in any respect preclude anyone, whether he has approved the standard or not, from manufacturing, marketing, purchasing, or using products, processes, or procedures not conforming to the standard. American National Standards are subject to periodic review, and users are cautioned to obtain the latest editions.

CAUTION NOTICE: This American National Standard may be revised or withdrawn at any time. The procedures of the American National Standards Institute require that action be taken to reaffirm, revise, or withdraw this standard no later than five years from the date of approval. Purchasers of American National Standards may receive current information on all standards by calling or writing the American National Standards Institute.

Approved June 19, 1987
American National Standards Institute, Inc.

Foreword

(This Foreword is not a part of American National Standard Quality Systems — Model for Quality Assurance in Design/Development, Production, Installation, and Servicing.)

Guidance concerning the selection of this standard or others in the ANSI/ASQC Q91-94 series is contained in ANSI/ASQC Q90-1987.

Rather than independently revising and extending its current *Generic Guidelines for Quality Systems* (ANSI/ASQC Z1.15-1979) the Standards Committee has elected to join other nations in adopting standards fully consistent with the "ISO 9000-9004 Series" of Quality Management and Quality Assurance Standards, since the latter were in agreement with the efforts of the ANSI/ASQC revision team .

These five ISO standards (ISO 9000-9004) were prepared by Technical Committee ISO/TC 176 on Quality Assurance in the interest of harmonizing the large number of national and international standards in this field. In addition to input from other countries, such U.S. standards as ANSI/ASQC Z1.15 and ANSI/ASQC Z1.8 were considered in the source material used in developing these ISO standards. The ANSI/ASQC Q90 through Q94 standards are technically equivalent to the ISO 9000-9004 series, but incorporate customary American language usage and spelling.

Users should note that all ANSI/ASQC standards undergo revision from time to time, and that any reference herein to any other standard implies the latest revision, unless otherwise stated.

Comments concerning this standard will be welcome. They should be sent to the standard's sponsor, American Society for Quality Control, 310 West Wisconsin Avenue, Milwaukee, Wisconsin 53203.

0.0 INTRODUCTION

This Standard is one of a series of three Standards dealing with quality systems that can be used for external quality assurance purposes. The alternative quality assurance models, set out in the three Standards listed below, represent three distinct forms of functional or organizational capability suitable for two-party contractual purposes:

- ANSI/ASQC Q91-1987, *Quality Systems — Model for Quality Assurance in Design/Development, Production, Installation, and Servicing.*

  For use when conformance to specified requirements is to be assured by the supplier during several stages which may include design/development, production, installation, and servicing.
- ANSI/ASQC Q92-1987, *Quality Systems — Model for Quality Assurance in Production and Installation.*

  For use when conformance to specified requirements is to be assured by the supplier during production and installation.
- ANSI/ASQC Q93-1987, *Quality Systems — Model for Quality Assurance in Final Inspection and Test.*

  For use when conformance to specified requirements is to be assured by the supplier solely at final inspection and test.

It is emphasized that the quality system requirements specified in this Standard, Standards Q92 and Q93 are complementary (not alternative) to the technical (product/service) specified requirements. These Standards are technically equivalent to the International Standards ISO 9001, 9002, and 9003, respectively.

It is intended that these Standards will normally be adopted in their present form, but on occasions they may need to be tailored for specific contractual situations. Q90 provides guidance on such tailoring as well as selection of the appropriate quality assurance model, namely Q91, Q92, or Q93.

1.0 SCOPE AND FIELD OF APPLICATION

1.1 Scope

This Standard specifies quality system requirements for use where a contract between two parties requires the demonstration of a supplier's capability to design and supply product. The requirements specified in this Standard are aimed primarily at preventing nonconformity at all stages from design to servicing.

1.2 Field of Application

This Standard is applicable in contractual situations when:

223

a) The contract specifically requires design effort and the product requirements are stated principally in performance terms or they need to be established.

b) Confidence in product conformance can be attained by adequate demonstration of certain supplier's capabilities in design, development, production, installation, and servicing.

2.0 REFERENCES

ANSI/ASQC A3, *Quality Systems Terminology.*

ISO 8402-1986, *Quality — Vocabulary.*

ANSI/ASQC Q90-1987, *Quality Management and Quality Assurance Standards — Guidelines for Selection and Use.*

ISO 9000-1987, *Quality Management and Quality Assurance Standards — Guidelines for Selection and Use.*

3.0 DEFINITIONS

For the purposes of this Standard, the definitions given in ANSI/ASQC A3 apply.

NOTE: For the purposes of this Standard, the term "product" is also used to denote "service," as appropriate.

4.0 QUALITY SYSTEM REQUIREMENTS

4.1 Management Responsibility

4.1.1 Quality Policy

The supplier's management shall define and document its policy and objectives for, and commitment to, quality. The supplier shall ensure that this policy is understood, implemented, and maintained at all levels in the organization.

4.1.2 Organization

4.1.2.1 Responsibility and Authority

The responsibility, authority, and the interrelation of all personnel who manage, perform, and verify work affecting quality should be defined; particularly for personnel who need the organizational freedom and authority to:

a) Initiate action to prevent the occurrence of product nonconformity.

b) Identify and record any product quality problems.
c) Initiate, recommend, or provide solutions through designated channels.
d) Verify the implementation of solutions.
e) Control further processing, delivery, or installation of nonconforming product until the deficiency or unsatisfactory condition has been corrected.

4.1.2.2 Verification Resources and Personnel

The supplier shall identify in-house verification requirements, provide adequate resources, and assign trained personnel for verification activities (see 4.18).

Verification activities shall include inspection, test, and monitoring of the design, production, installation, and servicing of the process and/or product; design reviews and audits of the quality system, processes, and/or product shall be carried out by personnel independent of those having direct responsibility for the work being performed.

4.1.2.3 Management Representative

The supplier shall appoint a management representative who, irrespective of other responsibilities, shall have defined authority and responsibility for ensuring that the requirements of this Standard are implemented and maintained.

4.1.3 Management Review

The quality system adopted to satisfy the requirements of this Standard shall be reviewed at appropriate intervals by the supplier's management to ensure its continuing suitability and effectiveness. Records of such reviews shall be maintained (see 4.16).

NOTE: Management reviews normally include assessment of the results of internal quality audits, but are carried out by, or on behalf of, the supplier's management, namely management personnel having direct responsibility for the system (see 4.17).

4.2 Quality System

The supplier shall establish and maintain a documented quality system as a means of ensuring that product conforms to specified requirements. This shall include:

a) The preparation of documented quality system procedures and instructions in accordance with the requirements of this Standard.
b) The effective implementation of the documented quality system procedures and instructions.

NOTE: In meeting specified requirements, timely consideration needs to be given to the following activities:

a) The preparation of quality plans and a quality manual in accordance with the specified requirements.
b) The identification and acquisition of any controls, processes, inspection equipment, fixtures, total production resources, and skills that may be needed to achieve the required quality.
c) The updating, as necessary, of quality control, inspection, and testing techniques, including the development of new instrumentation.
d) The identification of any measurement requirement involving capability that exceeds the known state of the art in sufficient time for the needed capability to be developed.
e) The clarification of standards of acceptability for all features and requirements, including those which contain a subjective element.
f) The compatibility of the design, the production process, installation, inspection and test procedures, and the applicable documentation.
g) The identification and preparation of quality records (see 4.16).

4.3 Contract Review

The supplier shall establish and maintain procedures for contract review and for the coordination of these activities.

Each contract shall be reviewed by the supplier to ensure that:

a) The requirements are adequately defined and documented.
b) Any requirements differing from those in the tender are resolved.
c) The supplier has the capability to meet contractual requirements.

Records of such contract reviews shall be maintained (see 4.16).

NOTE: The contract review activities, interfaces, and communication within the supplier's organization should be coordinated with the purchaser's organization, as appropriate.

4.4 Design Control

4.4.1 General

The supplier shall establish and maintain procedures to control and verify the design of the product to ensure that the specified requirements are met.

4.4.2 Design and Development Planning

The supplier shall draw up plans that identify the responsibility for each design and development activity. The plans shall describe or reference these activities and shall be updated as the design evolves.

4.4.2.1 Activity Assignment

The design and verification activities shall be planned and assigned to qualified staff equipped with adequate resources.

4.4.2.2 Organizational and Technical Interfaces

Organizational and technical interfaces between different groups shall be identified and the necessary information documented, transmitted, and regularly reviewed.

4.4.3 Design Input

Design input requirements relating to the product shall be identified, documented, and their selection reviewed by the supplier for adequacy.

Incomplete, ambiguous, or conflicting requirements shall be resolved with those responsible for drawing up these requirements.

4.4.4 Design Output

Design output shall be documented and expressed in terms of requirements, calculations, and analyses.

Design output shall:

a) Meet the design input requirements.
b) Contain or reference acceptance criteria.
c) Conform to appropriate regulatory requirements whether or not these have been stated in the input information.
d) Identify those characteristics of the design that are crucial to the safe and proper functioning of the product.

4.4.5 Design Verification

The supplier shall plan, establish, document, and assign to competent personnel functions for verifying the design.

Design verification shall establish that design output meets the design input requirement (see 4.4.4) by means of design control measures such as:

a) Holding and recording design reviews (see 4.16).
b) Undertaking qualification tests and demonstrations.
c) Carrying out alternative calculations.
d) Comparing the new design with a similar proven design, if available.

4.4.6 Design Changes

The supplier shall establish and maintain procedures for the identification, documentation, and appropriate review and approval of all changes and modifications.

4.5 Document Control

4.5.1 Document Approval and Issue

The supplier shall establish and maintain procedures to control all documents and data that relate to the requirements of this Standard. These documents shall be reviewed and approved for adequacy by authorized personnel prior to issue. This control shall ensure that:

a) The pertinent issues of appropriate documents are available at all locations where operations essential to the effective functioning of the quality system are performed.

b) Obsolete documents are promptly removed from all points of issue or use.

4.5.2 Document Changes/Modifications

Changes to documents shall be reviewed and approved by the same functions/organizations that performed the original review and approval unless specifically designated otherwise. The designated organizations shall have access to pertinent background information upon which to base their review and approval.

Where practicable, the nature of the change shall be identified in the document or the appropriate attachments.

A master list or equivalent document control procedure shall be established to identify the current revision of documents in order to preclude the use of nonapplicable documents.

Documents shall be reissued after a practical number of changes have been made.

4.6 Purchasing

4.6.1 General

The supplier shall ensure that purchased product conforms to specified requirements.

4.6.2 Assessment of Sub-Contractors

The supplier shall select sub-contractors on the basis of their ability to meet sub-contract requirements, including quality requirements. The supplier shall establish and maintain records of acceptable sub-contractors (see 4.16).

The selection of sub-contractors, and the type and extent of control exercised by the supplier, shall be dependent upon the type of product and, where appropriate, on records of subcontractors' previously demonstrated capability and performance.

The supplier shall ensure that quality system controls are effective.

228

4.6.3 Purchasing Data

Purchasing documents shall contain data clearly describing the product ordered, including, where applicable:

a) The type, class, style, grade, or other precise identification.
b) The title or other positive identification, and applicable issue of specifications, drawings, process requirements, inspection instructions, and other relevant technical data, incuding requirements for approval or qualification of product, procedures, process equipment and personnel.
c) The title, number, and issue of the quality system Standard to be applied to the product.

The supplier shall review and approve purchasing documents for adequacy of specified requirements prior to release.

4.6.4 Verification of Purchased Product

Where specified in the contract, the purchaser or the purchaser's representative shall be afforded the right to verify at source or upon receipt that purchased product conforms to specified requirements. Verification by the purchaser shall not absolve the supplier of the responsibility to provide acceptable product nor shall it preclude subsequent rejection.

When the purchaser or the purchaser's representative elects to carry out verification at the sub-contractor's plant, such verification shall not be used by the supplier as evidence of effective control of quality by the sub-contractor.

4.7 Purchaser Supplied Product

The supplier shall establish and maintain procedures for verification, storage, and maintenance of purchaser supplied product provided for incorporation into the supplies. Any such product that is lost, damaged, or is otherwise unsuitable for use shall be recorded and reported to the purchaser (see 4.16).

NOTE: Verification by the supplier does not absolve the purchaser of the responsibility to provide acceptable product.

4.8 Product Identification and Traceability

Where appropriate, the supplier shall establish and maintain procedures for identifying the product from applicable drawings, specifications, or other documents, during all stages of production, delivery, and installation.

Where, and to the extent that, traceability is a specified requirement, individual product or batches shall have a unique identification. This identification shall be recorded (see 4.16).

4.9 Process Control

4.9.1 General

The supplier shall identify and plan the production and, where applicable, installation processes which directly affect quality and shall ensure that these processes are carried out under controlled conditions. Controlled conditions shall include the following:

    a) Documented work instructions defining the manner of production and installation, where the absence of such instructions would adversely affect quality, use of suitable production and installation equipment, suitable working environment, compliance with reference standards/codes, and quality plans.

    b) Monitoring and control of suitable process and product characteristics during production and installation.

    c) The approval of processes and equipment, as appropriate.

    d) Criteria for workmanship which shall be stipulated, to the greatest practicable extent, in written standards or by means of representative samples.

4.9.2 Special Processes

These are processes, the results of which cannot be fully verified by subsequent inspection and testing of the product and where, for example, processing deficiencies may become apparent only after the product is in use. Accordingly, continuous monitoring and/or compliance with documented procedures is required to ensure that the specified requirements are met. These processes shall be qualified and shall also comply with the requirements of 4.9.1.

Records shall be maintained for qualified processes, equipment, and personnel, as appropriate.

4.10 Inspection and Testing

4.10.1 Receiving Inspection and Testing

4.10.1.1 The supplier shall ensure that incoming product is not used or processed (except in the circumstances described in 4.10.1.2) until it has been inspected or otherwise verified as conforming to specified requirements. Verification shall be in accordance with the quality plan or documented procedures.

4.10.1.2 Where incoming product is released for urgent production purposes, it shall be positively identified and recorded (see 4.16) in order to permit immediate recall and replacement in the event of nonconformance to specified requirements.

NOTE: In determining the amount and nature of receiving inspection, consideration should be given to the control exercised at source and documented evidence of quality conformance provided.

4.10.2 In-Process Inspection and Testing
The supplier shall:

a) Inspect, test , and identify product as required by the quality plan or documented procedures.
b) Establish product conformance to specified requirements by use of process monitoring and control methods.
c) Hold product until the required inspection and tests have been completed or necessary reports have been received and verified except when product is released under positive recall procedures (see 4.10.1). Release under positive recall procedures shall not preclude the activities outlined in 4.10.2 a).
d) Identify nonconforming product.

4.10.3 Final Inspection and Testing
The quality plan or documented procedures for final inspection and testing shall require that all specified inspection and tests, including those specified either on receipt of product or in-process, have been carried out and that the data meet specified requirements.

The supplier shall carry out all final inspection and testing in accordance with the quality plan or documented procedures to complete the evidence of conformance of the finished product to the specified requirements.

No product shall be dispatched until all the activities specified in the quality plan or documented procedures have been satisfactorily completed and the associated data and documentation is available and authorized.

4.10.4 Inspection and Test Records
The supplier shall establish and maintain records which give evidence that the product has passed inspection and/or test with defined acceptance criteria (see 4.16).

4.11 Inspection, Measuring, and Test Equipment
The supplier shall control, calibrate, and maintain inspection, measuring, and test equipment, whether owned by the supplier, on loan, or provided by the purchaser, to demonstrate the conformance of product to the specified requirements. Equipment shall be used in a manner which ensures that measurement uncertainty is known and is consistent with the required measurement capability.

The supplier shall:

a) Identify the measurements to be made, the accuracy required, and select the appropriate inspection, measuring, and test equipment.

b) Identify, calibrate, and adjust all inspection, measuring and test equipment, and devices that can affect product quality at prescribed intervals, or prior to use, against certified equipment having a known valid relationship to nationally recognized standards — where no such standards exist, the basis used for calibration shall be documented.

c) Establish, document, and maintain calibration procedures, including details of equipment type, identification number, location, frequency of checks, check method, acceptance criteria, and the action to be taken when results are unsatisfactory.

d) Ensure that the inspection, measuring, and test equipment is capable of the accuracy and precision necessary.

e) Identify inspection, measuring, and test equipment with a suitable indicator or approved identification record to show the calibration status.

f) Maintain calibration records for inspection, measuring, and test equipment (see 4.16).

g) Assess and document the validity of previous inspection and test results when inspection, measuring, and test equipment is found to be out of calibration.

h) Ensure that the environmental conditions are suitable for the calibrations, inspections, measurements, and tests being carried out.

i) Ensure that the handling, preservation, and storage of inspection, measuring, and test equipment is such that the accuracy and fitness for use is maintained.

j) Safeguard inspection, measuring, and test facilities, including both test hardware and test software, from adjustments which would invalidate the calibration setting.

Where test hardware (e.g., jigs, fixtures, templates, patterns) or test software is used as suitable forms of inspection, they shall be checked to prove that they are capable of verifying the acceptability of product prior to release for use during production and installation and shall be rechecked at prescribed intervals. The supplier shall establish the extent and frequency of such checks and shall maintain records as evidence of control (see 4.16). Measurement design data shall be made available, when required by the purchaser or his representative, for verification that is functionally adequate.

4.12 Inspection and Test Status
The inspection and test status of product shall be identified by using markings, authorized stamps, tags, labels, routing cards, inspection re-

cords, test software, physical location, or other suitable means, which indicate the conformance or nonconformance of product with regard to inspection and tests performed. The identification of inspection and test status shall be maintained, as necessary, throughout production and installation of the product to ensure that only product that has passed the required inspections and tests is dispatched, used, or installed.

Records shall identify the inspection authority responsible for the release of conforming product (see 4.16).

4.13 Control of Nonconforming Product

The supplier shall establish and maintain procedures to ensure that product that does not conform to specified requirements is prevented from inadvertent use or installation. Control shall provide for identification, documentation, evaluation, segregation when practical, disposition of nonconforming product, and for notification to the functions concerned.

4.13.1 Nonconformity Review and Disposition

The responsibility for review and authority for the disposition of nonconforming product shall be defined.

Nonconforming product shall be reviewed in accordance with documented procedures. It may be:

a) Reworked to meet the specified requirements.
b) Accepted with or without repair by concession.
c) Re-graded for alternative applications
d) Rejected or scrapped.

Where required by the contract, the proposed use or repair of product (see 4.13.1 b) which does not conform to specified requirements shall be reported for concession to the purchaser or the purchaser's representative. The description of nonconformity that has been accepted, and of repairs, shall be recorded to denote the actual condition (see 4.16).

Repaired and reworked product shall be reinspected in accordance with documented procedures.

4.14 Corrective Action

The supplier shall establish, document, and maintain procedures for:

a) Investigating the cause of nonconforming product and the corrective action needed to prevent recurrence.
b) Analyzing all processes, work operations, concessions, quality records, service reports, and customer complaints to detect and eliminate potential causes of nonconforming product.
c) Initiating preventative actions to deal with problems to a level

233

corresponding to the risks encountered.

d) Applying controls to ensure that corrective actions are taken and that they are effective.
e) Implementing and recording changes in procedures resulting from corrective action.

4.15 Handling, Storage, Packaging, and Delivery

4.15.1 General

The supplier shall establish, document, and maintain procedures for handling, storage, packaging, and delivery of product.

4.15.2 Handling

The supplier shall provide methods and means of handling that prevent damage or deterioration.

4.15.3 Storage

The supplier shall provide secure storage areas or stock rooms to prevent damage or deterioration of product, pending use, or delivery. Appropriate methods for authorizing receipt and the dispatch to and from such areas shall be stipulated. In order to detect deterioration, the condition of product in stock shall be assessed at appropriate intervals.

4.15.4 Packaging

The supplier shall control packing, preservation, and marking processes (including materials used) to the extent necessary to ensure conformance to specified requirements and shall identify, preserve, and segregate all product from the time of receipt until the supplier's responsibility ceases.

4.15.5 Delivery

The supplier shall arrange for the protection of the quality of product after final inspection and test. Where contractually specified, this protection shall be extended to include delivery to destination.

4.16 Quality Records

The supplier shall establish and maintain procedures for identification, collection, indexing, filing, storage, maintenance, and disposition of quality records.

Quality records shall be maintained to demonstrate achievement of the required quality and the effective operation of the quality system. Pertinent sub-contractor quality records shall be an element of these data.

All quality records shall be legible and identifiable to the product involved. Quality records shall be stored and maintained in such a way that they are readily retrievable in facilities that provide a suitable environment to minimize deterioration or damage and to prevent loss. Retention times of quality records shall be established and recorded. Where agreed contractually, quality records shall be made available for evaluation by the purchaser or the purchaser's representative for an agreed period.

4.17 Internal Quality Audits

The supplier shall carry out a comprehensive system of planned and documented internal quality audits to verify whether quality activities comply with planned arrangements and to determine the effectiveness of the quality system.

Audits shall be scheduled on the basis of the status and importance of the activity.

The audits and follow-up actions shall be carried out in accordance with documented procedures.

The results of the audits shall be documented and brought to the attention of the personnel having responsibility in the area audited. The management personnel responsible for the area shall take timely corrective action on the deficiencies found by the audit (see 4.1.3).

4.18 Training

The supplier shall establish and maintain procedures for identifying the training needs and provide for the training of all personnel performing activities affecting quality. Personnel performing specific assigned tasks shall be qualified on the basis of appropriate education, training, and/or experience, as required. Appropriate records of training shall be maintained (see 4.16).

4.19 Servicing

Where servicing is specified in the contract, the supplier shall establish and maintain procedures for performing and verifying that servicing meets the specified requirements.

4.20 Statistical Techniques

Where appropriate, the supplier shall establish procedures for identifying adequate statistical techniques required for verifying the acceptability of process capability and product characteristics.

Procurement Quality Control

AMERICAN NATIONAL STANDARD

ANSI/ASQC Q92-1987, *Quality Systems — Model for Quality Assurance in Production and Installation*

Abstract

Quality Systems — Model for Quality Assurance in Production and Installation specifies quality system requirements for use where a contract between two parties requires the demonstration of a supplier's capability to control the processes that determine the acceptability of a product supplied.

AMERICAN NATIONAL STANDARD: An American National Standard implies a consensus of those substantially concerned with its scope and provisions. An American National Standard is intended as a guide to aid the manufacturer, the consumer, and the general public. The existence of an American National Standard does not in any respect preclude anyone, whether he has approved the standard or not, from manufacturing, marketing, purchasing, or using products, processes, or procedures not conforming to the standard. American National Standards are subject to periodic review, and users are cautioned to obtain the latest editions.

CAUTION NOTICE: This American National Standard may be revised or withdrawn at any time. The procedures of the American National Standards Institute require that action be taken to reaffirm, revise, or withdraw this standard no later than five years from the date of approval. Purchasers of American National Standards may receive current information on all standards by calling or writing the American National Standards Institute.

Approved June 15, 1987
American National Standards Institute, Inc.

Foreword

(This Foreword is not a part of American National Standard Quality Systems — Model for Quality Assurance in Production and Installation.)

Guidance concerning the selection of this standard or others in the ANSI/ASQC Q91-94 series is contained in ANSI/ASQC Q90-1987.

Rather than independently revising and extending its current *Generic Guidelines for Quality Systems* (ANSI/ASQC Z1.15-1979) the Standards Committee has elected to join other nations in adopting standards fully consistent with the "ISO 9000-9004 Series" of Quality Management and Quality Assurance Standards, since the latter were in agreement with the efforts of the ANSI/ASQC revision team .

These five ISO standards (ISO 9000-9004) were prepared by Technical Committee ISO/TC 176 on Quality Assurance in the interest of harmonizing the large number of national and international standards in this field. In addition to input from other countries, such U.S. standards as ANSI/ASQC Z1.15 and ANSI/ASQC Z1.8 were considered in the source material used in developing these ISO standards. The ANSI/ASQC Q90 through Q94 standards are technically equivalent to the ISO 9000-9004 series, but incorporate customary American language usage and spelling.

Users should note that all ANSI/ASQC standards undergo revision from time to time, and that any reference herein to any other standard implies the latest revision, unless otherwise stated.

Comments concerning this standard will be welcome. They should be sent to the standard's sponsor, American Society for Quality Control, 310 West Wisconsin Avenue, Milwaukee, Wisconsin 53203.

0.0 INTRODUCTION

This Standard is one of a series of three Standards dealing with quality systems that can be used for external quality assurance purposes. The alternative quality assurance models, set out in the three Standards listed below, represent three distinct forms of functional or organizational capability suitable for two-party contractual purposes:

- ANSI/ASQC Q91-1987, *Quality Systems — Model for Quality Assurance in Design/Development, Production, Installation, and Servicing.*

  For use when conformance to specified requirements is to be assured by the supplier during several stages which may include design/development, production, installation, and servicing.
- ANSI/ASQC Q92-1987, *Quality Systems — Model for Quality Assurance in Production and Installation.*

  For use when conformance to specified requirements is to be assured by the supplier during production and installation.
- ANSI/ASQC Q93-1987, *Quality Systems — Model for Quality Assurance in Final Inspection and Test.*

  For use when conformance to specified requirements is to be assured by the supplier solely at final inspection and test.

It is emphasized that the quality system requirements specified in this Standard, Standards Q92 and Q93 are complementary (not alternative) to the technical (product/service) specified requirements. These Standards are technically equivalent to the International Standards ISO 9001, 9002, and 9003 respectively.

It is intended that these Standards will normally be adopted in their present form, but on occasions they may need to be tailored for specific contractual situations. Q90 provides guidance on such tailoring as well as selection of the appropriate quality assurance model, namely Q91, Q92, or Q93.

1.0 SCOPE AND FIELD OF APPLICATION

1.1 Scope

This Standard specifies quality system requirements for use where a contract between two parties requires the demonstration of a supplier's capability to control the processes that determine the acceptability of product supplied.

The requirements specified in this Standard aimed primarily at preventing and at detecting any nonconformity during production and installation, and implementing the means to prevent its recurrence.

1.2 Field of Application

This Standard is applicable in contractual situations when:

a) The specified requirements for product are stated in terms of an established design or specification.
b) Confidence in product conformance can be attained by adequate demonstration of a certain supplier's capabilities in production and installation.

2.0 REFERENCES

ANSI/ASQC A3, *Quality Systems Terminology.*

ISO 8402-1986, *Quality — Vocabulary.*

ANSI/ASQC Q90-1987, *Quality Management and Quality Assurance Standards — Guidelines for Selection and Use.*

ISO 9000-1987, *Quality Management and Quality Assurance Standards — Guidelines for Selection and Use.*

3.0 DEFINITIONS

For the purposes of this Standard, the definitions given in ANSI/ASQC A3 apply.

NOTE: For the purposes of this Standard, the term ''product'' is also used to denote ''service,'' as appropriate.

4.0 QUALITY SYSTEM REQUIREMENTS

4.1 Management Responsibility

4.1.1 Quality Policy

The supplier's management shall define and document its policy and objectives for, and commitment to, quality. The supplier shall ensure that this policy is understood, implemented, and maintained at all levels in the organization.

4.1.2 Organization

4.1.2.1 Responsibility and Authority

The responsibility, authority, and the interrelation of all personnel who manage, perform, and verify work affecting quality shall be defined; particularly for personnel who need the organizational freedom and authority to:

a) Initiate action to prevent the occurrence of product nonconformity.
b) Identify and record any product quality problems.
c) Initiate, recommend, or provide solutions through designated channels.
d) Verify the implementation of solutions.
e) Control further processing, delivery, or installation of nonconforming product until the deficiency or unsatisfactory condition has been corrected.

4.1.2.2 Verification Resources and Personnel

The supplier shall identify in-house verification requirements, provide adequate resources, and assign trained personnel for verification activities (see 4.17).

Verification activities shall include inspection, test, and monitoring of the production and installation processes and/or product; audits of the quality system, process, and/or product shall be carried out by personnel independent of those having direct responsibility for the work being performed.

4.1.2.3 Management Representative

The supplier shall appoint a management representative who, irrespective of other responsibilities, shall have defined authority and responsibility for ensuring that the requirements of this Standard are implemented and maintained.

4.1.3 Management Review

The quality system adopted to satisfy the requirements of this Standard shall be reviewed at appropriate intervals by the supplier's management to ensure its continuing suitability and effectiveness. Records of such reviews shall be maintained (see 4.15).

NOTE: Management reviews normally include assessment of the results of internal quality audits, but are carried out by, or on behalf of, the supplier's management, namely management personnel having direct responsibility for the system (see 4.16).

4.2 Quality System

The supplier shall establish and maintain a documented quality system as a means of ensuring that product conforms to specified requirements. This shall include:

a) The preparation of documented quality system procedures and instructions in accordance with the requirements of this Standard.
b) The effective implementation of the documented quality system procedures and instructions.

NOTE: In meeting specified requirements, timely consideration needs to be given to the following activities:

a)   The preparation of quality plans and a quality manual in accordance with the specified requirements.
b)   The identification and acquisition of any controls, processes, inspection equipment, fixtures, total production resources, and skills that may be needed to achieve the required quality.
c)   The updating, as necessary, of quality control, inspection, and testing techniques, including the development of new instrumentation.
d)   The identification of any measurement requirement involving capability that exceeds the known state of the art in sufficient time for the needed capability to be developed.
e)   The clarification of standards of acceptability for all features and requirements, including those which contain a subjective element.
f)   The compatibility of the production process, installation, inspection, and test procedures, and the applicable documentation.
g)   The identification and preparation of quality records (see 4.15).

4.3 Contract Review

The supplier shall establish and maintain procedures for contract review and for the coordination of these activities.

Each contract shall be reviewed by the supplier to ensure that:

a)   The requirements are adequately defined and documented.
b)   Any requirements differing from those in the tender are resolved.
c)   The supplier has the capability to meet contractual requirements.

Records of such contract reviews shall be maintained (see 4.15).

NOTE: The contract review activities, interfaces, and communication within the supplier's organization should be coordinated with the purchaser's organization, as appropriate.

4.4 Document Control

4.4.1 Document Approval and Issue

The supplier shall establish and maintain procedures to control all documents and data that relate to the requirements of this Standard. These documents shall be reviewed and approved for adequacy by authorized personnel prior to issue.

This control shall ensure that:

a)   the pertinent issues of appropriate documents are available at all locations where operations essential to the effective functioning of the quality system are performed.

b) Obsolete documents are promptly removed from all points of issue or use.

4.4.2 Document Changes/Modifications

Changes to documents shall be reviewed and approved by the same functions/organizations that performed the original review and approval unless specifically designated otherwise. The designated organizations shall have access to pertinent background information upon which to base their review and approval.

Where practicable, the nature of the change shall be identified in the document or the appropriate attachments.

A master list or equivalent document control procedure shall be established to identify the current revision of documents in order to preclude the use of non-applicable documents.

Documents shall be re-issued after a practical number of changes have been made.

4.5 Purchasing

4.5.1 General

The supplier shall ensure that purchased product conforms to specified requirements.

4.5.2 Assessment of Sub-Contractors

The supplier shall select sub-contractors on the basis of their ability to meet sub-contract requirements, including quality requirements. The supplier shall establish and maintain records of acceptable subcontractors (see 4.15).

The selection of sub-contractors, and the type and extent of control exercised by the supplier shall be dependent upon the type of product and, where appropriate, on records of sub-contractors' previously demonstrated capability and performance.

The supplier shall ensure that quality system controls are effective.

4.5.3 Purchasing Data

Purchasing documents shall contain data clearly describing the product ordered, including, where applicable:

a) The type, class, style, grade, or other precise identification.
b) The title or other positive identification, and applicable issue of specifications, drawings, process requirements, inspection instructions, and other relevant technical data, including requirements for approval or qualification of product, procedures, process equipment, and personnel.

c) The title, number, and issue of the quality system standard to be applied to the product.

The supplier shall review and approve purchasing documents for adequacy of specified requirements prior to release.

4.5.4 Verification of Purchased Products

Where specified in the contract, the purchaser or the purchaser's representative shall be afforded the right to verify at source or upon receipt that purchased product conforms to specified requirements. Verification by the purchaser shall not absolve the supplier of the supplier's responsibility to provide acceptable products nor shall it preclude subsequent rejection.

When the purchaser or the purchaser's representative elects to carry out verification at the sub-contractor's plant, such verification shall not be used by the supplier as evidence of effective control of quality by the sub-contractor.

4.6 Purchaser Supplied Product

The supplier shall establish and maintain procedures for verification, storage, and maintenance of purchaser supplied product provided for incorporation into the supplies. Any such product that is lost, damaged, or is otherwise unsuitable for use shall be recorded and reported to the purchaser (see 4.15).

NOTE: Verification by the supplier does not absolve the purchaser of the responsibility to provide acceptable product.

4.7 Product Identification and Traceability

Where appropriate, the supplier shall establish and maintain procedures for identifying the product from applicable drawings, specifications, or other documents, during all stages of production, delivery, and installation.

Where, and to the extent that, traceability is a specified requirement, individual product or batches shall have a unique identification. This identification shall be recorded (see 4.15).

4.8 Process Control

4.8.1 General

The supplier shall identify and plan the production and, where applicable, installation processes which directly affect quality and shall ensure that these processes are carried out under controlled conditions. Controlled conditions shall include the following:

a) Documented work instructions defining the manner of production and installation, where the absence of such instructions would adversely affect quality, use of suitable production and installation equipment, suitable working environment, compliance with reference standards/codes, and quality plans.

b)   Monitoring and control of suitable process and product characteristics during production and installation.

c)   The approval of processes and equipment, as appropriate.

d)   Criteria for workmanship which shall be stipulated, to the greatest practicable extent, in written standards or by means of representative samples.

4.8.2 Special Processes

These are processes, the results of which cannot be fully verified by subsequent inspection and testing of the product and where, for example, processing deficiencies may become apparent only after the product is in use. Accordingly, continuous monitoring and/or compliance with documented procedures is required to ensure that the specified requirements are met. These processes shall be qualified and shall also comply with the requirements of 4.8.1.

Records shall be maintained for qualified processes, equipment, and personnel, as appropriate.

4.9 Inspection and Testing

4.9.1 Receiving Inspection and Testing

4.9.1.1 The supplier shall ensure that incoming product is not used or processed (except in the circumstances described in 4.9.1.2) until it has been inspected or otherwise verified as conforming to specified requirements. Verification shall be in accordance with the quality plan or documented procedures.

4.9.1.2 Where incoming product is released for urgent production purposes, it shall be positively identified and recorded (see 4.15) in order to permit immediate recall and replacement in the event of nonconformance to specified requirements.

NOTE: In determining the amount and nature of receiving inspection consideration should be given to the control exercised at source and documented evidence of quality conformance provided.

4.9.2 In-Process Inspection and Testing

The supplier shall:

a)   Inspect, test, and identify product as required by the quality plan or documented procedures.

b)   Establish product conformance to specified requirements by use

245

of process monitoring and control methods.

c) Hold product until the required inspections and tests have been completed or necessary reports have been received and verified except when product is released under positive recall procedures (see 4.9.1). Release under positive recall procedures shall not preclude the activities outlined in 4.9.2 a.

d) Identify nonconforming product.

4.9.3 Final Inspection and Testing

The quality plan or documented procedures for final inspection and testing shall require that all specified inspection and tests, including those specified either on receipt of product or in-process, have been carried out and that the data meets specified requirements.

The supplier shall carry out all final inspection and testing in accordance with the quality plan or documented procedures to complete the evidence of conformance of the finished product to the specified requirements.

No product shall be dispatched until all the activities specified in the quality plan or documented procedures have been satisfactorily completed and the associated data and documentation is available and authorized.

4.9.4 Inspection and Test Records

The supplier shall establish and maintain records which give evidence that the product has passed inspection and/or test with defined acceptance criteria (see 4.15).

4.10 Inspection, Measuring, and Test Equipment

The supplier shall control, calibrate, and maintain inspection, measuring, and test equipment, whether owned by the supplier, on loan, or provided by the purchaser, to demonstrate the conformance of product to the specified requirements. Equipment shall be used in a manner which ensures that measurement uncertainty is known and is consistent with the required measurement capability.

The supplier shall:

a) Identify the measurements to be made, the accuracy required, and select the appropriate inspection, measuring, and test equipment.

b) Identify, calibrate, and adjust all inspection, measuring, and test equipment and devices that can affect product quality at prescribed intervals, or prior to use, against certified equipment having a known valid relationship to nationally recognized standards — where no such standards exist, the basis used for calibration shall be documented;

c) Establish, document, and maintain calibration procedures, including details of equipment type, identification number, location, frequency of checks, check method, acceptance criteria, and the action to be taken when results are unsatisfactory.

d) Ensure that the inspection, measuring, and test equipment is capable of the accuracy and precision necessary.

e) Identify inspection, measuring, and test equipment with a suitable indicator or approved identification record to show the calibration status.

f) Maintain calibration records for inspection, measuring, and test equipment (see 4.15).

g) Assess and document the validity of previous inspection and test results when inspection, measuring, and test equipment is found to be out of calibration.

h) Ensure that the environmental conditions are suitable for the calibrations, inspections, measurements, and tests being carried out.

i) Ensure that the handling, preservation, and storage of inspection, measuring, and test equipment is such that the accuracy and fitness for use is maintained.

j) Safeguard inspection, measuring, and test facilities, including both test hardware and test software, from adjustments which would invalidate the calibration setting.

Where test hardware (e.g., jigs, fixtures, templates, patterns) or test software is used as suitable forms of inspection, they shall be checked to prove that they are capable of verifying the acceptability of product prior to release for use during production and installation and shall be rechecked at prescribed intervals. The supplier shall establish the extent and frequency of such checks and shall maintain records as evidence of control (see 4.15). Measurement design data shall be made available, when required by the purchaser or his representative, for verification that it is functionally adequate.

4.11 Inspection and Test Status

The inspection and test status of product shall be identified by using markings, authorized stamps, tags, labels, routing cards, inspection records, test software, physical location, or other suitable means, which indicate the conformance or nonconformance of product with regard to inspection and tests performed. The identification of inspection and test status shall be maintained, as necessary, throughout production and installation of the product to ensure that only product that has passed the required inspection and test is dispatched, used, or installed.

Records shall identify the inspection authority responsible for the release of conforming product (see 4.15).

4.12 Control of Nonconforming Product

The supplier shall establish and maintain procedures to ensure that product that does not conform to specified requirements is prevented from inadvertent use or installation. Control shall provide for identification, documentaton, evaluation, segregation when practical, disposition of nonconforming product, and for notification to the functions concerned.

4.12.1 Nonconformity Review and Disposition

The responsibility for review and authority for the disposition of nonconforming product shall be defined.

Nonconforming product shall be reviewed in accordance with documented procedures. They may be:

a) Reworked to meet the specified requirements.
b) Accepted with or without repair by concession.
c) Regraded for alternative applications.
d) Rejected or scrapped.

Where required by the contract, the proposed use or repair of product, see 4.12.1 b, which does not conform to specified requirements shall be reported for concession to the purchaser or his representative. The description of nonconformity that has been accepted, and of repairs, shall be recorded to denote the actual condition (see 4.15).

Repaired and reworked product shall be re-inspected in accordance with documented procedures.

4.13 Corrective Action

The supplier shall establish, document, and maintain procedures for:

a) Investigating the cause of nonconforming product and the corrective action needed to prevent recurrence.
b) Analyzing all processes, work operations, concessions, quality records, service reports, and customer complaints to detect and eliminate potential causes of nonconforming product.
c) Initiating preventative actions to deal with problems to a level corresponding to the risks encountered.
d) Applying controls to ensure that corrective actions are taken and that they are effective.
e) Implementing and recording changes in procedures resulting from corrective action.

4.14 Handling, Storage, Packaging, and Delivery

4.14.1 General

The supplier shall establish, document, and maintain procedures for handling, storage, packaging, and delivery of product.

4.14.2 Handling

The supplier shall provide methods and means of handling that prevent damage or deterioriation.

4.14.3 Storage

The supplier shall provide secure storage areas or stock rooms to prevent damage or deterioration of product, pending use or delivery. Appropriate methods for authorizing receipt and the dispatch to and from such areas shall be stipulated. In order to detect deterioration, the condition of product in stock shall be assessed at appropriate intervals.

4.14.4 Packaging

The supplier shall control packing, preservation, and marking processes (including materials used) to the extent necessary to ensure conformance to specified requirements and shall identify, preserve, and segregate all product from the time of receipt until the supplier's responsibility ceases.

4.14.5 Delivery

The supplier shall arrange for the protection of the quality of the product after final inspection and test. Where contractually specified, this protection shall be extended to include delivery to destination.

4.15 Quality Records

The supplier shall establish and maintain procedures for identification, collection, indexing, filing, storage, maintenance, and disposition of quality records.

Quality records shall be maintained to demonstrate achievement of the required quality and the effective operation of the quality system. Pertinent sub-contractor quality records shall be an element of these data.

All quality records shall be legible and identifiable to the product involved. Quality records shall be stored and maintained in such a way that they are readily retrievable in facilities that provide a suitable environment to minimize deterioration or damage to prevent loss. Retention times of quality records shall be established and recorded. Where agreed contractually quality records shall be made available for evaluation by the purchaser or the purchaser's representative for an agreed period.

4.16 Internal Quality Audits

The supplier shall carry out internal quality audits to verify whether quality activities comply with planned arrangements and to determine the effectiveness of the quality system.

Audits shall be scheduled on the basis of the status and importance of the activity.

The audits and follow-up actions shall be carried out in accordance with documented procedures.

The results of the audits shall be documented and brought to the attention of the personnel having responsibility in the area audited. The management personnel responsible for the area shall take timely corrective action on the deficiencies found by the audit (see 4.1.3).

4.17 Training

The supplier shall establish and maintain procedures for identifying the training needs and provide for the training of all personnel performing activities affecting quality during production and installation. Personnel performing specific assigned tasks shall be qualified on the basis of appropriate education, training, and/or experience, as required. Appropriate records of training shall be maintained (see 4.15).

4.18 Statistical Techniques

Where appropriate, the supplier shall establish procedures for identifying adequate statistical techniques required for verifying the acceptability of process capability and product characteristics.

AMERICAN NATIONAL STANDARD

ANSI/ASQC Q93-1987 *Quality Systems — Model for Quality Assurance in Final Inspection and Test*

Abstract

Quality Systems — Model for Quality Assurance in Final Inspection and Test specifies quality system requirements for use where a contract between two parties requires the demonstration of a supplier's capability to detect and control the disposition of any product nonconformity during final inspection and test.

AMERICAN NATIONAL STANDARD: An American National Standard implies a consensus of those substantially concerned with its scope and provisions. An American National Standard is intended as a guide to aid the manufacturer, the consumer, and the general public. The existence of an American National Standard does not in any respect preclude anyone, whether he has approved the standard or not, from manufacturing, marketing, purchasing, or using products, processes, or procedures not conforming to the standard. American National Standards are subject to periodic review, and users are cautioned to obtain the latest editions.

CAUTION NOTICE: This American National Standard may be revised or withdrawn at any time. The procedures of the American National Standards Institute require that action be taken to reaffirm, revise, or withdraw this standard no later than five years from the date of approval. Purchasers of American National Standards may receive current information on all standards by calling or writing the American National Standards Institute.

Approved June 15, 1987
American National Standards Institute, Inc.

Foreword

(This Foreword is not a part of American National Standard *Quality Systems — Model for Quality Assurance in Final Inspection and Test.*)

Guidance concerning the selection of this standard or others in the ANSI/ASQC Q91-94 series is contained in ANSI/ASQC Q90-1987.

Rather than independently revising and extending its current *Generic Guidelines for Quality Systems* (ANSI/ASQC Z1.15-1979) the Standards Committee has elected to join other nations in adopting standards fully consistent with the "ISO 9000-9004 Series" of Quality Management and Quality Assurance Standards, since the latter were in agreement with the efforts of the ANSI/ASQC revision team.

These five ISO standards (ISO 9000-9004) were prepared by Technical Committee ISO/TC 176 on Quality Assurance in the interest of harmonizing the large number of national and international standards in this field. In addition to input from other countries, such U.S. standards as ANSI/ASQC Z1.15 and ANSI/ASQC Z1.8 were considered in the source material used in developing these ISO standards. The ANSI/ASQC Q90 through Q94 standards are technically equivalent to the ISO 9000-9004 series, but incorporate customary American language usage and spelling.

Users should note that all ANSI/ASQC standards undergo revision from time to time, and that any reference herein to any other standard implies the latest revision, unless otherwise stated.

Comments concerning this standard will be welcome. They should be sent to the standard's sponsor, American Society for Quality Control, 310 West Wisconsin Avenue, Milwaukee, Wisconsin 53203.

0.0 INTRODUCTION

This Standard is one of a series of three Standards dealing with quality systems that can be used for external quality assurance purposes. The alternative quality assurance models, set out in the three Standards listed below, represent three distinct forms of "functional or organizational capability" suitable for two-party contractual purposes:

- ANSI/ASQC Q91-1987, *Quality Systems — Model for Quality Assurance in Design/Development, Production, Installation, and Servicing.*

  For use when conformance to specified requirements is to be assured by the supplier during several stages which may include design/development, production, installation, and servicing.
- ANSI/ASQC Q92-1987, *Quality Systems — Model for Quality Assurance in Production and Installation.*

  For use when conformance to specified requirements is to be assured by the supplier during production and installation.
- ANSI/ASQC Q93-1987, *Quality Systems — Model for Quality Assurance in Final Inspection and Test.*

  For use when conformance to specified requirements is to be assured by the supplier solely at final inspection and test.

It is emphasized that the quality system requirements specified in this Standard, Standards Q91 and Q92 are complementary (not alternative) to the technical (product/service) specified requirements. These Standards are technically equivalent to the International Standards ISO 9001, 9002, and 9003 respectively.

It is intended that these Standards will normally be adopted in their present form, but on occasions they may need to be tailored for specific contractual situations. Q90 provides guidance on such tailoring as well as selection of the appropriate quality assurance model, namely Q91, Q92, or Q93.

1.0 SCOPE AND FIELD OF APPLICATION

1.1 Scope

This Standard specifies quality system requirements for use where a contract between two parties requires the demonstration of a supplier's capability to detect and control the disposition of any product nonconformity during final inspection and test.

1.2 Field of Application

This Standard is applicable in contractual situations when the conformance of the product to specified requirements can be shown with adequate confidence providing that certain supplier's capabilities for inspection and tests conducted on the product supplied can be satis-factorily demonstrated on completion.

2.0 REFERENCES

ANSI/ASQC A3, *Quality Systems Terminology.*

ISO 8402-1986, *Quality — Vocabulary.*

ANSI/ASQC Q90-1987, *Quality Management and Quality Assurance Standards — Guidelines for Selection and Use.*

ISO 9000-1987, *Quality Management and Quality Assurance Standards — Guidelines for Selection and Use.*

3.0 DEFINITIONS
For the purposes of this Standard, the definitions given in ANSI/ASQC A3 apply.

NOTE: For the purposes of this Standard, the term "product" is also used to denote "service," as appropriate.

4.0 QUALITY SYSTEM REQUIREMENTS

4.1 Management Responsibility

4.1.1 Quality Policy
The supplier's management shall define its policy and objectives for, and commitment to, quality.

4.1.2 Organization

4.1.2.1 Responsibility and Authority
The responsibility, authority, and the interrelation of all personnel engaged in final inspection and/or tests shall be defined.

4.1.2.2 Verification Resources and Personnel
The supplier shall identify in-house verification requirements, pro-vide adequate resources and assign trained and/or experienced personnel for verifying that product conforms to specified requirements (see 4.11).

4.1.2.3 Management Representative
The supplier shall appoint a management representative who, irre-spective of other responsibilities, shall have defined authority and responsibility for ensuring that the requirements of this Standard are implemented and maintained.

4.1.3 Management Review

The quality system adopted to satisfy the requirements of this Standard shall be reviewed at appropriate intervals by the supplier's management to ensure its continuing suitability and effectiveness. Records of such reviews shall be maintained (see 4.10).

4.2 Quality System

The supplier shall establish and maintain an effective quality system for inspection and tests of product on completion. This shall include documented procedures for final inspection and test operations, including workmanship standards and quality records.

4.3 Document Control

Documented procedures for final inspection and testing shall be reviewed and approved for adequacy by authorized personnel prior to issue. The document control shall ensure that only valid documents are available for final inspection and testing.

4.4 Product Identification

Where contractually specified, individual product or batches shall be marked for identification. The identification shall be recorded on related records (see 4.10).

4.5 Inspection and Testing

The supplier shall carry out all final inspection and testing in accordance with the documented procedures and maintain appropriate records to complete the evidence of conformance of product to the specified requirements. The final inspection shall include a verification of acceptable results of other necessary inspection and tests performed previously for the purpose of verifying requirements (see 4.10).

4.6 Inspection, Measuring, and Test Equipment

The supplier shall calibrate and maintain inspection, measuring, and test equipment to demonstrate the conformance of product to the specified requirements.

All inspection, measuring, and test equipment used by the supplier for final inspection and testing shall be calibrated and adjusted against certified equipment having a known valid relationship to nationally recognized standards. The supplier shall maintain calibration records for inspection, measuring, and test equipment (see 4.10).

4.7 Inspection and Test Status

The inspection and test status of product shall be identified by using markings, authorized stamps, tags, labels, inspection records, test software, physical location, or other suitable means, which indicate the conformance or nonconformance of product with regard to inspection and tests performed. Records shall identify the inspection authority responsible for the release of conforming product (see 4.10).

4.8 Control of Nonconforming Product

The supplier shall maintain control of product that does not conform to the specified requirements.

All nonconforming product shall be clearly identified and segregated, when practical, to prevent unauthorized use, delivery, or mixing with conforming product.

Repaired or reworked product shall be reinspected in accordance with documented procedures.

4.9 Handling, Storage, Packaging, and Delivery

The supplier shall arrange for the protection of the quality of product and its identification after final inspection and test. Where contractually specified, this protection shall be extended to include delivery to destination.

4.10 Quality Records

The supplier shall maintain appropriate inspection and test records to substantiate conformance with specified requirements. Quality records shall be legible and identifiable to the product involved. Quality records that substantiate conformance with the specified requirements shall be retained for an agreed period and made available on request.

4.11 Training

Personnel performing final inspection and tests shall have appropriate experience and/or training.

4.12 Statistical Techniques

Where appropriate, the supplier shall establish procedures for identifying adequate statistical techniques required for verifying the acceptability of product characteristics.

AMERICAN NATIONAL STANDARD

ANSI/ASQC Q94-1987 *Quality Management and Quality System Elements — Guidelines*

Abstract

Quality Management and Quality System Elements — Guidelines describes a basic set of elements by which a Quality Management System can be developed and implemented internally.

AMERICAN NATIONAL STANDARD: An American National Standard implies a consensus of those substantially concerned with its scope and provisions. An American National Standard is intended as a guide to aid the manufacturer, the consumer, and the general public. The existence of an American National Standard does not in any respect preclude anyone, whether he has approved the standard or not, from manufacturing, marketing, purchasing, or using products, processes, or procedures not conforming to the standard. American National Standards are subject to periodic review, and users are cautioned to obtain the latest editions.

CAUTION NOTICE: This American National Standard may be revised or withdrawn at any time. The procedures of the American National Standards Institute require that action be taken to reaffirm, revise, or withdraw this standard no later than five years from the date of approval. Purchasers of American National Standards may receive current information on all standards by calling or writing the American National Standards Institute.

Approved June 15, 1987
American National Standards Institute, Inc.

Foreword

(This Foreword is not a part of American National Standard *Quality Management and Quality System Elements — Guidelines.*)

Guidance concerning the selection of this standard or others in the ANSI/ASQC Q91-94 series is contained in ANSI/ASQC Q90-1987.

Rather than independently revising and extending its current *Generic Guidelines for Quality Systems* (ANSI/ASQC Z1.15-1979) the Standards Committee has elected to join other nations in adopting standards fully consistent with the ''ISO 9000-9004 Series'' of Quality Management and Quality Assurance Standards, since the latter were in agreement with the efforts of the ANSI/ASQC revision team.

These five ISO standards (ISO 9000-9004) were prepared by Technical Committee ISO/TC 176 on Quality Assurance in the interest of harmonizing the large number of national and international standards in this field. In addition to input from other countries, such U.S. standards as ANSI/ASQC Z1.15 and ANSI/ASQC Z1.8 were considered in the source material used in developing these ISO standards. The ANSI/ASQC Q90 through Q94 standards are *technically equivalent* to the ISO 9000-9004 series, but incorporate customary American language usage and spelling. Appendices A and B from ANSI/ASQC Z1.15 have been added to this standard, but were not included in ISO 9004.

Users should note that all ANSI/ASQC standards undergo revision from time to time, and that any reference herein to any other standard implies the latest revision, unless otherwise stated.

Comments concerning this standard will be welcome. They should be sent to the standard's sponsor, American Society for Quality Control, 310 West Wisconsin Avenue, Milwaukee, Wisconsin 53203.

0.0 INTRODUCTION

0.1 General
A primary concern of any company or organization must be the quality of its products and services.

In order to be successful, a company must offer products or services that:

a) Meet a well-defined need, use, or purpose.
b) Satisfy customers' expectations.
c) Comply with applicable standards and specifications.
d) Comply with statutory (and other) requirements of society (see 3.3).
e) Are made available at competitive prices.
f) Are provided at a cost which will yield a profit.

0.2 Organizational Goals
In order to meet its objectives, the company should organize itself in such a way that the technical, administrative, and human factors affecting the quality of its products and services will be under control. All such control should be oriented towards the reduction, elimination, and most importantly, prevention of quality deficiencies.

A quality management system should be developed and implemented for the purpose of accomplishing the objectives set out in a company's quality policies.

Each element (or requirement) in a quality management system will vary in importance from one type of activity to another and from one product or service to another.

In order to achieve maximum effectiveness and to satisfy customer expectations, it is essential that the quality management system be appropriate to the type of activity and to the product or service being offered.

0.3 Meeting Company/Customer Needs
A quality management system has two interrelated aspects:

a) **The company's needs and interests**
For the company, there is a business need to attain and to maintain the desired quality at an optimum cost; the fulfillment of this quality aspect is related to the planned and efficient utilization of the technological, human, and material resources available to the company.

b) **The customer's needs and expectations**
For the customer, there is a need for confidence in the ability of the company to deliver the desired quality as well as the consistent maintenance of that quality.

Each of the above aspects of a quality management system requires objective evidence in the form of information and data concerning the quality of the system and the quality of the company's products.

0.4 Risks, Costs, and Benefits

0.4.1 General
Risk, cost, and benefit considerations have great importance for both company and customer. These considerations are inherent aspects of most products and services. The possible effects and ramifications of these considerations are given in 0.4.2 to 0.4.4.

0.4.2 Risk Considerations

0.4.2.1 For the Company
Consideration has to be given to risks related to deficient products or services which lead to loss of image or reputation, loss of market, complaints, claims, liability, and waste of human and financial resources.

0.4.2.2 For the Customer
Consideration has to be given to risks such as those pertaining to the health and safety of people, dissatisfaction with goods and services, availability, marketing claims, and loss of confidence.

0.4.3 Cost Considerations

0.4.3.1 For the Company
Consideration has to be given to costs due to marketing and design deficiencies, including unsatisfactory materials, rework, repair, replacement, reprocessing, loss of production, warranties, and field repair.

0.4.3.2 For the Customer
Consideration has to be given to safety, acquisition cost, operating, maintenance, downtime and repair costs, and possible disposal costs.

0.4.4 Benefit Considerations

0.4.4.1 For the Company
Consideration has to be given to increased profitability and market share.

0.4.4.2 For the Customer
Consideration has to be given to reduced costs, improved fitness for use, increased satisfaction, and growth in confidence.

0.4.5 Conclusion

An effective quality management system should be designed to satisfy customer needs and expectations while serving to protect the company's interests. A well-structured quality system is a valuable management resource in the optimization and control of quality in relation to risk, cost, and benefit considerations.

1.0 SCOPE AND FIELD OF APPLICATION

This Standard describes a basic set of elements by which quality management systems can be developed and implemented.

The selection of appropriate elements contained in this Standard and the extent to which these elements are adopted and applied by a company depends upon factors such as market being served, nature of product, production processes, and consumer needs.

NOTES:
1. This Standard is not intended to be used as a checklist for compliance with a set of requirements.
2. The American Society for Quality Control is in the process of developing a separate Standard on the subject of service.
3. This Standard is technically equivalent to the International Standard ISO 9004-1987.

2.0 REFERENCES

ANSI/ASQC A3, *Quality Systems Terminology.*

ISO 8402-1986, *Quality-Vocabulary.*

ANSI/ASQC Q90-1987, *Quality Management and Quality Assurance Standards — Guidelines for Selection and Use.*

ANSI/ASQC Q91-1987, *Quality Systems — Model for Quality Assurance in Design/Development, Production, Installation, and Servicing.*

ANSI/ASQC Q92-1987, *Quality Systems — Model for Quality Assurance in Production and Installation.*

ANSI/ASQC Q93-1987, *Quality Systems — Model for Quality Assurance in Final Inspection and Test.*

ISO 9000-1987, *Quality Management and Quality Assurance Standards — Guidelines for Selection and Use.*

ISO 9001-1987, *Quality Systems — Model for Quality Assurance in*

Design/Development, Production, Installation and Servicing.

ISO 9002-1987, *Quality Systems — Model for Quality Assurance in Production and Installation.*

ISO 9003-1987, *Quality Systems — Model for Quality Assurance in Final Inspection and Test.*

3.0 DEFINITIONS
For the purposes of this Standard, the definitions given in ANSI/ASQC A3 and the following definitions apply.

3.1 Organization
A company, corporation, firm, or enterprise, whether incorporated or not, public or private.

3.2 Company
Term used primarily to refer to a business first party, the purpose of which is to supply a product or service.

3.3 Requirements of Society
Requirements including laws, statutes, rules and regulations, codes, environmental considerations, health and safety factors, and conservation of energy and materials.

3.4 Customer
Ultimate consumer, user, client, beneficiary, or second party.

4.0 MANAGEMENT RESPONSIBILITY

4.1 General
The responsibility for and commitment to a quality policy belongs to the highest level of management. Quality management is that aspect of the overall management function which determines and implements quality policy.

4.2 Quality Policy
The management of a company should develop and state its corporate quality policy. This policy should be consistent with company policies. Management should take all necessary measures to ensure that its corporate quality policy is understood, implemented, and maintained.

4.3 Quality Objectives

4.3.1 For the corporate quality policy, management should define objectives pertaining to key elements of quality, such as fitness for use, performance, safety, and reliability.

4.3.2 The calculation and evaluation of costs associated with all quality elements and objectives should always be an important consideration, with the objective of minimizing quality losses.

4.3.3 Appropriate levels of management, where necessary, should define specialized quality objectives consistent with corporate quality policy as well as other corporate objectives.

4.4 Quality System

4.4.1 A quality system is the organizational structure, responsibilities, pro--cedures, processes, and resources for implementing quality management.

4.4.2 Management should develop, establish, and implement a quality system as the means by which stated policies and objectives might be accomplished.

4.4.3 The quality system should be structured and adapted to the company's particular type of business and should take into account the appropriate elements outlined in this Standard.

4.4.4 The quality system should function in such a manner as to provide proper confidence that:

    a)   The system is well understood and effective.
    b)   The products or services actually do satisfy requirements and customer expectations.
    c)   Emphasis is placed on problem prevention rather than dependence on detection after occurrence.

5.0 QUALITY SYSTEM PRINCIPLES

5.1 Quality Loop

5.1.1 The quality system typically applies to, and interacts with, all activities pertinent to the quality of a product or service. It involves all phases from initial identification to final satisfaction of requirements and customer expectations. These phases and activities may include the following:

    a)   Marketing and market research.
    b)   Design/specification engineering and product development.
    c)   Procurement.

d) Process planning and development.
e) Production.
f) Inspection, testing, and examination.
g) Packaging and storage.
h) Sales and distribution.
i) Installation and operation.
j) Technical assistance and maintenance.
k) Disposal after use.

See the figure (page 265) for a schematic representation of the quality loop, which is similar in concept to the quality spiral.

5.1.2 In the context of interacting activities within a company, marketing and design should be emphasized as especially important for:

a) Determining and defining customer needs, expectations, and the product requirements.
b) Providing the concepts (including back-up data) for producing a product or service to defined specifications at optimum cost.

5.2 Structure of the Quality System

5.2.1 General
Management is ultimately responsible for establishing the quality policy and for decisions concerning the initiation, development, implementation, and maintenance of the quality system.

5.2.2 Quality Responsibility and Authority
Activities contributing to quality, whether directly or indirectly, should be identified and documented, and the following actions taken:

a) General and specific responsibilities should be explicitly defined.
b) Responsibility and authority delegated to each activity contributing to quality should be clearly established; authority and responsibility should be sufficient to attain the assigned quality objectives with the desired efficiency.
c) Interface control and coordination measures between different activities should be defined.
d) Management may choose to delegate the responsibility for internal quality assurance and for external quality assurance where necessary; the persons so delegated should be independent of the activities reported on.
e) In organizing a well structured and effective quality system, emphasis should be placed on the identification of actual or potential quality problems and the initiation of remedial or preventive measures.

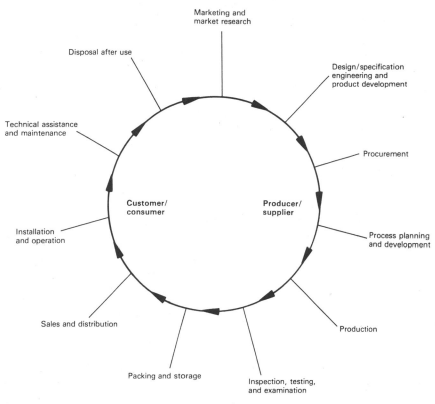

Figure   Quality Loop

5.2.3 Organizational Structure

The organizational structure pertaining to the quality management system should be clearly established within the overall management of a company. The lines of authority and communication should be defined.

5.2.4 Resources and Personnel

Management should provide sufficient and appropriate resources essential to the implementation of quality policies and the achievement of quality objectives. These resources may include:

a)   Human resources and specialized skills.
b)   Design and development equipment.
c)   Manufacturing equipment.
d)   Inspection, test, and examination equipment.
e)   Instrumentation and computer software.

Management should determine the level of competence, experience, and training necessary to ensure the capability of personnel (see 18).

265

Management should identify quality factors affecting market position and objectives relative to new products, processes, or services (including new technologies) in order to allocate company resources on a planned and timely basis.

Programs and schedules covering these resources and skills should be consistent with the company's overall objectives.

5.2.5 Operational Procedures

The quality system should be organized in such a way that adequate and continuous control is exercised over all activities affecting quality.

The management system should emphasize preventive actions that avoid occurrence of problems, while not sacrificing the ability to respond to and correct failures should they occur.

Operational procedures coordinating different activities with respect to an effective quality system should be developed, issued, and maintained to implement corporate quality policies and objectives. These procedures should lay down the objectives and performance of the various activities having an impact on quality, e.g., design, development, procurement, production, and sales.

All written procedures should be stated simply, unambiguously, and understandably, and should indicate methods to be used and the criteria to be satisfied.

5.3 Documentation of the System

5.3.1 Quality Policies and Procedures

All the elements, requirements, and provisions adopted by a company for its quality management system should be documented in a systematic and orderly manner in the form of written policies and procedures. Such documentation should ensure a common understanding of quality policies and procedures (i.e., quality programs, plans, manuals, and records).

The quality management system should include adequate provision for the proper identification, distribution, collection, and maintenance of all quality documents and records. However, care should be taken to limit documentation to the extent pertinent to the application (see 17).

5.3.2 Quality Manual

5.3.2.1 The typical form of the main document used in drawing up and implementing a quality system is a ''Quality Manual.''

5.3.2.2 The primary purpose of a quality manual is to provide an adequate description of the quality management system while serving as a permanent reference in the implementation and maintenance of that system.

5.3.2.3 Methods should be established for making changes, modifications, revisions, or additions to the contents of a quality manual.

5.3.2.4 In larger companies, the documentation relating to the quality management system may take various forms, including the following:

a) A corporate quality manual.
b) Divisional quality manuals.
c) Specialized quality manuals (e.g., design, procurement, project, work instructions).

5.3.3 Quality Plans

For projects relating to new products, services, or processes, management should prepare, as appropriate, written quality plans consistent with all other requirements of a company's quality management system.

Quality plans should define:

a) The quality objectives to be attained.
b) The specific allocation of responsibilities and authority during the different phases of the project.
c) The specific procedures, methods, and work instructions to be applied.
d) Suitable testing, inspection, examination, and audit programs at appropriate stages (e.g., design, development).
e) A method for changes and modifications in a quality plan as projects proceed.
f) Other measures necessary to meet objectives.

5.3.4 Quality Records

Quality records and charts pertaining to design, inspection, testing, survey, audit, review, or related results are important constituents of a quality management system (see 17.2 and 17.3).

5.4 Auditing the Quality System

5.4.1 General

All elements, aspects, and components pertaining to a quality system should be internally audited and evaluated on a regular basis. Audits should be carried out in order to determine whether various elements within a quality management system are effective in achieving stated quality objectives. For this purpose, an appropriate audit plan should be formulated and established by company management.

5.4.2 Audit Plan

The format of the audit plan should cover the following points:

a) The specific activities and areas to be audited.
b) Qualifications of personnel carrying out audits.
c) The basis for carrying out audits (e.g., organizational changes, reported deficiencies, routine checks, and surveys).
d) Procedures for reporting audit findings, conclusions, and re-commendations.

5.4.3 Carrying Out the Audit

Objective evaluations of quality system elements by competent personnel may include the following activities or areas:

a) Organizational structures.
b) Administrative and operational procedures.
c) Personnel, equipment, and material resources.
d) Work areas, operations, and processes.
e) Items being produced (to establish degree of conformance to standards and specifications).
f) Documentation, reports, and record-keeping.

Personnel carrying out audits of quality system elements should be independent of the specific activities or areas being audited.

5.4.4 Reporting and Follow-up of Audit Findings

Audit findings, conclusions, and recommendations should be submitted in documentary form for consideration by appropriate members of company management.

The following items should be covered in the reporting and follow-up of audit findings:

a) Specific examples of noncompliance or deficiencies should be documented in the audit report; possible reasons for such deficiencies, where evident, may be included.
b) Appropriate corrective actions may be suggested.
c) Implementation and effectiveness of corrective actions suggested in previous audits should be assessed.

5.5 Review and Evaluation of the Quality Management System

Provision should be made by company management for independent review and evaluation of the quality system. Such reviews should be carried out by appropriate members of company management or by competent independent personnel as decided on by company management.

Reviews should consist of well structured and comprehensive evaluations which include:

a) Findings of audits centered on various elements of the quality

268

system (see 5.4.3).

b) The overall effectiveness of the quality management system in achieving stated quality objectives.

c) Considerations for updating the quality management system in relation to changes brought about by new technologies, quality concepts, market strategies, and social or environmental conditions.

Findings, conclusions, and recommendations reached as a result of review and evaluation should be submitted in documentary form for necessary action by company management.

6.0 ECONOMICS — QUALITY-RELATED COST CONSIDERATIONS

6.1 General

The impact of quality upon the profit and loss statement can be highly significant, particularly in the long term. It is, therefore, important that the effectiveness of a quality system be measured in a business-like manner. The main objective of quality cost reporting is to provide means for evaluating effectiveness and establishing the basis for internal improvement programs.

6.2 Selecting Appropriate Elements

A portion of total business costs is earmarked for meeting the quality objectives. In practice, the combination of selected elements from this portion of total costs can provide the necessary information for marshalling efforts towards achieving quality goals. It is now common practice to identify and measure "quality costs." Both costs of activities directed at achieving appropriate quality and resultant costs from inadequate control should be identified.

6.3 Types of Quality-Related Costs

6.3.1 General

Quality costs can be broadly divided into operating quality costs (see 6.3.2) and external assurance quality costs (see 6.3.3).

6.3.2 Operating Quality Costs

Operating quality costs are those costs incurred by a business in order to attain and ensure specified quality levels. These include the following:

a) Prevention and appraisal costs (or investments)
-prevention: Costs of efforts to prevent failures
-appraisal: Costs of testing, inspection, and examination to assess whether specified quality is being maintained;

b) Failure costs (or losses)
   -internal failure: Costs resulting from a product or service failing to meet the quality requirements prior to delivery (e.g., reperforming of service, reprocessing, rework, retest, scrap)
   -external failure: Costs resulting from a product or service failing to meet the quality requirements after delivery (e.g., product service, warranties and returns, direct costs and allowances, product recall costs, liability costs).

6.3.3 External Assurance Quality Costs

External assurance quality costs are those costs relating to the demonstration and proof required as objective evidence by customers, including particular and additional quality assurance provisions, procedures, data, demonstration tests, and assessments (e.g., the cost of testing for specific safety characteristics by recognized independent testing bodies).

6.4 Management Visibility

Quality costs should be regularly reported to and monitored by management and be related to other cost (ration) measures, such as "sales," "turnover," or "added value" so as to:

a) Evaluate the adequacy and effectiveness of the quality management system.
b) Identify additional areas requiring attention.
c) Establish quality and cost objectives.

7.0 QUALITY IN MARKETING

7.1 Marketing Requirements

The marketing function should take the lead in establishing quality requirements for the product. It should:

a) Determine the need for a product or service.
b) Accurately define the market demand and sector, since doing so is important in determining the grade, quantity, price, and timing estimates for the product or service.
c) Accurately determine customer requirements by a review of contract or market needs: actions include an assessment of any unstated expectations or biases held by customers.
d) Communicate all customer requirements clearly and accurately within the company.

7.2 Product Brief

The marketing function should provide the company with a formal statement or outline of product requirements, e.g., a product brief. The product brief translates customer requirements and expectations into a preliminary set of specifications as the basis for subsequent design work. Among the elements that may be included in the product brief are the following requirements:

a) Performance characteristics (e.g., environmental and usage conditions and reliability).
b) Sensory characteristics (e.g., style, color, taste, smell).
c) Installation configuration or fit.
d) Applicable standards and statutory regulations.
e) Packaging.
f) Quality assurance/verification.

7.3 Customer Feedback Information

The marketing function should establish an information monitoring and feedback system on a continuous basis. All information pertinent to the quality of a product or service should be analyzed, collated, interpreted, and communicated in accordance with defined procedures. Such information will help to determine the nature and extent of product or service problems in relation to customer experience and expectations. In addition, feedback information may provide clues to possible design changes as well as appropriate management action (see also 8.8, 8.9, and 16.3).

8.0 QUALITY IN SPECIFICATION AND DESIGN

8.1 Contribution of Specification and Design to Quality

The specification and design function should provide for the translation of customer needs from the product brief into technical specifications for materials, products, and processes. This should result in a product that provides customer satisfaction at an acceptable price that enables a satisfactory return on investment for the enterprise. The specification and design should be such that the product or service is producible, verifiable, and controllable under the proposed production, installation, commissioning, or operational conditions.

8.2 Design Planning and Objectives (Defining the Project)

8.2.1 Management should specifically assign responsibilities for various design duties to activities inside and/or outside the organization and ensure that all those who contribute to design are aware of their responsibilities for achieving quality.

8.2.2 In its delegation of responsibilities for quality, management should ensure that design functions provide clear and definitive technical data for procurement, the execution of work, and verification of conformance of products and processes to specification requirements.

8.2.3 Management should establish time-phased design programs with checkpoints appropriate to the nature of the product. The extent of each phase and the stages at which design reviews or evaluations will take place may depend upon the product's application, its design complexity, the extent of innovation and technology being introduced, the degree of standardization, and similarity with past proven designs.

8.2.4 In addition to customer needs, the designer should give due consideration to the requirements relating to safety, environmental, and other regulations, including items in the company's quality policy which may go beyond existing statutory requirements.

8.2.5 The quality aspects of the design should be unambiguous and adequately define characteristics important to quality, such as the acceptance and rejection criteria. Both fitness for purpose and safeguards against misuse should be considered. Product definition may also include reliability, expectancy, including benign failure and safe disposability, as appropriate.

8.3 Product Testing and Measurement

The methods of measurement and test, and the acceptance criteria applied to evaluate the product and processes during both the design and production phases should be specified. Parameters should include the following:

a) Performance target values, tolerances, and attribute features.
b) Acceptance and rejection criteria.
c) Test and measurement methods, equipment, bias and precision requirements, and computer software considerations.

8.4 Design Qualification and Validation

The design process should provide periodic evaluation of the design at significant stages. Such evaluation can take the form of analytical methods, such as FMEA (Failure Mode and Effects Analysis), fault tree analysis, or risk assessment, as well as inspection or test of prototype models and/or actual production samples. The amount and degree of testing should be related to the risks identified in the design plan (see 8.2). Independent evaluation may be employed, as appropriate, to verify original calculations, provide alternative calculations, or perform tests. Adequate numbers of samples should be examined by tests and/or inspection to provide adequate statistical confidence in the results. The tests should include the following activities:

a) Evaluation of performance, durability, safety, reliability, and maintainability under expected storage and operational conditions.

b) Inspections to verify that all design features are as intended and that all authorized design changes have been accomplished and recorded.

c) Validation of computer systems and software.

The results of all tests and evaluations should be documented regularly throughout the qualification test cycle. Review of test results should include defect and failure analysis.

8.5 Design Review

8.5.1 General

At the conclusion of each phase of design development, a formal, documented, systematic, and critical review of the design results should be conducted. This should be distinguished from a project progress meeting, which is primarily concerned with time and cost. Participants at each design review should include representatives of all functions affecting quality as appropriate to the phase being reviewed. The design review should identify and anticipate problem areas and inadequacies, and initiate corrective actions to ensure that the final design and supporting data meet customer requirements.

8.5.2 Elements of Design Reviews

As appropriate to the design phase and product, the following elements outlined below should be considered:

a) Items pertaining to customer needs and satisfaction

1) Comparison of customer needs expressed in the product brief with technical specifications for materials, products, and processes.

2) Validation of the design through prototype tests.

3) Ability to perform under expected conditions of use and environment.

4) Considerations of unintended uses and misuses.

5) Safety and environmental compatibility.

6) Compliance with regulatory requirements, national and international standards, and corporate practices.

7) Comparisons with competitive design.

8) Comparison with similar designs, especially analysis of internal and external problem history to avoid repeating problems.

b) Items pertaining to product specification and service requirements

1) Reliability, serviceability, and maintainability requirements.
2) Permissible tolerances and comparison with process capabilities.
3) Product acceptance/rejection criteria.
4) Installability, ease of assembly, storage needs, shelf life, and disposability.
5) Benign failure and fail-safe characteristics.
6) Aesthetic specifications and acceptance criteria.
7) Failure modes and effects analyses, and fault tree analysis.
8) Ability to diagnose and correct problems.
9) Labeling, warnings, identification, traceability requirements, and user instructions.
10) Review and use of standard parts.

c) Items pertaining to process specifications and service requirements

1) Manufacturability of the design, including special process needs, mechanization, automation, assembly, and installation of components.
2) Capability to inspect and test the design, including special inspection and test requirements.
3) Specification of materials, components, and subassemblies, including approved supplies and suppliers as well as availability.
4) Packaging, handling, storage, and shelf life requirements, especially safety factors relating to incoming and outgoing items.

8.5.3 Design Verification

Design verification may be undertaken independently or in support of design reviews by applying the following methods:

a) Alternative calculations, made to verify the correctness of the original calculations and analyses.
b) Testing, e.g., by model or prototype tests — if this method is adopted, the test programs should be clearly defined and the results documented.
c) Independent verification, to verify the correctness of the original calculations and/or other design activities.

8.6 Design Baseline and Production Release

The results of the final design review should be appropriately documented in specifications and drawings that define the design baseline. Where appropriate, this should include description of qualification test units "as built" and modified to correct deficiencies during the qualifications test programs for configuration control throughout the production cycle. The total document package that defines the design baseline should require approval at appropriate levels of management affected by or contributing to the product. This "approval" constitutes the production release and signifies concurrence that the design can be realized.

8.7 Market Readiness Review

The quality system should provide for a review to determine whether production capability and field support are adequate for the new or redesigned product. Depending upon the type of product, the review may cover the following points:

a) Availability and adequacy of installation, operation, maintenance, and repair manuals.
b) Existence of an adequate distribution and customer service organization.
c) Training of field personnel.
d) Availability of spare parts.
e) Field trials.
f) Certification of the satisfactory completion of qualification tests.
g) Physical inspection of early production units and their packaging and labeling.
h) Evidence of process capability to meet specification on production equipment.

8.8 Design Change Control (Configuration Management)

The quality system should provide a procedure for controlling the release, change, and use of documents that define the design baseline (resultant product configuration) and for authorizing the necessary work to be performed to implement changes that may affect product during its entire life cycle. The procedures should provide for various necessary approvals, specified points and times for implementing changes, removing obsolete drawings and specifications from work areas, and verification that changes are made at the appointed times and places. This control process is referred to as "configuration management." These procedures should handle emergency changes necessary to prevent production of nonconforming product. Consideration should be given to instituting formal design reviews and validation testing when the magnitude, complexity, or risk associated with the change warrant such actions.

8.9 Design Requalification

Periodic reevaluation of product should be performed in order to ensure that the design is still valid with respect to all specified requirements. This should include a review of customer needs and technical specifications in the light of field experiences, field performance surveys, or new technology and techniques. This review should also consider process modifications. The quality system should ensure that any production and field experience indicating the need for design change is fed back for analysis. Care should be taken that design changes do not cause product quality degradation and that proposed changes are evaluated for their impact on all product characteristics in the design baseline definition.

9.0 QUALITY IN PROCUREMENT

9.1 General

Purchase materials, components, and assemblies become part of the company's product and directly affect the quality of its product. Quality of services such as calibration and special processes should also be considered. The procurement of purchased supplies should be planned and controlled. The purchaser should establish a close working relationship and feedback system with each supplier. In this way, a program of continual quality improvements can be maintained and quality disputes avoided or settled quickly. This close working relationship and feedback system will benefit both the purchaser and the supplier.

The procurement quality program should include the following elements as a minimum:

a) Requirements for specification, drawings, and purchase orders (see 9.2).
b) Selection of qualified suppliers (see 9.3).
c) Agreement on quality assurance (see 9.4).
d) Agreement on verification methods (see 9.5).
e) Provisions for settlement of quality disputes (see 9.6).
f) Receiving inspection plans (see 9.7).
g) Receiving controls (see 9.7).
h) Receiving quality records (see 9.8).

9.2 Requirements for Specifications, Drawings, and Purchase Orders

The successful procurement of supplies begins with a clear definition of the requirements. Usually these requirements are contained in the contract specifications, drawings, and purchase orders which are provided to the supplier.

The procuring activity should develop appropriate methods to ensure that the requirements for the supplies are clearly defined, communicated, and most importantly, are completely understood by the supplier. These methods may include written procedures for the preparation of specifications, drawings, and purchase orders, vendor/purchaser conferences prior to purchase order release, and other methods appropriate for the supplies being procured.

Purchasing documents should contain data clearly describing the product or service ordered. Elements that may be included are as follows:

a) Precise identification of style and grade.
b) Inspection instructions and applicable specifications.
c) Quality system standard to be applied.

Purchasing documents should be reviewed for accuracy and completeness before release.

9.3 Selection of Qualified Suppliers
Each supplier should have a demonstrated capability to furnish supplies which can meet all the requirements of the specifications, drawings, and purchase order.
The methods of establishing this capability may include any combination of the following:

a) On-site assessment and evaluation of supplier's capability and/or quality system.
b) Evaluation of product samples.
c) Past history with similar supplies.
d) Test results of similar supplies.
e) Published experience of other users.

9.4 Agreement on Quality Assurance
A clear understanding should be developed with the supplier on quality assurance for which the supplier is responsible. The assurance to be provided by the supplier may vary as follows:

a) The purchaser relies on supplier's quality assurance system.
b) Submission of specified inspection/test data or process control records with shipments.
c) One hundred percent inspection/testing by the supplier.
d) Lot acceptance inspection/testing by sampling by the supplier.
e) Implementation of a formal quality assurance system as specified by the purchaser.
f) None — the purchaser relies on receiving inspection or in-house sorting.

The assurance provisions should be commensurate with the needs of the purchaser's business and should avoid unnecessary costs. In certain cases, formal quality assurance systems may be involved (see Q90, Q91, Q92, and Q93). This may include periodic assessment of supplier quality system assurance by the purchaser.

9.5 Agreement on Verification Methods

A clear agreement should be developed with the supplier on the methods by which conformance to purchaser's requirements will be verified. Such agreements may also include the exchange of inspection and test data with the aim of furthering quality improvements. Reaching agreement can minimize difficulties in the interpretation of requirements as well as inspection, test, or sampling methods.

9.6 Provisions for Settlement of Quality Disputes

Systems and procedures should be established by which settlement of disputes regarding quality can be reached with suppliers. Provisions should exist for dealing with routine and nonroutine matters.

A very important aspect of these systems and procedures is the provision of improved communication channels between the purchaser and the supplier on matters affecting quality.

9.7 Receiving Inspection Planning and Controls

Appropriate measures should be established to ensure that supplies which have been received are properly controlled. These procedures should include quarantine areas or other appropriate methods to prevent unqualified supplies from being inadvertently used (see 14.4).

The extent to which receiving inspection will be performed should be carefully planned. The level of inspection, when inspection is deemed necessary, should be selected with overall cost being borne in mind.

In addition, when the decision has been made to perform an inspection, it is necessary to select with care the characteristics to be inspected.

It is also necessary to ensure, before the supplies arrive, that all the necessary tools, gauges, meters, instruments, and equipment are available and properly calibrated, along with adequately trained personnel.

9.8 Receiving Quality Records

Appropriate receiving quality records should be maintained to ensure the availability of historical data to assess supplier performance and quality trends.

In addition, it may be useful and, in certain instances, essential to maintain records of lot identification for purposes of traceability.

10.0 QUALITY IN PRODUCTION

10.1 Planning for Controlled Production

10.1.1 Planning of production operations should ensure that these proceed under controlled conditions in the specified manner and sequence. Controlled conditions include appropriate controls for materials, production equipment, processes and procedures, computer software, personnel, and associated supplies, utilities, and environments.

Production operations should be specified to the necessary extent by documented work instructions.

Process capability studies should be conducted to determine the potential effectiveness of a process (see 10.2).

Provisions for common practice that apply throughout the production facility should be similarly documented and referenced in individual work instructions. These instructions should describe the criteria for determining satisfactory work completion and conformity to specification and standards of good workmanship. Workmanship standards should be defined to the necessary extent by written standards, photographs, and/or physical samples.

10.1.2 Verification of the quality status of a product, process, software, material, or environment should be considered at important points in the production sequence to minimize effects of errors and to maximize yields. The use of control charts and statistical sampling procedures and plans are examples of techniques employed to facilitate production/process control (see also 12.1).

10.1.3 Verifications at each stage should relate directly to finished product specifications or to an internal requirement, as appropriate. If verification of characteristics of the process itself is not physically or economically practical or feasible, then verification of the product should be utilized. In all cases, relationships between in-process controls, their specifications, and final product specifications should be developed, communicated to production and inspection personnel, and documented.

10.1.4 All in-process and final inspections should be planned and specified. Documented test and inspection procedures should be maintained, including the specific equipment to perform such checks and tests, as well as the specified requirement(s) and/or workmanship standard(s) for each quality characteristic to be checked.

10.1.5 Efforts to develop new methods for improving production quality and process capability should be encouraged.

10.2 Process Capability

Production processes should be verified as capable of producing in accordance with product specifications. Operations associated with product or process characteristics that can have a significant effect on product quality should be identified. Appropriate control should be established to ensure that these characteristics remain within specification or that appropriate modifications or changes are made.

Verification of production processes should include material, equipment, computer system and software, procedures, and personnel.

10.3 Supplies, Utilities, and Environments

Where important to quality characteristics, auxiliary materials and utilities, such as water, compressed air, electric power, and chemicals used for processing, should be controlled and verified periodically to ensure uniformity of effect on the process. Where a production environment, such as temperature, humidity, and cleanliness, is important to product quality, appropriate limits should be specified, controlled, and verified.

11.0 CONTROL OF PRODUCTION

11.1 General

The quality loop involves the control of quality in a manufacturing cycle (see also 5.1 in which the interaction of various quality system functions is outlined).

11.2 Material Control and Traceability

All materials and parts should conform to appropriate specifications and quality standards before being introduced into production. However, in determining the amount of test and/or inspection necessary, consideration should be given to cost impact and the effect that substandard material quality will have on production flow (see 9). Materials should be appropriately stored, segregated, handled, and protected during production to maintain their suitability. Special consideration should be given to shelf-life and deterioration control. Where in-plant traceability of material is important to quality, appropriate identification should be maintained throughout the production process to ensure traceability to original material identification and quality status (see 11.7 and 16.1.3).

11.3 Equipment Control and Maintenance

All production equipment, including fixed machinery, jigs, fixtures, tooling, templates, patterns, and gauges, should be proved for bias and precision prior to use. Special attention should be paid to computers used in controlling processes, and especially the maintenance of the related software (see 13.1).

Equipment should be appropriately stored and adequately protected between use, and verified or recalibrated at appropriate intervals to ensure control of bias and precision.

A program of preventive maintenance should be established to ensure continuing process capability. Special attention should be given to equipment characteristics that contribute to key product quality characteristics.

11.4 Special Processes

Special considerations should be given to production processes in which control is particularly important to product quality. Such special consideration may be required for product characteristics that are not easily or economically measured, for special skills required in their operation or maintenance, or for a product or process the results of which cannot be fully verified by subsequent inspection and test. More frequent verification of special processes should be made to keep a check on:

a) The accuracy and variability of equipment used to make or measure product, including settings and adjustments.
b) The skill, capability, and knowledge of operators to meet quality requirements.
c) Special environments, time, temperature, or other factors affecting quality.
d) Certification records maintained for personnel, processes, and equipment, as appropriate.

11.5 Documentation

Work instructions, specifications, and drawings should be controlled as specified by the quality system (see 5.3 and 17.2).

11.6 Process Change Control

Those responsible for authorization of process changes should be clearly designated and, where necessary, customer approval should be sought. As with design changes, all changes to production tooling or equipment, materials, or processes should be documented. The implementation should be covered by defined procedures.

A product should be evaluated after any change to verify that the change instituted had the desired effect upon product quality. Any changes in the relationships between process and product characteristics resulting from the change should be documented and appropriately communicated.

11.7 Control of Verification Status

Verification status of material and assemblies should be identified throughout production. Such identification may take the form of stamps, tags, or notations on shop travelers, or inspection records that accompany the product. The identification should include the ability to distinguish between verified and unverified material and indication of acceptance at the point of verification. It should also provide traceability to the unit responsible for the operation.

11.8 Control of Nonconforming Materials

Provision should be made for the positive identification and control of all nonconforming material (see 14).

12.0 PRODUCT VERIFICATION

Procurement Quality Control

12.1 Incoming Materials and Parts

The method used to ensure quality of purchased materials, component parts, and assemblies that are received into the production facility will depend on the importance of the item to quality, the state of control and information available from the supplier, and impact on costs (see 9.7 and 9.8).

12.2 In-Process Inspection

Inspections or tests should be considered at appropriate points in the process to verify conformity. Location and frequency will depend on the importance of the characteristics and ease of verification at the stage of production. In general, verification should be made as close as possible to the point of production of the feature or characteristic.

Verifications may include the following checks:

a) Setup and first piece inspection.
b) Inspection or test by machine operator.
c) Automatic inspection or test.
d) Fixed inspection stations at intervals through the process.
e) Patrol inspection by inspectors monitoring specified operations.

12.3 Completed Product Verification

To augment inspections and tests made during production, two forms of final verification of completed product are available. Either or both of the following may be used, as appropriate:

a) Acceptance inspections or tests may be used to ensure that items or lots produced have met performance and other quality requirements. Reference may be made to the purchase order to verify that product to be shipped agrees in type and quantity. Examples include screening (100 percent of items), lot sampling, and continuous sampling.
b) Product quality auditing of sample units selected as representative of completed production lots may be either continuous or periodic.

Acceptance inspection and product quality auditing may be used to provide rapid feedback for corrective action of product and process. Deficiencies or deviations should be reported, taken out, and reworked or repaired. Modified products should be reinspected or retested.

13.0 CONTROL OF MEASURING AND TEST EQUIPMENT

13.1 Measurement Control

Sufficient control should be maintained over all measurement systems used in the development, manufacture, installation, and servicing of a product to provide confidence in decisions or actions based on measurement data. Control should be exercised over gages, instruments, sensors, special test equipment, and related computer software. In addition, manufacturing jigs, fixtures, and process instrumentation that can affect the specified characteristics of a product, process, or service should be suitably controlled (see 11.3). Procedures should be established to monitor and maintain the measurement process itself under statistical control, including equipment, procedures, and operator skills. Measurement error should be compared with requirements and appropriate action taken when precision and/or bias requirements are not achieved.

13.2 Elements of Control

The control of measuring and test equipment and test methods should include the following factors, as appropriate:

a) Correct specification and acquisition, including range, bias, precision, robustness, and durability under specified environmental conditions for the intended service.

b) Initial calibration prior to first use in order to validate the required bias and precision; the software, and procedures controlling automatic test equipment, should also be tested.

c) Periodic recall for adjustment, repair, and recalibration, considering manufacturer's specification, the results of prior calibration, the method and extent of use, to maintain the required accuracy in use.

d) Documentary evidence covering identification of instruments, frequency of recalibration, calibration status, and procedures for recall, handling, and storage, adjustment, repair, calibration, installation, and use.

e) Traceability to reference standards of known accuracy and stability, preferably to national or international standards, or, in industries or products where such do not exist, to specially developed criteria.

13.3 Supplier Measurement Controls

The control of measuring and test equipment and procedures extend to all suppliers furnishing goods and services.

13.4 Corrective Action

Where measuring processes are found to be out of control or where measuring and test equipment is found to be outside the required calibration limits, corrective action is necessary. Evaluation should be made to determine the effects on completed work and to what extent reprocessing, retesting, recalibration, or complete rejection may be necessary. In addition, investigation of cause is important in order to avoid recurrence. This may include review of calibration methods and frequency, training, and adequacy of test equipment.

13.5 Outside Testing

The facilities of outside organizations may be used for measurement, testing, or calibration services to avoid costly duplication or additional investment, provided that the requirements given in 13.2 and 13.4 are satisfied.

14.0 NONCONFORMITY

14.1 General

The steps outlined in 14.2 to 14.7 should be taken as soon as indications occur that materials, components, or completed product do not or may not meet the specified requirements.

14.2 Identification

Suspected nonconforming items or lots should be immediately identified and the occurrence(s) recorded. Whenever possible, provision should be made as necessary to examine previous production lots.

14.3 Segregation

The nonconforming items should be segregated, wherever possible, from conforming items and adequately identified to prevent further use of them until the appropriate disposition is decided.

14.4 Review

Nonconforming items should be subjected to review by designated persons to determine whether they can be used as they are or whether they shall be repaired, reworked, reclassified, or scrapped. Persons carrying out the review should be competent to evaluate the effects of nonconformity on interchangeability, further processing, performance, reliability, safety, and esthetics (see 9.7 and 11.8).

14.5 Disposition

Disposition of nonconforming items should be taken as soon as practicable in accordance with decisions made in 14.4. Decisions to "pass" an item should be accompanied by authorized concessions/waivers, with appropriate precautions (see 15.8).

14.6 Documentation

The steps for dealing with nonconforming items should be set out in documented procedures with examples of the format of markers, forms, and reports (see 17.2).

14.7 Prevention of Recurrence

Appropriate steps should be taken to prevent the recurrence of nonconformity (see 15.5 and 15.6). Consideration should be given to establishing a file listing nonconformities to help identify those problems having a common source, contrasted with those that are unique occurrences.

15.0 CORRECTIVE ACTION

15.1 General

The implementation of corrective action begins with the detection of a quality-related problem and involves taking measures to eliminate or minimize the recurrence of a problem. Corrective action also presupposes the repair, reworking, recall, or scrapping of unsatisfactory materials or items.

15.2 Assignment of Responsibility

The responsibility and authority for instituting corrective action should be defined as part of the quality system. The coordination, recording, and monitoring of corrective action related to all aspects of the organization or a particular product should be assigned to a particular function within the organization. However, the analysis and execution may involve a variety of functions, such as sales, design, production engineering, production, and quality control.

15.3 Evaluation of Importance

The significance of a problem affecting quality should be evaluated in terms of its potential impact on such aspects as production costs, quality costs, performance, reliability, safety, and customer satisfaction.

15.4 Investigation of Possible Causes

The relationship of cause and effect should be determined, with all potential causes considered. Important variables affecting the capability of the process to meet required standards should be identified.

15.5 Analysis of Problem

In the analysis of a quality-related problem, the root cause should be determined before the preventive measures are planned. Often the root cause is not obvious, thus requiring careful analysis of the product or service specifications and of all related processes, operations, quality records, service reports, and customer complaints. Statistical methods can be useful in problem analysis (see 20).

15.6 Preventive Action

In order to prevent a future recurrence of a nonconformity, it may be necessary to change a manufacturing packing, transit, or storage process, revise a product specification and/or revise the quality system. Preventive action should be initiated to a degree appropriate to the magnitude of potential problems.

15.7 Process Controls

Sufficient control of processes and procedures should be implemented to prevent recurrence of the problem. When the preventive measures are implemented, their effect should be monitored in order to ensure that desired goals are met.

15.8 Disposition of Nonconforming Items

For work in progress, remedial action should be instituted as soon as practical in order to limit the costs of repair, reworking, or scrapping. In addition, it may be necessary to recall completed items, whether these items are in a finished goods warehouse, in transit to distributors, in their stores, or already in field use (see 16.1.3). Recall decisions are affected by considerations of safety, product liability, and customer satisfaction (see 14.5).

15.9 Permanent Changes

Permanent changes resulting from corrective action should be recorded in work instructions, manufacturing processes, product specifications, and/or the quality system. It may also be necessary to revise the procedures used to detect and eliminate potential problems.

16.0 HANDLING AND POST-PRODUCTION FUNCTIONS

16.1 Handling, Storage, Identification, Packaging, Installation, and Delivery

16.1.1 General

The handling of materials requires proper planning, control, and a documented system for incoming materials, materials in process, and finished goods; this applies not only during delivery but up to the time of being put into use.

16.1.2 Handling and Storage

The method of handling and storage of materials should provide for the correct pallets, containers, conveyors, and vehicles to prevent damage due to vibration, shock, abrasion, corrosion, temperature, or any other conditions occurring during handling and storage. Items in storage should be checked periodically to detect possible deterioration.

16.1.3 Identification

The marking and labeling of materials should be legible, durable, and in accordance with the specifications. Identifications should remain intact from the time of initial receipt to delivery to final destination. Marking should be adequate to identify a particular product in the event that a recall or special inspection becomes necessary.

16.1.4 Packaging

The methods of cleaning and preserving, and the details of packing, including moisture elimination, cushioning, blocking, and crating, should be detailed in written instructions, as appropriate.

16.1.5 Installation

Instructional documents should contribute to proper installations and should include provisions which preclude improper installation or factors degrading the quality, reliability, safety, and performance of any product or material.

16.1.6 Delivery

Items with limited shelf life or requiring special protection during transport or storage should be identified, and procedures should be maintained to ensure that deteriorated items are not put into use. Provision for protection of the quality of product is important during all phases of delivery.

16.2 After-Sales Servicing

16.2.1 Special-purpose tools or equipment for handling and servicing products during or after installation should have their design and function validated, as for any new product.

16.2.2 Measuring and test equipment used in field installation and tests should be controlled (see 13).

16.2.3 Instructions for use dealing with the assembly and installation, commissioning, operation, spares or parts lists, and servicing of any product should be comprehensive and supplied in a timely manner. The suitability of instructions for the intended reader should be verified.

16.2.4 Assurance should be provided for an adequate logistic back-up, to include technical advice, spares or parts supply, and competent servicing. Responsibility should be clearly assigned and agreed among suppliers, distributors, and users.

16.3 Marketing Reporting and Product Supervision

An early warning system may be established for reporting instances of product failure or shortcomings, as appropriate, particularly for newly introduced products, to ensure rapid corrective action.

A feedback system regarding performance in use should exist to monitor the quality characteristics of the product throughout its life cycle. This system should be designed to analyze, as a continuing operation, the degree to which the product or service satisfies customer expectations on quality, including safety and reliability.

Information on complaints, the occurrence and modes of failure, customer needs and expectations, or any problem encountered in use should be made available for design review and corrective action in the supply and/or use of the item.

17.0 QUALITY DOCUMENTATION AND RECORDS

17.1 General

The quality management system should establish, and require the maintenance of, a means for identification, collection, indexing, filing, storage, maintenance, retrieval, and disposition of pertinent quality documentation and records. Policies should be established concerning availability and access of records to customers and suppliers. Policies should also be established concerning availability and access of records to customers and suppliers. Policies should also be established concerning procedures for changes and modifications in various types of documents.

17.2 Quality Documentation

The system should require that sufficient documentation be available to follow the achievement of the required product quality and the effective operation of the quality management system. Appropriate sub-contractor documentation should be included. All documentation should be legible, dated (including revision dates), clean, readily identifiable, and maintained in an orderly manner. Data may be hard copy or stored in a computer.

In addition, the quality management system should provide a method for removing and/or disposing of documentation used in the manufacture of products when that documentation has become out-of-date.

The following are examples of the types of documents requiring control:

- Drawings.
- Specifications.
- Blueprints.
- Inspection instructions.
- Test procedures.
- Work instructions.
- Operation sheets.
- Quality manual (see 5.3.2).
- Operational procedures.
- Quality assurance procedures.

17.3 Quality Records

The system should require that sufficient records be maintained to demonstrate achievement of the required quality and verify effective operation of the quality management system.

The following are examples of the types of quality records requiring control:

- Inspection reports.
- Test data.
- Qualification reports.
- Validation reports.
- Audit reports.
- Material review reports.
- Calibration data.
- Quality cost reports.

Quality records should be retained, for a specified period, in such a manner as to be retrievable for analysis in order to identify quality trends and the need for, and effectiveness of, corrective action.

While in storage, quality records should be protected from damage, loss, and deterioration due to environmental conditions.

18.0 PERSONNEL

18.1 Training

18.1.1 General
The need for training of personnel should be identified and a method for providing that training should be established. Consideration should be given to providing training to all levels of personnel within the organization. Particular attention should be given to the selection and training of recruited personnel and personnel transferred to new assignments.

18.1.2 Executive and Management Personnel
Training should be considered which will provide executive management with an understanding of the quality system together with the tools and techniques needed for full executive management participation in the operation of the system. Executive management should also understand the criteria available to evaluate the effectiveness of the system.

18.1.3 Technical Personnel
Training should be given to the technical personnel to enhance their contribution to the success of the quality system. Training should not be restricted to personnel with primary quality assignments, but should include assignments such as marketing, procurement, and process and product engineering. Particular attention should be given to training in statistical techniques, such as process capability studies, statistical sampling, data collection and analysis, problem identification, problem analysis,

and corrective action.

18.1.4 Production Supervisors and Workers

All production supervisors and workers should be thoroughly trained in the methods and skills required to perform their tasks, i.e., the proper operation of instruments, tools, and machinery they have to use, reading and understanding the documentation provided, the relationship of their duties to quality, and safety in the work place. As appropriate, operators should be certified in their skills, such as welding. Training in basic statistical techniques should also be considered.

18.2 Qualification

The need to require formal qualification of personnel performing certain specialized operations, processes, tests, or inspections should be evaluated and implemented where necessary. Consideration should be given both to experience and demonstrated skills.

18.3 Motivation

18.3.1 General

Motivation of personnel begins with their understanding of the tasks they are expected to perform and how those tasks support the overall activities. Employees should be made aware of the advantages of proper job performance at all levels, and of the effects of poor job performance on other employees, customer satisfaction, operating costs, and the economic well-being of the company.

18.3.2 Application

Efforts to motivate employees towards quality of performance should not be directed only at production workers, but also at personnel in marketing, design, documentation, purchasing, inspection, test, packing and shipping, and after-sale services. Management, professional, and staff employees should be included.

18.3.3 Quality Awareness

The need for quality should be emphasized through an awareness program which may include introduction and elementary programs for new employees, periodic refresher programs for long-standing employees, provision for employees to initiate corrective actions, and other methods.

18.3.4 Measuring Quality

Accurate, definitive measures of quality achievement attributable to individuals or groups may be publicized to let employees and production line supervisors see for themselves what they, as a group or as individuals, are achieving and to encourage them to produce satisfactory quality. Management should provide recognition of performance when satisfactory quality levels are attained.

19.0 PRODUCT SAFETY AND LIABILITY

The safety aspects of product or service quality should be identified with the aim of enhancing product safety and minimizing product liability. Steps should be taken both to limit the risk of product liability and to minimize the number of cases by:

a) Identifying relevant safety standards in order to make the formulation of product or service specifications more effective.
b) Carrying out design evaluation tests and prototype (or model) testing for safety and documenting the test results.
c) Analyzing instructions for warnings to the user, maintenance manuals and labeling, and promotional material in order to minimize misinterpretation.
d) Developing a means of traceability to facilitate product recall if features are discovered compromising safety and to allow a planned investigation of products or services suspected of having unsafe features (see 15.4 and 16.1.3).

NOTE: See Appendix II (page 297), *Product Liability and User Safety,* for a more extensive presentation of this subject.

20.0 USE OF STATISTICAL METHODS

20.1 Applications

Correct application of modern statistical methods is an important element at all stages in the quality loop and is not limited to the post-production (or inspection) stages. Applications may be for purposes such as:

a) Market analysis.
b) Product design.
c) Reliability specification, longevity/durability prediction.
d) Process control/process capability studies.
e) Determination of quality levels/inspection plans.
f) Data analysis/performance assessment/defect analysis.

20.2 Statistical Techniques

Specific statistical methods and applications available include, but are not limited to, the following:

a) Design of experiments/factorial analysis.
b) Analysis of variance/regression analysis.

291

c)   Safety evaluation/risk analysis.
d)   Tests of significance.
e)   Quality control charts/cusum techniques.
f)   Statistical sampling inspection.

NOTE: See Appendix I (page 293) for a more extensive presentation of *Sampling and Other Statistical Methods.*

NOTE: Attention is drawn to the activities of the ASQC Divisions and Technical Committees as well as ASQC Standards and to ISO/TC 69, *Applications of Statistical Methods* (see ISO Standards Handbook 3, *Statistical Methods*) and IEC/TC 56, *Reliability and Maintainability,* which have published several standard guides (or codes of practice) to assist in this sphere.

Appendix I — Sampling and Other Statistical Methods

This Appendix is not a part of American National Standard ANSI/ASQC Q94-1987 *Quality Management and Quality System Elements — Guidelines,* and was not contained in ISO 9004, but is included for information purposes only.

1. BACKGROUND. Effective data analysis is a keystone to efficient, economic control of quality. The correct application of modern statistical approaches is therefore an important element in a sound quality control program. There are available a wide range of statistical methods for applications such as process control, evaluation of alternatives, experiment design, market research, and inspection procedures. This appendix is restricted to a brief description of the principles of, advantages of, and types of sampling and of such tools as process control charts and acceptance sampling.

2. SAMPLING INSPECTION. Sampling inspection involves drawing a random sample from a lot of the product, or, in continuous sampling, drawing sample units from the stream of product. This is done either to evaluate the process or to make a decision regarding disposition of the lot, or, in continuous sampling, to make decisions relative to disposition of sampled units and severity of inspection frequency.

3. USES OF SAMPLING INSPECTION. Properly employed, statistical sampling procedures are valuable to:

3.1 Estimate level of quality objectively.

3.2 Achieve control of a process.

3.3 Economically attain assurance regarding average or long-run quality by:

3.3.1 (a) Shifting to tightened inspection and thus accentuating lot rejections, which will put increased pressure on a producer to correct deterioration in quality to a level worse than a given acceptable quality level (AQL), and (b) discontinuing inspection when tightened inspection does not improve the quality.

3.3.2 Performing 100 percent inspection of rejected lots in lot-by-lot sampling to attain a designated average outgoing quality limit (AOQL).

3.3.3 In continuous sampling, performing 100 percent inspection of alternate periods of output to attain a given AOQL (see 6.2.2, this Appendix).

4. ADVANTAGES OF SAMPLING. Sampling has the advantage of economically using manpower and enabling more careful examination of those items in the sample. It is the only practical way when the test makes the item unusable for its end purpose. When there is cumulative evidence that a process is running at a high quality level, a shift may be made to reduce sampling inspection to attain further savings in inspection costs.

5. TYPES OF SAMPLING.

5.1 Statistical sampling procedures for giving assurance regarding a lot or process average percent nonconforming may be classed generally into one of two types, attribute sampling and variables sampling.

5.1.1 ATTRIBUTE SAMPLING. Each sampled unit of product is classified as conforming or nonconforming with possibly some indication of the seriousness of the nonconformity being checked.

5.1.2 VARIABLES SAMPLING FOR PERCENT NONCONFORMING. In this case the determination of lot acceptability comes from considering the actual measurements made on sample items and a decision is based on certain functions of these measurements, e.g., their mean and standard deviation. While variables sampling requires fewer observations for a given degree of assurance, it is generally more costly to administer and considers only a single quality characteristic. Determination of precise risks depends on the validity of the assumptions that must be made regarding the nature of the distribution of product quality.

5.2 Statistical sampling procedures are also used to give assurance regarding a lot or process mean quality or a lot or process standard deviation. These usually make use of a sample mean and/or a sample standard deviation.

6. BASIC STATISTICAL METHODS. The two most common statistical methods used in quality control are process control charts and acceptance sampling.

6.1 PROCESS CONTROL CHARTS. Statistical quality control charts are used to attain and maintain a state of statistical control of a process. Process control charts permit identification and analysis of causes of significant variations in manufacturing operations. A commonly used attribute control chart is the p-chart and a commonly used variables control chart is the $\overline{X}$-R chart combination. For definitions and terminology for a variety of control charts, see ANSI/ASQC A1.

6.1.1 P-CHART. This chart records the percent nonconforming in samples taken from the process at more or less regular intervals.

6.1.2 $\overline{X}$-R CHART COMBINATION. This chart records jointly the mean and range of samples taken from the process at more or less regular intervals.

6.2 ACCEPTANCE SAMPLING. This is a procedure that may be applied to individual lots or to continuous production.

6.2.1 LOT-BY-LOT SAMPLING. Units of product typically are selected randomly from a lot and a decision reached whether to accept or reject the lot based on the quality of the sample examined. Acceptance sampling may be single, double, multiple, or unit sequential sampling depending on whether additional stages of sample selection are to be made before an acceptance decision is reached. Special sampling procedures include chain sampling and skip-lot sampling. Sampling plans are available for both attributes and variables.* They generally relate sample size to lot size. A single sampling plan for attributes specifies a sample size and acceptance/rejection numbers, which defines the acceptance criteria for lot acceptance. The sample size normally does not increase in proportion to the lot size.

6.2.2 CONTINUOUS SAMPLING. Continuous sampling plans consist of alternate periods of sampling inspection of individual items and 100 percent inspection (at the beginning of the inspection process or when loss of control has been observed), the aim being to assure a given average outgoing quality limit (AOQL). These may be used when production is continuous and the formation of lots is not a normal part of production, or where the volume or weight of multiple units is so great as to preclude lot formation.* *

---

*The most widely used lot acceptance sampling references are MIL-STD-105D (ANSI Z1.4), for attribute sampling, and MIL-STD-414 (ANSI Z1.9), for variables sampling. These are AQL indexed schemes, but both standards give charts of operating characteristic curves and MIL-STD-105D gives tables of LQ (LQL) values. Economical AOQL plans and LTPD (LQL) plans are given in H. F. Dodge and H. G. Romig, Sampling Inspection Tables. Plans that are indexed with respect to a process (or individual lot) limiting quality level (LQL) with a designated probability of lot acceptance (Pa) at the specified LQL give an assurance that lots from a process with average quality (or an individual lot with quality) worse than the LQL will have a probability of acceptance no greater than Pa. For terminology used in acceptance sampling see ANSI/ASQC A2.

* *See MIL-STD-1235A. This standard lists AQLs as well as AOQLs, but the AQLs are simply indexes to facilitate coordination with lot-by-lot plans. With reference to a continuous sampling plan, an AQL has no meaning.

7. OTHER STATISTICAL METHODS. In addition to the basic methods of statistical quality control mentioned previously, there is a wide range of statistical techniques available for the analysis and control of quality, not only in the production process and in finished lot evaluation, as above, but also in reliability analysis, as a part of design review and control. These techniques include regression analysis, tests of significance, risk analysis, design of experiments, and analysis of variance. For discussion of these techniques see a textbook on statistics.

8. SAMPLING RISK. When critical requirements are of significant importance, 100 percent inspection, or even 200 percent or more complete inspection may be called for, but will not assure 100 percent certainty because of equipment and personnel variability. It may be necessary to use other techniques for more complete assurance.*** All statistical sampling involves an element of risk. These risks apply both to producers and consumers, and cannot be completely eliminated, although they can be accurately assessed by statistical techniques. Risks of sampling depend not only on the size of the sample taken, and the acceptance criteria, but also in the case of variables sampling, on the particular distribution of quality measurements that exists.

9. EFFECTIVE USE OF STATISTICAL METHODS. Using statistical sampling requires proper application with adequate knowledge of the limitations and protection of the plans being used. It is advisable that statistical sampling methods be administered by someone who has formal training in their use. To assure effective use of sampling, there should be:

1. Stated quality objectives (for example, AQL, LQL, consumer's risk, and producer's risk).
2. Lot and sample identification, including the provision for segregating accepted and unaccepted items and lots.
3. Adherence to rules for selection of random samples.
4. Specified test, inspection, and measurement procedures.
5. A procedure for correcting rejected lots, such as sorting inspection and rework of defectives, or submittal to a board of review.
6. Provision for corrective action to be taken to avoid or minimize the opportunity for recurrence.

***To assure critical requirements some people view 100 percent, 200 percent, or more complete inspections of a lot as inspection of a sample (of lot size) from the process and will accept the lot only if the complete inspection(s) yield zero (0) or at the most only one (1) nonconforming item.

Appendix II — Product Liability and User Safety

This Appendix is not a part of American National Standard ANSI/ASQC Q94-1987 *Quality Management and Quality System Elements — Guidelines,* and was not contained in ISO 9004, but is included for information purposes only.

1. GENERAL. Exposure to product liability can be minimized by following, where applicable, the quality system outlined in this document.

2. COMPANY POLICY STATEMENT ON PRODUCT SAFETY. The essential element in the continuous development, design, production, marketing, and service of safe products is total and organized commitment to the task by all management levels. This starts with a documented statement of policy on product safety.

2.1 SCOPE. The policy statement defines product safety objectives and assigns responsibility for accomplishing these objectives.

2.2 SAFETY STANDARDS. Voluntary safety standards from industry and concensus standardization bodies, domestic and international, are often incorporated into a company statement of policy to simplify the formulation of objectives and detailed specifications.

2.3 LEGISLATION. Federal, state, local, international, and other national safety requirements affecting products are, of necessity, considered, as well as rulings affecting their interpretation.

2.4 PRODUCT SAFETY COUNCIL. Where applicable, an internal council may be established to guide and monitor activities related to the company's product safety policy. The council usually consists of representatives from all functional elements concerned with safety aspects of the product. Specific responsibilities of the council should include:

1. Periodic audits of company procedures related to product safety, including design validation (see 8.5) and design requalification (see 8.9).
2. Review and appraisal of legislation and the actions of regulatory agencies related to product liability and product safety.
3. Review and appraisal of standards related to the safety and reliability of company products.

2.5 USE OF THIRD PARTIES. Where applicable, evaluation and testing of production prototypes internally may be supplemented by independent third parties that validate compliance with applicable product safety standards and authorize the use of a marking to that effect. The marking should serve also as evidence that the system used to assure quality conformance of production items is acceptable.

3. DESIGN AND DESIGN REVIEWS RELATED TO PRODUCT SAFETY. New products developed with a well-planned design and documented analysis of safety factors can be defended more readily in product liability law suits. The company that can prove to a court of law that it has a "design for safety" function is in a better position to prove that it has met its legal and moral obligations to society (see 8.5.2).

4. DOCUMENTATION OF TEST RESULTS. Documentation of test methods, procedures, and results is advisable. Legal questions concerning product safety often are answered best by presenting results of development and/or design evaluation tests, product qualification, and product testing. Retention of test results should follow the guidelines of paragraph 8 of this Appendix.

5. SAFETY REVIEW OF USER'S MANUALS AND PROMOTIONAL MATERIAL. Analysis and demonstration of user's instructions, maintenance and manuals and promotional material by the appropriate functional departments can predict their impact on safety. Counsel, versed in product liability law, then can review these items to determine if any statements may be subject to misinterpretation in product liability claims.

6. FIELD PERFORMANCE REPORTING SYSTEM. A well formulated field performance feedback system can supply pertinent information on details of failures affecting safety that can assist in design improvements.

7. HAZARD WARNINGS. Important to a "design for safety" program are the written warnings to users for hazardous or potentially dangerous conditions in the installation, operation, maintenance, repair, storage, or discarding of products. Legal, service, and engineering departments can analyze the express and implied obligations that their companies may be assuming through their publication. Words that are clear, precise, conspicuous, and neither overstated nor understated, whether on a label or in literature furnished with the product, will be most effective.

8. RETENTION OF RECORDS. All inspection and production records pertaining to the product's safety requirements should be retained for a minimum time in accordance with regulations, standards, and good practice stated by law. This includes not only new but also reworked and repaired parts. Good loss control practice considers anticipated product life as a factor in determining record retention time plus the requirements of statute of limitation and repose.

9. PRODUCT LIABILITY INFORMATION. Many firms retain a reference library with current copies of regulations, codes, standards, technical literature, periodicals, insurance company reports, and international standards and application requirements applicable to the firms' product liability considerations.

10. PRODUCT IDENTIFICATION SYSTEMS FOR TRACEABILITY DURING RECALL. The possibility of a product recall involving safety or a planned investigation of products suspected of having unsafe features affirms the need and use for an identification and traceability system as outlined in 16.1.3.

11. PRODUCT LIABILITY INSURANCE. The services of product liability insurers or risk managers should be utilized into the corporate task of safety improvements.

AMERICAN NATIONAL STANDARD

ANSI/ASQC C1-1985 *Specification of General Requirements for a Quality Program*

Abstract

Specification of General Requirements for a Quality Program concerns the establishment and maintenance of a quality program by a contractor to assure compliance with contract requirements in the areas of quality management, design information, procurement, manufacture, acceptance, and documentation.

AMERICAN NATIONAL STANDARD: An American National Standard implies a consensus of those substantially concerned with its scope and provisions. An American National Standard is intended as a guide to aid the manufacturer, the consumer, and the general public. The existence of an American National Standard does not in any respect preclude anyone, whether he has approved the standard or not, from manufacturing, marketing, purchasing, or using products, processes, or procedures not conforming to the standard. American National Standards are subject to periodic review, and users are cautioned to obtain the latest editions.

CAUTION NOTICE: This American National Standard may be revised or withdrawn at any time. The procedures of the American National Standards Institute require that action be taken to reaffirm, revise, or withdraw this Standard no later than five years from the date of publication. Purchasers of American National Standards may receive current information on all standards by calling or writing the American National Standards Institute.

Approved November 1985
Revision ANSI/ASQC Standard C1-1968
ANSI Std. Z1.8-1971
Approved November 18, 1971
American National Standards Institute, Inc.

Foreword

(This Foreword is not a part of the American National Standard *General Requirements for a Quality Program.*)

The Standards Committee of the American Society for Quality Control was formed in 1947, being "authorized to study and select symbols, concepts, terms, procedures, and other matters which it feels the Society might standardize to advantage and to make recommendations to the Board of Directors regarding such standardization."

The Standards Committee requires periodic review and reaffirmation or revision of ASQC standards at regular intervals. This revision of the 1968 standard includes extensive editorial changes to bring terminology up-to-date with common usage. Wording has been broadened throughout to clarify the intended application of the standard internally as a management document and externally as a sales and purchase specification. Applicability of the standard to services as well as products has been emphasized. A section on interpretation of limits has been added, and the sections on quality records and audits have been expanded.

Writing Committee

The following individuals were members of the Writing Commmittee for this revision to ANSI/ASQC C1-1968:

David L. Field, chairman	Charles V. Leach
William Anderson	Richard A. Maass
Andrew B. Andreason	John A. Malatesta
Arthur R. Blank	Don McNeil
Dr. C. L. Carter	Charles E. Meadows
Robert C. Cloutier	Meril Monashkin
J. Dol	Robert A. Morris
Thomas F. Frongillo	August B. Mundel
Charles W. Gaw	Paul E. Ruhling
Alfred Gieser	Ben Silver
H. D. Greiner	Walter Uhorchak
Robert E. Jouppi	Richard Weber
Richard J. Laford	Quitman White, Jr.
Roger G. Langevin	James C. Wilson
Barry Lawrimore	Howard N. Wilson

Marvin Weir

1. DEFINITION OF TERMS

1.1 Quality Program
The documented plans for implementing the quality system.

1.2 Quality System
The organizational structure, responsibilities, procedures, processes, and resources for implementing quality management.

1.3 Inspection
Activities, such as measuring, examining, testing, gauging one or more characteristics of a product or service, and comparing these with specified requirements to determine conformity.

1.4 Affected Organization
A term used herein to designate the individual or organization on whom this Standard is imposed.

1.5 Specifying Organization
A term used herein to designate the individual or organization that imposes this Standard on a contractor, vendor, supplier, or an internal organization.

1.6 Other ANSI/ASQC Definitions
Attention is called to the existence of additional ASQC definitions, including "Quality Plan," which are contained in ANSI/ASQC A3, *Quality Systems Terminology.*

2. SCOPE

2.1 Applicability
When this standard is prescribed or specified by contract or management directive, it provides a specification of the general requirements to be met by the quality program of a contractor or other organization. All the requirements apply except to the extent that they are specifically deleted, supplemented, or amended in the contract or directive.

2.2 General Purpose
This Standard was designed to provide a description of the basic quality principles essential to the assurance of quality. It is intended that it be imposed internally by management and externally through both sales and purchase contracts. Broad use of this Standard is intended to minimize the number of nonstandard and conflicting quality requirements that otherwise will be found in sales and purchase contracts.

This Standard requires the establishment and maintenance of a quality program by the Affected Organization and by its contractors and subcontractors to assure adequate control and assurance of quality. The quality program, including its procedures and operations, shall be documented and shall be subject to review by the Specifying Organization. The program shall apply to the control of quality throughout all areas of performance, including as appropriate, the design, procurement, identification, stocking, and issue of material; the entire process of manufacture; and the packaging, storing, and shipping of material.

The program shall provide that, as early as possible, discrepancies (product nonconformities and program deficiencies) shall be discovered, reported, and corrective action taken.

2.3 Other ANSI/ASQC Quality System Standards

Attention is called to the existence of other systems standards, including ANSI/ASQC Q90-1987 through Q94-1987, quality management and quality assurance standards. These are the technical equivalents to the International Standards Organziation (ISO) 9000 Standards.

3. REQUIREMENTS

3.1 Quality Management

3.1.1 General. There shall be planning, direction, and control in the sense of measurement and evaluation of the effectiveness of the quality system and the quality program.

3.1.2 Organization. Administration of the quality program shall be vested in a responsible, authoritative element of the organization, with unhindered access to senior management. This organization shall be staffed by technically competent personnel with freedom to make decisions without pressure or bias. It shall also have authority to ensure that quality requirements are consistently applied and maintained.

3.1.3 Procedures. Written quality control, test, and inspection procedures shall be used for all pertinent operations and for material, process, and product evaluations.

These procedures shall be kept current and shall be available at all locations where they will be used.

3.2 Design Information

3.2.1 General. Design information for a product (such as drawings, specifications, and standards) shall be maintained to ensure that the products are manufactured, inspected, and tested to the latest applicable requirements. In like manner, task definitions for a service shall be maintained to ensure that the services are performed and inspected to the latest applicable requirements.

3.2.2 Change Control. The Affected Organization will have a change control program acceptable to the Specifying Organization.All changes to design information or task definition shall be processed in a manner that will ensure accomplishment as specified, and a record of acutal incorporation points (by date, batch, lot, unit, or other specific identification) shall be maintained.

3.3 Procurement

3.3.1 General. Control over procurement sources shall be maintained to ensure that services and supplies conform to specified requirements, including this Standard. Purchase orders (or contracts) shall be controlled to ensure timely incorporation of pertinent technical and quality requirements, including authorized changes. Adequate records of inspections and tests performed on purchased material shall be maintained.

3.3.2 Source Inspection. The buyer and his authorized representatives reserve the right to inspect, at the source, any supplies furnished or services rendered under the contract. Inspection at the source shall not necessarily constitute acceptance, nor shall it relieve the seller of his responsibility to furnish acceptable product. When it is not practical, cost effective, or feasible to determine quality conformance of purchased items upon receipt, inspection at the source may be performed.

3.3.3 Purchased Material. All purchased material shall be evaluated to assure conformance with the requirements of applicable standards and specifications. When required, shipment of materials shall be accompanied by verifiable objective evidence that demonstrates the conformance of material and processes to the requirements stated in the purchase order or product specification. The validity of objective evidence of quality shall be verified periodically by the buyer. Provisions will be made for withholding from use all incoming supplies pending completion of each required inspection and test or receipt of necessary test reports. The seller shall be notified whenever nonconforming materials are received and corrective action shall be initiated when warranted.

3.3.4 Raw Materials. Raw material shall normally be tested to determine conformance to applicable specifications. Unless otherwise specified by the purchase order or the product specification, certified test reports identifiable with the material may be accepted as evidence of such tests. When certifications are used as a basis for acceptance, the test results shall be compared with specification requirements. Furthermore, the validity of certifications shall be periodically verified by the buyer through independent testing.

3.4 Material Control

3.4.1 General. Methods and facilities shall be established for controlling the identification, handling, and storage of purchased and fabricated material. The identification shall include indications of the inspection status of the material. These controls shall be maintained from the time of receipt of the material, through all processing or assembly until delivery to the customer in order to protect the material from damage, deterioration, loss, or unauthorized substitution, etc.

3.5 Production

3.5.1 General. Control shall be maintained over production processes to prevent product or service nonconformity and excessive variability, and to assure conformance of the characteristics of product and processes which can be verified at the time and point of manufacture.

3.5.2 Process Control. Evaluations and controls shall be implemented and maintained at appropriately located points in the production process to assure continuous control of product and service quality.

3.5.3 Special Processes. Methods and facilities shall be provided to assure conformance with requirements for special process specifications, such as welding, plating, anodizing, nondestructive testing, heat-treating, soldering, sterilizing, polymerizing, homogenizing, drying, carding, and testing of materials. Certifications for personnel, processes, and equipment shall be maintained.

3.6 Acceptance

3.6.1 General. Inspection and testing of completed products and services shall be performed as necessary to assure that contract requirements have been met. Surveillance shall be maintained over handling, preservation, storage, marking, packing, and shipping operations to assure compliance with requirements and to prevent damage, deterioration, loss, or substitutions.

3.6.2 Sampling Inspection. Any acceptance sampling procedures that differ from those required by the contract or specificaton shall afford adequate assurance that the quality meets acceptable levels. Such procedures are subject to approval by the Specifying Organization.

3.6.3 Nonconforming Material. Procedures and facilities for the handling of nonconforming material shall require prominent identification of the material and prompt removal (if practical) from the work area. Unless otherwise provided in the product specification or contract, the Affected Organization has the option of scrapping the material or requesting disposition instructions from the Specifying Organization.

3.7 Measuring Instruments

3.7.1 General. Validity of measurements and tests shall be assured through the use of suitable inspection measuring and test equipment of the range, accuracy, and precision necessary to determine conformance of articles. Calibration procedures shall be utilized and measurements shall be performed by qualified personnel in an environment controlled to the extent necessary to assure the required accuracy. At intervals established to ensure continued validity, measuring devices shall be verified or calibrated against certified standards that are traceable to national standards or naturally occurring physical constants. Tooling used as media of inspection shall be included in this program. Furthermore, every device so verified shall bear an indication attesting to the current status and showing the date (or other basis) on which inspection or recalibration is required next.

3.8 Interpretation of Limits

3.8.1 General. All limits are considered to be absolute. Limits, regardless of the number of places, are to be considered as being continued with zeros. For purposes of determining conformance with limits, the measured value is compared directly with the specified value without rounding. Any deviation, however small, outside the specified limiting value signifies nonconformance with that limit.

3.9 Quality Information

3.9.1 General. Information from control areas described in paragraphs 3.1 through 3.7 of this Standard shall be systematically utilized for the prevention, detection, and correction of deficiencies in the program that affect quality.

3.9.2 Quality Records. Inspection and test records shall be maintained for both conforming and nonconforming product. Unless otherwise required by the Specifying Organization (or by law), the Affected Organization shall retain all quality records for a period of three years after the final delivery under an order or contract. Such records shall be available to the Specifying Organization upon request.

A continuing review of these records and internal auditing records shall be made, and summary information shall be reported periodically to responsible management. All records shall be mechanically generated or handwritten in ink, dated, and traceable to the originator of the data.

3.9.3 Corrective Action. Prompt action shall be taken to correct conditions that cause nonconforming materials and program problems. Use shall be made of feedback data generated by the customer as well as data generated internally.

4. QUALITY PROGRAM AUDITS

4.1 Internal Audits
Internal quality audits shall be conducted by the Affected Organization to assure the adequacy of the program and the quality of the product.

4.2 External Audits
Quality programs will be audited by the Specifying Organization for conformance to the intent of this Standard. Disapproval of the program or major portions thereof may be cause for withholding acceptance of product or disqualification from future business considerations.

APPENDIX C

ADDITIONAL READING

1. Aljian, G.W., ed. *Purchasing Handbook*. New York: McGraw-Hill Book Company, 1986.

2. Feigenbaum, A.B. *Total Quality Control*. New York: McGraw-Hill Book Company, 1951.

3. Johnson, R.H., and R.T. Weber. *Buying Quality*. New York: Franklin Watts, 1985.

4. Juran, J.M. *Quality Control Handbook*. New York: McGraw-Hill Book Company, 1951.

5. Juran, J.M., and F.M. Gryna. *Quality Planning and Analysis*. New York: McGraw-Hill Book Company, 1970.

6. Laford, R.J. *Ship-to-Stock*. Milwaukee: ASQC Quality Press, 1986.

7. Western Electric Company. *Statistical Quality Control Handbook*. Western Electric, 1956 (6th printing 1982).

Procurement Quality Control

APPENDIX D

BIBLIOGRAPHY

Aquino, Michael A. "Improving Purchased Material Quality." *Purchasing World* 29, No. 5 (May 1985): 100-102.

Bain, William Jr. "Total-Value Management: The New Road to Competitive Advantage." *Chief Executive,* No. 33 (Autumn 1985): 46-49.

Barks, Joseph V. "Holland: More Strategies for International Distribution." *Distribution* 85, No. 5 (May 1985): 64-72.

Beels, Gregory. "Strategy for Survival." *Quality* 24, No. 4 (April 1985): 16.

Berry, Bryan H. "Now Chrysler Wants to Take on the World." *Iron Age* 229, No. 22 (November 1986): 45-48.

Bertrand, Kate. "Crafting 'Win-Win' Situations in Buyer-Supplier Relations." *Business Marketing* 76, No. 6 (June 1986): 42-50.

Boyer, Edward. "Are Japanese Managers Biased Against Americans?" *Fortune* 114, No. 5 (September 1986): 72-75.

Bridges, Linda. "LAN Leasing." *PC Week* 3 (January 1986): 51.

Brooks, Sandra. "Defiance is Termed 'World Class.' " *Production* 3, No. 2 (February 1986): 13.

Brush, Gary G., Thomas C. Hsiang, William McKeown, and Thomas Rogers. "After the Bell System Break Up: Bellcore Supplier Quality." *Quality Progress* 17, No. 11 (November 1984): 16-18.

Burgess, John A. "Developing a Supplier Certification Program." *Quality,* No. 1 (January 1987): 36.

Burgess, John A. "RIP: A Rejection Improvement Program." *Quality Progress* 17, No. 11 (November 1984): 70-72.

Burke, Jane. "Changing Systems: Who is Abandoning Whom?" *Library Journal* 111 (February 1986): 55.

Cherry, Joseph V. "Vendor's Viewpoint: Quality, Response, and Delivery." *Quality Progress* 17, No. 11 (November 1984): 40-42.

Cloer, W.C. "Objective: Zero Defects Suppliers." *Quality Progress* 17, No. 11 (November 1984): 20-22.

Debacco, Tom. "Integrate to Sell." *Systems International* 14, No. 11 (November 1986): 119-120.

Derose, Louis J. "Assuring Supplier Quality." *Purchasing World* 27, No. 11 (November 1983): 40.

Devlin, James M. "Weaker $ Turns Nordic Customers to U.S. Suppliers." *Business America* 9 (March 1986): 13.

Ealey, Lance. "World-Class Suppliers: How They Make the Grade." *Automotive Industries* (January 1987): 1-87.

Ergas, Henry. "Information Technology Standards: The Issues." *Telecommunications* 20, No. 9 (September 1986): 127-133.

Faillace, Joseph N. "Managing the QA Database." *Quality Progress* 19, No. 11 (November 1986): 13-16.

Farrell, Paul V. "Is There a Role for Purchasing in Improving U.S. Productivity?" *Purchasing World* 29, No. 9 (September 1985): 42.

Feldman, Allen W. "Vendor Quality Rating and Customer Perception." *Quality Progress* 17, No. 11 (November 1984): 64-66.

"Glossary of Selected Terms Related to Testing and Inspection." *1983 Buyer's Guide and Directory* 1. Metals Park, Ohio: American Society for Metals, 1983.

Goodman, Jeffrey S. "Future Resistance: Setting Standards for Software Vendors." *Credit and Financial Management* 88, No. 5 (May 1986): 17-18, 21.

Gordon, Howard, "The Multivendor Muddle." *Network World* 3, No. 35 (November 1986): 43-44.

Greenburg, Harold, and Paul Huppenbaur. "Ship to Stock — A Quality Partnership Success Story." *ASQC 38th Annual Quality Congress Transactions.* Milwaukee: American Society for Quality Control, May 1984. 46-51.

Grenier, Robert. "Total Quality Assurance, Part V." *Quality* 25, No. 4 (April 1986): 38-41.

Hagan, John T. "The Management of Quality: Preparing for a Competitive Future." *Quality Progress* 17, No. 11 (November 1984): 12-15.

Harbour, Jim. "Is New-Tech Really the Answer?" *Automotive Industries* (July 1986): 9.

Bibliography

Harper, Doug. "Value Added, the Key to Distributor Survival." *Industrial Distribution* 75, No. 11 (November 1986): 58.

Hart, Robert F. "Letter...To All Single Source Suppliers." *Quality* 25, No. 4 (April 1986): 64-65.

Hayes, Glenn E. "World-Class Vendor Quality." *Quality* 25, No. 6 (June 1986): 14-18.

Hoeffer, E. "How Ford Makes Quality Happen." *Purchasing* 90, No. 5 (March 1981): 51, 53.

Holmes, Donald. "A Quality Portfolio Management Chart." *Quality* 25, No. 12 (December 1986): 67.

Houston, Jerry. "Torque Auditing for SPC." *Quality* 25, No. 11 (November 1986): 29-33.

Huber, Robert F. "Assembly Gives a Perspective on Costs." *Production Week* 95, No. 5 (May 1985): 34-38.

Hunt, Robert O. "Quality from the Source." *Quality* 21, No. 4 (April 1982): 54-56.

Karabatsos, Nancy A. "World-Class Quality." *Quality* 23, No. 1 (January 1986): 14-18.

Kimber, Raymond J. "Chrysler's Renaissance." *Quality* 23, No. 6 (June 1984): 80-81.

Kirland, Carl. "JIT Manufacturing — What You Need to Know." *Plastics Technology* (August 1984): 63-68.

Krepchin, Ira P. "How MRP II and JIT Work Together at DuPont." *Modern Material Handling* 41, No. 15 (December 1986): 73-76.

Laford, Richard. "Cut Inspection Costs and Improve Quality with Ship-to-Stock." *Bureau of Business Practice Production Bulletin* 606 (March 1986): 1-4.

Laford, Richard. "Ship-to-Stock." *Quality Progress* 17, No. 11 (November 1984): 52-54.

Laford, Richard. "Ship-to-Stock." *30th EOQC Annual Conference Proceedings.* Stockholm: European Organization for Quality Control, June 1986. pp. 147-154.

Laford, Richard. *Ship-to-Stock: An Alternative to Incoming Inspection.* Milwaukee: ASQC Quality Press, 1986.

Laford, Richard, and Robert Steers. "Receiving Inspection Ship to Stock, Part 1 and Part 2." *33rd ASQC Annual Quality Congress Transactions.* Milwaukee: American Society for Quality Control, May 1979. 68-72.

Lindenmuth, Richard. "Stabilizing Volatile Telephone Instrument Market." *Telephony* 208, No. 6 (February 1985): 126-132.

Maass, Richard A. *For Goodness' Sake, Help.* Milwaukee: ASQC Quality Press, 1986.

Maass, Richard A. "World Class Quality — An Innovative Rx for Survival." *ASQC 39th Annual Quality Congress Transactions.* Milwaukee: American Society for Quality Control, May 1985. 258-274.

MacDonald, Roger, Paul Saacke, and Gary Brush. "The Bottom Line on Quality: Training Reaches Beyond QA Personnel." *Quality Progress* 18, No. 11 (November 1985): 59-61.

Maraschiello, Bill. "JIT and the Receiving Room." *Handling Shipping and Management* 27, No. 8 (August 1986): 36-38.

Matthews, Joseph R. "Boy Scouts from Missouri." *Library Journal* 111, (February 1986): 51.

McBryde, Vernon E. "In Today's Market, Quality's Best Focus for Upper Management." *IE* (July 1986): 51-55.

McCasland, Charles. "JIT + SPC = Q(uality)." *Manufacturing Systems* 3, No. 7 (July 1985): 47-48.

Moskal, B.S. "Just-in-Time — Putting the Squeeze on Suppliers." *Industry Week* 222, No. 1 (July 1984): 59-60, 62.

O'Neal, Charles. "New Operating Philosophy Means Smart Supplier Selection is a Must." *Marketing News* 20, No. 23 (November 1986): 31.

Palda, Kristina S. "Technological Insensitivity: Concept and Measurement." *Netherlands Research Policy* 15, No. 4 (August 1986): 187-198.

Pantases, Angeline. "Vendors Hunt for the Key to Success." *Datamation* 32 (May 1986): 82.

Pelchat, Raymond. "Quest — Quality Enhanced Supplier Test." *ASQC 39th Annual Quality Congress Transactions.* Milwaukee: American Society for Quality Control, May 1985. 41-46.

Pennucci, Nicholas. "Assuring Vendor Process Control to Reduce Incoming Sampling." *Quality Progress* 17, No. 11 (November 1984): 56-57.

Schonberger, Richard J. *Japanese Manufacturing Techniques.* New York: The Free Press, 1982.

Bibliography

Schonberger, Richard J. *World Class Manufacturing.* New York: The Free Press, 1986.

Sehnert, Tim. "Getting Suppliers Involved in Purchasing Quality Improvement." *Purchasing World* 30, No. 3 (March 1986): 68-69.

Serchuk, Alan. "Rate Supplier Quality Openly." *Purchasing* 74, No. 1 (January 1973): 53-54.

Shaw, Donald R. "Determining Package Quotient-Supplier Quality: User Needs." *Data Management* 17, No. 3 (March 1979): 16-19.

Shortell, Ann. "The Auditors." *Canadian Business* 59, No. 11 (November 1986): 38-44.

Shrabek, Quentin R. "Process Diagnostics — Seven Steps for Problem Solving." *Quality Progress* 19, No. 11 (November 1986): 40-44.

Stone, Robert B. "What Major Companies Expect from a Supplier and His Product." *Production* 91, No. 5 (May 1983): 29, 31.

"Supplier Quality Improvement Today." *Quality Progress* 17, No. 11 (November 1984): 48-51.

"Supplier Quality Improvement Today — Part II. *Quality Progress* 17, No. 12 (December 1984): 35-38.

Sullivan, Kristina. "Users Turn to LAN Vendors for Multiuser Databases." *PC Week* 3, (February 1986): 127.

Talley, Dorsey J. "Cost Cutting with the Lone Ranger Concept." *Manage* 34, No. 4 (October 1982): 12-14.

Teja, Edward. "PC Board Vendors Rush to Fill EGA Standards." *Mini-Micro Systems* 19, No. 9 (July 1986): 69-81.

Temkin, Robert H. "Automating Auditing: Auditing Will Never be the Same." *Corporate Accounting* 4, No. 4 (Fall 1986): 56-59.

Tolan, Thomas. "Provider Quality: Long Distance Inspection Services." *Quality Progress* 17, No. 11 (November 1984): 74-75.

Unger, Harlow. "Car Makers Force Steel Industry Turnaround." *Industrial Management* 9, No. 10 (November 1985): 11.

Wortham, William A. "Problem-Solving in the QC Area Creates a 'Ripple Effect.' " *Industrial Engineering* 18, No. 7 (July 1986): 78-82.

INDEX

Index

Statistical process control (SPC), 10, 113, 115, 205

Strategy, 9-11

Supplier certification, 45, 78, 107-111, 121, 205

Supplier survey, 191-194
    preparation, 129-130
    site, 4, 129-148
    team, 5, 130-132

Survey, 205

System:
    audit, 205
    survey, 205

Test Capability Index (TCI), 21

Variable measurement, 206

Variation, 206

Vendor rating, 53-103, 206

Verification, 206

About the Editor

James L. Bossert is a quality consultant for Eastman Kodak Company. He is currently working in the Customer Quality Assessment Organization which evaluates Kodak and competitive products from the customer's viewpoint. Mr. Bossert received his Master's degree in statistics from the Rochester Institute of Technology and is a member of its adjunct faculty at the Center for Quality and Applied Statistics. He teaches courses on statistical process control, experimental design, and basic statistics. A member of the ASQC Vendor-Vendee Technical Committee, Mr. Bossert is the current chair of the ASQC Rochester Section and the vice chair of the Technical Media Committee.